THE FIRST BLITZ

THE FIRST BLITZ

THE GERMAN BOMBER CAMPAIGN AGAINST BRITAIN IN THE FIRST WORLD WAR

Andrew P Hyde

LEO COOPER

First published in Great Britain 2002 by
LEO COOPER
an imprint of Pen & Sword Books Ltd
47 Church Street, Barnsley, S. Yorkshire, S70 2AS

ISBN 0 85052 812 7

A catalogue record for this book is
available from the British Library

Typeset in 11/13 Sabon by
Pen & Sword Books, Barnsley, South Yorkshire

Printed and Bound in England by
CPI UK

CONTENTS

Introduction and Acknowledgements

Travelling on holiday to our uncle and aunt in Dorset during the 1960s was always a daunting prospect. It was a lengthy, gruelling slog and, before the advent of the M25 Motorway, involved among other feats of endurance, a long-winded grind through the London suburbs. Boredom remains the overriding memory of those tortuous trips, sometimes alleviated only when we got lost or missed a turning and my parents rounded on one another in their customary way.

There was however one other, fleeting diversion from the ennui. Part of the journey through London took us along the East India Dock Road in Tower Hamlets, or what used to be known as Poplar and where both my parents were born and brought up. Every year we covered the same ground, and at this point, every year, we would pass Poplar Memorial Park, at which juncture my father unfailingly took his left hand off the steering wheel and pointed over towards the left with his thumb. With hardly a fraction of a second to register it in my head, the barely discernible figure of an off-white stone angel would come briefly into view. 'Your uncle's name's on that,' he would pronounce intriguingly. Then the car would be too far ahead to take a second look and we would be back on our way – the welcome distraction awaiting our return the following year.

On this went until finally, my curiosity pricked, I decided I wanted to know more about this enigmatic angel and the story behind it. Finally it transpired that my uncle, George Albert Hyde, was one of eighteen children killed when a German bomb demolished their school in Upper North Street Poplar, during the First World War, just round the corner from where the memorial which bears their names stands.

It was one of hundreds of incidents to occur in the British Home Front during the Great War, when German airships and occasionally lone aircraft, flew over towns and cities to unload their cargoes of bombs. Then, on Wednesday, 13 June 1917 – in a complete change of tack – a squadron of German purpose-built bombers flew above London and scattered their payloads over the capital in what would arguably prove to be the world's first ever strategic air raid.

Naturally, I did not appreciate, much less understand too much of it at first. I was only a youngster in the 1960s. The deepest my grasp of the past went then was to absorb the war stories in sixpenny editions of the comics *Battle* or *Commando*, or tales of derring-do in the *Victor*. However, my love of history had begun to develop by the time I was nine or ten-years-old and I started looking the period up in books. There were indeed, accounts of the airship raids and even brief mentions of the short summer campaign which included the raid in which Uncle George died when he was just five-years-old.

There was though, never more than a passing mention of this and the other raids which became the Gotha Campaign. Many books had been written about the period, but with one or two notable exceptions, only a brief mention was ever given of the children who died at Upper North Street or any of the other incidents which occurred in that fateful summer of 1917.

By the time I was in my late teens and early twenties I had developed and honed my relationship with the subject of history to the extent that I fancied myself as something of a very amateur historian. I therefore decided to compensate for the fact that the raid coverage seemed incomplete and research it. This book is the result. In embarking upon this project one cannot, however, assume that the reader will be aware of all the circumstances surrounding the air raids. I have, therefore, extended my research beyond the immediate circumstances of the attacks to take in the relevant events leading up to, and surrounding, the devastating raids which took place as part of the campaign. These will include the attack on Folkestone on 25 May 1917, which shook the south-east of the country, and the almost unknown attack on Sheerness a week later.

I have been anxious not to repeat what could be found in other works, but in order to clarify just how this and the other tragedies were allowed to occur in the first place I have drawn in a number of strands. I have gone back to the days when men could only dream of flying, and trace developments from there to the time when that dream became a reality. I have examined other relevant details connected to the story of the actual raids, so as to describe to the reader how political and military decisions both in Britain and Germany combined to make what occurred inevitable.

My aim has been to provide a rounded account of both the raids and the historical events which were inexorably wound up with them, led up to them, and eventually caused them.

This book has taken me the best part of twenty years to write, and I have many people to thank for their time, effort and patience in the help they have given me. In that time I have visited the Public Record Office at Kew many times, finding the reports written by the British defenders, pilots and commanders of the anti-aircraft gun stations, official reports by military intelligence and leads for further study and investigation. I secured the assistance of local and national newspapers in the UK and abroad; I have visited libraries and had letters from people who witnessed, or knew people who had been present at the events which have been described here. As these incidents occurred nearly eighty years ago, that has been no mean feat. Most people have long since passed-on even if they were only children at the time but, despite this, I have received numerous letters from eyewitnesses over the years, some from as far afield as Australia and New Zealand, whose accounts have still been vivid so long after the events they describe. To the many other people who corresponded with me and spoke over the phone I am very, very grateful.

To supplement the letters, I have found old newspaper articles and quotations from printed material which I have used to fill in gaps where otherwise the story would have been incomplete. I have also referred to a book written in the 1960s, entitled *The Sky on Fire* by Raymond H Fredette. Mr Fredette's work includes interviews with some of the original German Gotha crews, something I could not have hoped to achieve after all this time. But in the 1960s there were still a few old survivors left, and he managed to use their recollections to enrich his book. I have also consulted many other works covering the First World War and the people who helped to influence its progress – or perhaps lack of it. I have travelled around the places described and searched for and sometimes found, relics and evidence of what happened. From this wealth of disparate information and research material I have produced this book.

Where sources have been quoted in any form, I have endeavoured to contact the author, his publisher or their successor. I found no successors to the defunct *Women's Dreadnought*, *Star* and *Daily News*, but am grateful to original writers for their observations. Some assorted quotes come from lines found in books, papers or periodicals which I hastily scribbled down without the foresight of noting the source. I therefore humbly apologize to, and belatedly thank who or whatsoever recognizes itself as such.

A special thank you to Mr John Hook, who gave me free and open access to his labour of love, *They Come, They Come* and which I found indispensable. John spent many years researching the raids on London during the period 1915-1918, and his research uncovered some very interesting and useful material, which he kindly gave me permission to use. Thanks also to Orion Publishing for allowing me to refer to *Vickers, A History* on my description of the Mayfly debacle, and the Oxford University Press for permission to quote from

Echoes from the Great War. Lionel Leventhal of Greenhill Books generously allowed me to quote from the Greenhill editions of *Flying Fury, 5 Years in the Royal Flying Corps* by Captain James McCudden and *Sagittarius Rising* by Cecil Lewis. Both contain priceless first-hand pilots' accounts of the raids which took place, and give readers an invaluable insight into the war from their point of view. My thanks to the *Evening Standard* for allowing me to quote from contemporary reports of the defunct *Evening News*, and similarly to the *Express* and *Daily Mail* for giving me permission to quote from their newspapers of the time. Thanks to Joan Blake of the Shepherd's Bush Local History Society, who allowed me to quote in full from the late Bill Goble's account of the raid of 13 June, which he put down in his autobiography *Bill Goble - Lifelong Rebel*. Sadly, Bill died a few years ago. The staff of the Imperial War Museum Department of Photographs, and also the Guildhall Library Department of Prints also deserve my thanks in assisting me in sourcing photographs from the period, as does the editorial staff of the *Folkestone Herald* for printing an appeal for witnesses and accounts from the Folkestone raid. The *Evening Standard* letters page also did me a similar service many years ago. I would also like to mention Mr Bill Church who was the only child casualty of the bomb on Upper North Street School I had the privilege of meeting. He kindly gave his time and allowed me to tape his account. He narrowly escaped death that day, and when I met him many years ago, was a fine sprightly old gentlemen with a healthy attitude to life. He is also now a dedicated pacifist.

I am also grateful to Richard Romang and Martin Curran who, of the many people who offered to read the early versions of the manuscript and give me their views, were two who actually did so. Reading something for the author is an onerous task sometimes, so their help and comments is much appreciated.

I found Martin Gilbert's awesome biography of Winston Churchill invaluable in giving me an insight into the man's contribution to creating an effective defence against the air ships. I believe it has given another view of this many faceted man, and demonstrates just how much his long and distinguished life meant to his country.

Last, but certainly not least, I wish to record a very great debt of gratitude to Max Anderson, who has taken valuable time away from his proper job, at time of writing that of editor of the *Sunday Times* Travel Section, to help me edit this tome. Over a period of three years he has gone through several re-writes with me, offered advice and urged where necessary merciless editing and different ways of approaching large parts of this book. He is one of the reasons I am glad it has taken me all these years to finish the job – it has meant that I have got it right. I'm sure it would have been all the poorer for him not being involved. We cooperated, as they say.

My thanks too, to the following libraries and publications which assisted me in my research, printed appeals and helped identify relevant archive material from their records. Bancroft Road Library, Tower Hamlets London, Folkestone Central Library, Greater London Records Office, Clerkenwell London, The Island History Trust, The Library Association, The London Hospital, Whitechapel, Margate Central Library, Southend Reference Library.

I received a number of letters as a result of various appeals to newspapers and relevant periodicals. I am greatly indebted to the following individuals who kindly responded to those appeals, and who generously gave me their time, and the benefit of their first-hand knowledge of the events covered in this book. If my disorderly filing has resulted in my leaving anybody off the list, my sincere apologies: Colonel D R Bennett, Janice Booker, Mrs R A Bray, George A Bregenzer, F H Buenfeld, D Bynoth, L J Clarke, Helen Cobden, Mrs I Collings, Robert Connell, James W Cook, Mrs G Courtney, D F Cowers, Joyce Crew, John Cutten, Mrs M J Drayton, B K Eastwell, Mrs H Fazzani, S A Francis, Doris Frank, H Freedman, Stella Furnival, Winifred Harris, Edward Harrison, E R Herrington, Ivy Inch, Phyllis Jones, Stanley Lambert, Maureen Lewsey, A D Lidderdale, Mrs G Marshall, G Mills, Mrs J Mills, W C Mitchell, Arthur Parsons, Mr G Perrott, Helen Perry, L Piper, Stanley Pickering, Elsie Podewin, T J Reader, Lilly Richards, C L Saville, Mrs A V Sharman, H J Shepherd, Alfred E Smith, Martha Stimson, Marie Stimson, Frank Tanner, Mrs L Thirkell, A J Thompson, E S Tucker, G H Weeks, Doreen Whitehead, Marjorie Whyman, Geoffrey Yeo.

In conclusion, I make no apologies for wishing to dedicate the work firstly to my Uncle George who was denied the rest his life, secondly to the other children who died in the school and last but not least, my own beautiful daughters Deandre and Clöe.

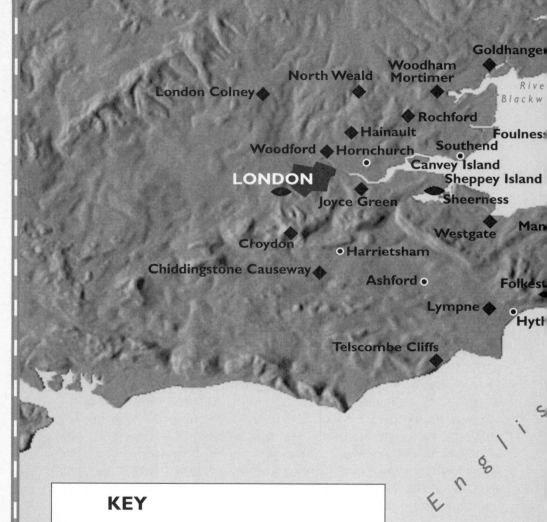

Goldhanger

Woodham
Mortimer

North Weald

London Colney

River
Blackw

Rochford

Foulness

Hainault

Southend

Woodford ◆ Hornchurch

Canvey Island

LONDON

Sheppey Island

Joyce Green

Sheerness

Croydon

Westgate

Man

Harrietsham

Chiddingstone Causeway

Ashford

Folkes

Lympne

Hyth

Telscombe Cliffs

Englis

KEY

◆ Home Defence Airfields

✠ Gotha Airfields

✈ RNAS/RFC Airfields in France/Belgium

⚓ Observation Lightships

⬗ Major Air Raid Targets

SE ENGLAND, FRANCE & BELGIUM IN 1917

xstowe

N o r t h   S e a

Middles LS

Edinburgh LS

er LS

Tongue LS

largate

C h a n n e l

OVER

Zeebrugge

Nieumunster

Ostend

BRUGES

Oostacker

Nieuport

Mariakerke

Ghistelles

Bray Dunes

Thielt

GENT

Dunkirk

Furnes

St Denis Westrem

Calais

Melle-Gontrode

FRONT LINE

BELGIUM

BELGIAN BORDER

FRANCE

Estree
Blanche

CHAPTER 1

A POWER WHICH CONTROLS THE FATE OF NATIONS

When H G Wells' doom-laden vision of a London under attack, as depicted in his *War of the Worlds*, was published in 1898 it took the world by storm. *War of the Worlds* was not only a work which showed a fertile mind with a genius for story-telling, but also one which could see far beyond the comfortable closing days of the century.

Although it was conceived and written even before man had achieved mastery of powered-flight, it nevertheless served as a cautionary tale of the consequences should London ever be confronted by a form of warfare that it was unable to face on equal terms.

Yet only the previous year, the world had witnessed a magnificent Jubilee designed to impress upon it the primacy of the British Empire, celebrating the sixtieth year of Queen Victoria's rule over an empire of 387 million people and ten million square miles of territory. A quarter of the globe was under British influence and control and Britain's power traditionally supported by one single instrument of force, the Royal Navy.

Serving as the grand finale of the Jubilee was a review at Spithead where 170 warships of the Home Fleet paid homage to the Queen. It was claimed to be the largest assembly ever which, if laid end-to-end would have stretched thirty miles. One American correspondent who witnessed the spectacle bravely declared that the United States itself was but 'a part, and a great part, of the Greater Britain which seems so plainly destined to dominate this planet'.

Not everyone was impressed however. To seasoned cynics such as the author Mark Twain it was 'no more than embroidery'. Yet, apparently assured of supremacy on land and sea, the average Victorian would have dismissed the Wellsian hypothesis as preposterous.

Ever since the crushing victory against the combined fleets of France and Spain at Trafalgar in 1805, British naval might remained unchallenged. By observing the 'Two-Power Standard' she was able in theory at least to field a force ten per cent larger than the combined navies of any two potential enemies. The oceans had given Britain the means by which to defend its own shores whilst providing it with the tools with which to violate others. The sea was not merely a part of her history, it was her history. Drake, Frobisher and Nelson, the men who had helped write the greatest chapters, had done so from the decks of ships hewn from English oak. The romanticized, idealized view of the Royal Navy was bound up in the British people's self-confidence. It was all perhaps still too good to be true. A tiny island off the coast of Europe being at the epicentre of things sat well with the Victorians. But Britain, sleepy and self-confident in her 'Splendid Isolation', was due for a rude awakening.

In a different history, this complacency could have been undone centuries before, when men such as the humble Jesuit priest, Francesca Lana, conceived machines that floated in the sky, destroying foes who scampered helplessly on the ground. Before Trafalgar and the 'Two-Power Standard', the author Thomas Gray wrote in 1757 of how:

> The time will come, when thou shalt lift up thine eyes to watch a long-drawn battle in the skies, while aged peasants, too amazed for words, stare at the flying fleets of wond'rous birds. England, so long the mistress of the sea, where winds and waves confess her sovereignty, her ancient triumphs yet on this shall bear, and reign, the sovereign of the conquered air.

Nevertheless, since no nation had met and outmatched her supremacy in the oceans, history would continue to give England an advantage based on this strength for 100 years after Trafalgar.

Whilst some sat and dreamt of things to come, others began to turn ideas and words into deeds. Men like the French Montgolfier brothers who in 1783, built the first balloon, unveiling their innovation before their King, and earning sufficient patronage to continue their work. Though scoffed at by numerous detractors, the brothers built bigger and better craft, each in turn demonstrating enhanced performance. Eleven years after their first flight, a balloon detachment was established within the French Army to be used to spy on enemy troop movements. It proved its mettle in June of 1794 when, at the Battle of Fleurus during one of the sporadic wars of the Napoleonic era, one Capitaine Coutelle clambered aboard his rasping air-filled monster and spent the battle observing what the Austrians were up to.

Whether the noble captain helped his side one way or the other remains unrecorded, but the French commander Napoleon Bonaparte had dismissed balloons as so much hot air and swiftly dispensed with their services.

Contemporary men of foresight, however, saw things differently. One was a Prussian officer, Julius Voss who, in 1810, wrote how in future wars:

> The enemy, eager to conceal his intentions, did not hesitate to send up his own light craft in order to drive back the enemy balloons, and so in the heavens above skirmishes developed between advanced patrols.

Adventurers meanwhile took the balloon even further afield. Individuals like Charles Green who, in 1836 piloted his craft 500 miles from London to Weilburg in Germany; and John La Mountain who added 300 miles to the record by flying from St Louis to Henderson, New York, in the United States. And, without one *Oberleutnant* Franz Uchatius, the Austrian Army of 1849 might never have known that they had the wherewithal to perform the first ever aerial bombardment.

Their achievement was made during the bitter war with Italy, which was fighting to secede from its bigger neighbour. The hapless Italians were pushed back until finally they sought safety in the walled city of Venice where the Austrians could pummel the fragile city with round after round of artillery shell.

Eventually young Uchatius suggested the outrageous alternative of bombing the enemy from above their heads. The terror and fear it would unleash, he insisted, would have them unfurling their white flags in no time. Though no doubt dubious, his superiors decided that they had little to lose and so listened. He described how they could launch a number of paper balloons, carrying 22lb each of explosives, let them drift slowly with the wind until, in accordance with a predetermined time fuse, they would hit the ground, to send the defenders of Venice running in all directions.

The day came, and the balloons were launched. At first it seemed as if the Austrians had provoked the very reaction they wanted, the first few explosions causing dreadful panic among the Italians. But as time wore on, the defenders realized that, although they were capable of killing, the small bombs were no greater danger than the cholera and starvation which also plagued the city. Venice eventually did fall, but it was not due to assault from the air.

3

It is hardly surprising Uchatius' invention received scant attention, no doubt being dismissed by most contemporaries as, at best, a novel improvisation. However, whether or not they were prompted by the Austrians, or by some other phenomena, twelve years after the events above Venice, the United States' Army of the Potomac formed a Balloon Corps during the American Civil War, under the command of one Thaddeus Loew. The same year John La Mountain took up a balloon from the deck of the ingloriously named USS *Fanny*, effectively the world's first aircraft carrier, to observe Confederate troop movements over Virginia. The Confederacy also employed balloons from the tug *Teaser*.

Across the Atlantic, the value of these devices was also being demonstrated. During the Franco-Prussian War of 1870-71, balloons were effectively employed to carry dispatches and VIPs out of Paris. The besieging Prussians succeeded in shooting down some of the sixty-six launched from the capital, but most reached safety. One of them succeeded in a flight of 1,400 miles to Narvik in Norway.

By 1879, even the conservative British War Office approved a budget of £150, with which the Royal Engineers were to set up a balloon detachment at Woolwich Arsenal in London. Three years later, an establishment of one officer and fifteen men took three balloons to serve as scouts with the ill-fated expedition under General Hicks to recover the Sudan. However, the entire column was wiped out in the Battle of El Obeid. Whatever other services they may have provided, they clearly failed to anticipate tens of thousands of whirling Dervishes descending upon them.

In 1884 three more balloons accompanied a British Expeditionary Force dispatched to annex Bechuanaland in southern Africa. In 1887, Major Templar became the British Army's first Director of Ballooning, and three years on an Army Balloon Section was officially sanctioned. In 1899, the Second war against the errant Boer farmers presented the new unit with an ideal opportunity to show what it could do. It was used with some success at Lombard's Kop and Magersfontein, where 'Filled Balloon Titania', under the command of one Captain Jones, reported enemy movements and directed artillery fire. Meanwhile, over a hundred miles away Kimberley was being besieged by Boer troops. The British outflanked them in their attempt to relieve the town, and then the enemy withdrew to Paardeburg twenty-three miles south-east, where they established defensive positions in a dry river bed. Despite numerous British assaults, the farmers held firm. The British commander, Lord Kitchener, decided to blast them out. Here the balloons came into their own, directing the gunfire until, after nine days of relentless pounding, the enemy finally succumbed and surrendered.

This distant triumph in a far-flung corner of the world created little more than a ripple beyond the veld of South Africa. And in any case, as the stuffy generals in Whitehall would confirm, no ungainly gas bag would ever successfully usurp the graceful cavalry in the unique role of scout. The horse had provided the British Army with all the intelligence it needed for as long as any of them could remember and they saw no good reason to change now.

The Royal Navy was also otherwise occupied, watching with justifiable concern the growth of the Imperial German Navy. With little hope of any air borne interest or investment from the British it seemed that, in the short term at least, amateurs and adventurers would have to be relied upon to take technology another step.

⸺⸺✦⸺⸺

By the end of the nineteenth century the work of men like Count Ferdinand Zeppelin had firmly superseded the concept of the balloon with the 'airship'.

Born in 1838, Zeppelin joined the Prussian Cavalry in 1852, serving in the American Civil War as a volunteer in their Balloon Corps, and later in the Austrian and Franco-Prussian Wars. He had been persuaded that the balloon had proved itself as a capable resource during that conflict, and in the Austro-Prussian War was further convinced of its efficacy. His love of flying soon became a near obsession, and before long his mind was directed towards the fulfilment of a single goal - mastery of the air. Upon retiring from the cavalry he was able to pursue his dream with vigour. Following up on the work of men like Charles Renard and Otto Krebs, Zeppelin spent days hidden away from family and friends struggling to produce what he knew would be the natural successor to the balloon. Although Zeppelin was not the only man toiling towards this end, his name would become synonymous with the end result.

This was the age of science. All over Europe men were tinkering in workshops and poring over drawing boards to secure what had thus far eluded them. Many experiments were doomed to failure, like the petrol-engined airship designed by Karl Wolfert. This was flown in 1888, using what was known as a 'hot-tube' ignition Daimler engine.

His efforts not only failed, they sent him plunging to his death in a ball of flame.

The world's first proper rigid airship was the result of the work done by an Austrian engineer called David Schwartz, and complemented by an aluminium frame developed by Frenchman, P Heroult, and American, C M Hall. It was given its test flight in November 1897 but a strong wind blew up, tossing the machine like a child's toy. It barely managed to return to the ground intact.

Meanwhile, Zeppelin had produced a multitude of drafts and early prototypes, until in July 1900 he rolled out LZ1. It had a modest beginning with a range of ten and a half miles and an endurance of twenty-three minutes, but was merely the small shape of greater things to come.

— ⸰ —

Entrepreneurs were also venturing into the field of what was being referred to as 'heavier-than-air-machines'. Few trials and experiments would lead further than their imagination or the wastepaper basket, but they were spurred on by the coming of a new century and continued to happily give vent to wild ideas.

One of these was Hiram Maxim who between 1889 and 1894 had been experimenting with a steam-powered aeroplane. He built a biplane weighing some 3.5 tons, powered by two 180hp steam engines and carrying a crew of three. It cost £20,000 to develop, and was finally unveiled in Baldwyn's Park in Kent on 31 July 1894. Maxim watched his £20,000 go up in smoke as it crashed moments after it took to the air, and humiliated by the experience, took a long sabbatical before he endeavoured to repeat the exercise.

Others persevered, alternatively grasping and failing to master the laws of aerodynamics. Then two bicycle repairers from Dayton, Ohio, USA, Orville and Wilbur Wright, stumbled upon the beginnings of a solution. Captivated by the search for the secret of powered flight, they studied every aspect of the subject and, on 17 December 1903, achieved the first controlled powered flight at Kill Devil Hill. English Boer-War hero Lord Baden-Powell declared with admiration that, 'they were in possession of a power which controls the fate of nations'.

Another Briton who shared these sentiments was Lieutenant Colonel J E Capper, then Commandant of the Royal Engineers Balloon School and Depot at Aldershot and later, Superintendent of

Balloon Battalion of Royal Engineers 1890 ?

the Balloon Factory at Farnborough. Because early interest by the US military in the Wrights' achievement had waned, they were forced to look elsewhere for a market for their aeroplanes. Capper invited them to England, where they generated a certain amount of interest in the War Office but none where it counted, in the Treasury, where they were met with a cool response.

Capper was not to be deterred however. Observing how matters were developing in Europe, he was moved to comment in a speech to the United Services Institute in November 1909 that:

> In a few years we may expect to see men moving swiftly through the air... such machines will move very rapidly... up to a hundred miles per hour... they will be small and difficult to hit... their range will be very large.

Despite the Wrights' early achievements, the concept of an aeroplane as anything other than an aberration still held sway. The airship seemed a far more tangible manifestation of scientific advance.

Zeppelin, now a man in his sixties, was still working unstintingly towards his own goal. Zeppelin LZ3 made several successful flights in 1906 and 1907 and the Imperial German Army was becoming attracted by their potential. They eventually approached him with a brief to build a vessel capable of flying for twenty-four hours non-stop with a ceiling of 10,000 feet to enable it to avoid ground fire.

The resulting labours produced LZ4, but it was wrecked during trials, and with waning interest, it looked like Zeppelin might never realize his ambition to make Germany master of the air. It was the public no less, who, enthusing of his endeavours, held collections to finance further work. By 1909 the name had become a byword for Teutonic industrial might and prestige. The Kaiser, Wilhelm II, had embraced the project and, at one airship trial, was driven to hyperbole:

> Our Fatherland may well be proud of possessing such a son, the greatest German of the twentieth century who, by this invention has opened a new epoch in the development of mankind.

Zeppelin appeared to warrant fully such an accolade. LZ5 achieved the specifications originally set by the Army and was duly commissioned, but few military orders followed. The Count turned his eyes increasingly towards commercial designs and his LZ10 of 1910 proved very successful, carrying 1,500 passengers in twelve months. The German Navy did not want to be left in the shade by its more august brother-in-arms, however and in the following year took possession of its first machine L1. Still things refused to go all the Count's way. Nine of the twenty-five commercial airships constructed between 1900 and the outbreak of the First World War came to unfortunate ends.

⸻ ⸙ ⸻

By now, the die had been well and truly cast. Gradually, rumblings of interest had worked their way through to Whitehall where it was finally accepted that European developments might very well warrant closer scrutiny. In 1908, the same year that Zeppelin hauled LZ4 out of its shed, the Committee of Imperial Defence (CID), formed in 1904 and designed to give the impression of cohesion in matters relevant to the defence of the Empire, charged one Lord Esher with the task of undertaking a thorough review of any danger airships might pose to the security of the Empire and Britain in particular.

Armed with its brief, the CID set to work to see if there was indeed any threat to Britain and perhaps more appropriately, anything to be gained from possessing an airship fleet themselves. The CID ground through the task with leaden zeal, interviewing scores of individuals who could claim an interest or some knowledge of the subject.

Not everyone, however, wanted or could wait for the findings of the Committee. Capper for one, eager to see what his own men could do, was embarking upon airship trials. In September 1907, *Nulli Secundus* made a successful flight of three-and-a-half hours from Farnborough to Crystal Palace, a distance of around fifty miles. This was followed by *Nulli Secundus II* a year later. Both airships were, however still small fry compared with the Zeppelin to which they definitely came a very distant second.

There was now a growing clique in the Admiralty who appreciated the German airship as a potential serious threat, and not all were junior officers faced with the impossible task of persuading older, more traditional, superiors. One in particular who needed little convincing was the then First Sea Lord, Admiral John Fisher. His long career had begun in the days of sail but he was, nevertheless, a keen sponsor of such modern developments as the torpedo and submarine, even flying in the face of the Royal Navy's complacent attitude towards the need to modernize the ageing Fleet, and calling for the Admiralty to 'Scrap the lot!' Furthermore, he saw in the airship an ideal scout, supporting the Navy in its primary role, that of defending

8

the United Kingdom from attack.

His enthusiasm ran concurrent to the efforts being made by the Director of Naval Ordnance, R.H.S. Bacon, to create an air arm for the Navy. In 1908 Bacon submitted detailed proposals which included the suggestion that a Naval Air Assistant be appointed at the Admiralty and that the War Office should ask Colonel Capper to liaise between them and the Army. He had also suggested that the well-respected engineering firm of Vickers be approached and asked to design a rigid airship. Bacon's ideas were submitted to the CID which, in January 1909 recommended to the Cabinet that £35,000 be included in the Naval Estimates (budget) for 1909-10 to finance the project – a trifling figure compared to the £13,000,000 allocated to the construction of warships, but a budget nonetheless.

The same month, Esher's Committee reported its findings to the Government. They saw in the airship a comprehensive range of potential threats, from the ability to bomb dockyards and naval installations, to the carrying of small raiding parties to attack special objectives. Of the aeroplane however, there was no similar endorsement. Despite the fact that both the French and the Germans had been undertaking major programmes by comparison, the committee felt that they were too small to be able to carry any meaningful bomb load and that in the act of flying 'the physical strain on the driver' meant that the machine was of very limited value.

Others were even less compromising in their views. Colonel J E B Seely, Parliamentary Private Secretary to War Minister Lord Haldane, stated that 'we do not consider that aeroplanes will be of any possible use for war purposes'. Other observers fought strongly in favour of the aeroplane. Pioneer aviator Charles Stewart Rolls, attested to the potential of the new phenomena and voiced the fears shared by many of his contemporaries. All such entreaties however, fell on deaf ears. While the CID debated the pros and cons of the aeroplane in England, a French entrepreneur, Louis Blériot, who had amassed a fortune from the manufacture of motor car lamps, had developed a fascination with the flying machine. He had worked closely with Robert Esnault-Pelterie in the field of box-kites, and in 1907 was undertaking modest flights of almost a mile. By the summer of 1909 the team had graduated to aeroplanes, and finally the Frenchmen felt ready to put their experiments to the test. Blériot also decided to extract the greatest amount of publicity he could from his debut. Thus, on a misty morning in July, he climbed aboard his monoplane in a field near

Calais. The machine spluttered reluctantly to life and eventually edged forward, finally gaining sufficient speed to lift skywards. It lurched awkwardly into the air and thirty-seven minutes later was touching down in Kent.

The huge moat that had fended off Dutchmen, Spanish and Frenchmen alike had been breached. Those who listened hard enough would have been able to hear Lord Nelson turning in his grave.

While this single-handed act of bravado finally caused heads to turn, other endeavours were furthering the possibilities of the aeroplane. In the United States, Brigadier General James Allen had issued a specification in 1907 for an armed reconnaissance machine with a crew of two, a speed of 40mph and an endurance of one hour; in August 1909, a Wright machine (interest had grown slightly by now) was delivered and submitted for trials. 1909 also saw the first flights in Germany by aircraft designed by Hans Gaede. The Austrian-designed Taube monoplane of Igo Etrich and F Wels was first flown at Wiener-Neustadt in November.

Only one year after Blériot had ably demonstrated that it was possible for an aircraft to violate the airspace of a potential enemy, others were showing that it was even possible to sink Britain's first line of defence – the mighty Dreadnoughts of the Home Fleet. In June 1910 American Glen Curtiss practised dropping dummy bombs on a 'battleship' marked out by buoys on a lake. The following year, Lieutenant Riley Scott succeeded in developing a crude combined bombsight and bomb rack. That August, another American, Jacob Fickel, became the first man to use an aeroplane as a platform from which to fire a weapon. Fast on his tail was Eugene Ely, the first to take off from a warship's deck in December 1910. In 1911, Myron Crissey and Phillip Parmalee became the first pilots to drop explosive bombs from an aircraft, while an Italian, Captain Guidone, also carried out trials with aeroplanes employed as bombers, launching a torpedo from a Henry Farman biplane. Charles de Forest Chandler was the first man to arm an aircraft with a machine gun in June 1912, when he took a Lewis Gun aloft. The first cannon to be fired successfully was a Vickers-made 37mm gun in July 1913.

⟫⟩⊰○⊱⟨⟪

During May and June of 1910, an international conference on Aerial Navigation was convened in Paris. It reflected the growing recognition that aircraft – both heavier-than-air and lighter-than-air, as aeroplanes and airships respectively were known, was becoming increasingly relevant to world geopolitics. High on the agenda was the threat the aircraft posed as an instrument of war. Even the British sent a delegation, which returned convinced that airships did indeed have a potentially critical military role to play, though the aircraft still seemed a rather poor cousin. Despite Curtiss' demonstrations in America, its perceived inability to bomb accurately served as a major drawback, whilst its superior speed did little to encourage confidence in its capacity to pursue airships.

So, although aircraft were still in the shadows, the airship had a chance, if it could prove itself. With Bacon now retired, the Vickers Project fell into the lap of Captain Murray Sueter RN. Under his unhappy tutelage there would occur one of the most farcical episodes in the history of flight.

Officially designated Airship No.1, the vessel was to be constructed at the Cavendish Dock in Barrow. The entire project was suspect from the start, as no one, either in Vickers or in Britain generally had the slightest idea how to build an airship of the quite unreasonable dimensions commissioned. The Admiralty brief included the requirement for a vessel 512 feet long and 48 feet in diameter, with a gas capacity of 64,000 cubic feet. It was to have a speed of 40 knots sustainable for twenty-four hours. She would have to be capable of climbing to 1,500 feet (although the Germans were already thinking in terms of 10,000 feet and above) and be able to carry a heavy, powerful wireless set should distress alerts need to be sent.

Mayfly (as the project was christened) was strongly influenced by the work of an American, Professor Albert Zahm, who wrongly favoured the concept of a twelve-sided hull, with different bow and stern shape to the Zeppelin. Later experiments would reveal that a ship of this design was only two-fifths as resistant to wind and air pressure as the Zeppelin. It also transpired that C G Roberton, the Marine Manager at Barrow, did not have the know-how to undertake a project of this scope and scale. His lack of mathematics, the defect in the Zahm design, boded ill.

More and more weight was added to accommodate changing requirements, until Roberton was forced to compensate by removing some of the superstructure, including the main keel member. One of his assistants, H B Pratt, whose mathematics was better than those of his boss, made his own calculations and concluded that such drastic measures severely undermined the integrity of the airship. His warnings were dismissed however, and time and again the vessel was changed

11

until, two years after her conception, she was due for her inaugural flight.

She was admittedly, an inspiring sight as she emerged from her shed at Cavendish Dock in late spring 1911, stirring the heart of many an Englishman. However, deprived of the shelter and protection of its concrete chrysalis, the structure fared badly as it found itself battered by 40mph winds for four days. Attempts to get her airborne were finally abandoned, and she was unceremoniously returned to her shed, where her tormentors imposed more drastic modifications. On 24 September, she was once again eased out, only to be caught in another gust of wind which promptly broke her back.

Her defenders claimed she had bounced against her shed, but most were in agreement with Admiral Sturdee, presiding over the subsequent enquiry, who called the entire enterprise 'the work of a lunatic'; a conclusion eagerly seized upon by all those convinced that airships and aircraft alike were a total waste of time and money.

Instead, the Admiralty had been gleefully planning its secret weapon to counter the growing threat posed by the German Navy. The wasteful search for a challenger to the Zeppelin had been a mere diversion while they developed the *Dreadnought* battleship, the most advanced and powerful example of naval technology the world had ever seen. Launched amid a panoply of pomp in February 1906, she was the fastest, largest and most powerful vessel in the world. She boasted ten 12-inch guns, twenty-seven 12-pounder quick firing anti-torpedo boat guns, five submerged torpedo tubes and had a speed of 21 knots. She could out range and outrun any other ship in the world.

Dreadnought was also proof positive that the Admiralty had steadfastly declined to take an aerial threat seriously enough to consider the need for counter measures. Not a single anti-aircraft weapon had been installed on the awesome vessel.

—≈⊷⊰⊱⊷≈—

But events were fast catching up. A small war in North Africa was to provide the first real opportunity for the aeroplane to prove its value in warfare. After protracted diplomatic posturing, war had broken out between Turkey and Italy for possession of the North African Ottoman province of Tripolitania. In order to establish their claim, the Italians dispatched an expeditionary force to the territory, which consisted of an air corps commanded by Captain Carlo Piazza. It included nine 50hp aeroplanes, two French Blériots, three

12

Nieuports, two Farmans and two Austrian Taubes, along with a handful of airships.

On 22 October, Piazza had decided to break the monotony of the fighting and venture towards the Turkish lines. He made a one-hour scouting flight in a Blériot around the town of Azizzia, collecting intelligence and observing enemy troop movements. On 1 November, a more audacious pilot, Sub Lieutenant Giulio Gavaotti, took to the air armed with 2kg 'Cipelli' grenades, and scattered a few over enemy forces in Ain Zara and Taguira. Helpless to respond, all the Turkish authorities could do was table a protest, claiming that a hospital had been hit and innocent patients killed and maimed. However, many observers appreciated the significance of the events, one being persuaded of 'the practical value of aeroplanes in time of war'.

The September 1912 issue of the British magazine *Central News* saw one journalist moved to comment in prophetic terms on the implications of the Italians' operations in Tripolitania, concluding that 'a great British air fleet needs to be created.'

Ironically, these sentiments were penned just three years after the aeroplane had been dismissed as useless. And Italy's foray over North Africa resulted in the action being singled out for breach of international law, embodied in two articles of the Hague Convention, signed in 1899 and 1907. In 1899, the signatories agreed to prohibit bombing from balloons and, in 1907, the bombing of 'undefended places' by 'any means whatsoever' was forbidden. Thus, the Italian air raids were deemed to have breached the 'usages' of war.

This technicality did not stop more and more men from contributing their own visions of future combat. In 1911 Bertram Dickson, a captain of the Royal Field Artillery, wrote to the technical sub-committee of the CID with an appraisal which mirrored that of Von Voss almost exactly 100 years before:

> In the event of a European war between two countries, both sides would be equipped with large corps of aeroplanes, each trying to obtain information on the other and to hide its own movements. The efforts which each would exert in order to hinder or prevent the enemy from obtaining information would lead to the inevitable result of war in the air. This fight for supremacy of the air in future wars will be of the first and greatest importance, and when it has been won the land and sea forces of the loser will be at such a disadvantage that the war will certainly have to terminate at a much smaller loss in men and money to both sides.

13

In Europe, the fashion for using aircraft in war was beginning to take hold. A year after the campaign in North Africa, the French employed aircraft to suppress the regular revolts by Moroccan tribesmen – two pilots sustaining rifle wounds when they flew too low over adversaries who ungraciously declined to be frightened off. In 1912, trouble flared up in the Balkans, when Bulgaria, Greece and Montenegro squared up against Turkey in order to tear Macedonian lands from Ottoman suzerainty. The Bulgarians deployed what, for the time, was a large number of aircraft to complement their ground forces. Even the British were waking up to the kudos being attributed to the aeroplane. The CID grudgingly concluded in July 1912 that:

> It is possible that aeroplanes, owing to their superior mobility, may be found capable of destroying airships, but this has yet to be proved. Having respect to the great speed of airships (47mph), to the great rapidity with which they can rise, to the fact that they carry guns and firearms for the purposes of defence, and to the difficulty of destroying them by shells and explosives, it is by no means proved that aeroplanes are likely to have the better of an encounter, though they can travel faster and ultimately rise higher than the present type of airship, which is some compensation for the greater time taken in rising... It appears probable that, for the immediate present, the surest method of attacking airships would be by a superior force of airships.

Air Battalion of Royal Engineers 1908

Whilst the War Office and the politicians prevaricated, private individuals, seeing the aeroplane as a 'wizard toy' if nothing else, pursued their own private and commercial experiments, giving birth to a fledgling air industry.

Contests such as that won by Henry Farman on 13 January 1908 brought to public attention the first machine capable of flying a kilometre round a closed circuit. A year later the world's first international flying meeting was convened at Reims in France. Thousands were attracted to such spectacles, curious to see for themselves the crazy men risking life and limb to raise wood and wire into the air. In England, Brooklands in Surrey became a magnet for aspiring aviators wanting to purchase a machine from one of the small companies springing up with their designs. By 1910, the embryonic British aircraft industry was supplying the growing civilian market, but no doubt waiting for the day when the War Office would wake from its stupor and start to place orders.

Despite affecting public aloofness, the Royal Balloon Factory was privately carrying out trials under the recently appointed Superintendent Mervyn O'Gorman. He sanctioned 'secret' work with aircraft he procured from any source he could find, and even employed civilian staff to help him. One was Geoffrey de Havilland, who under O'Gorman's tutelage would produce the prototype models which would lead eventually to the Blériot Experimental (B.E.) series of machines.

In 1911, the Vickers Company, no doubt still smarting from its ignominious dabbling with airships, was breaking a number of records with their Robert Esnault-Pelterie (R.E.P) series of aeroplanes. Incredibly, bearing in mind that war was just three years away, the Admiralty was still disinterested. Vickers however, persevered, and wrote to them pointing out that the R.E.P. two-seater could easily be adapted so as to make it 'capable of ascending from any of HM ships'. In January 1911, the Admiralty replied that they did not 'propose to acquire any aeroplanes for the Naval Service at present'. An attitude that was to be turned on its head just a few months later.

Undeterred, Vickers proceeded with production of their model at the Erith works and their first monoplane was completed in July 1911. This was taken by Sir Douglas Mawson on his expedition to the Antarctic, where it was left to wither amid the icy wastes when the expedition set off back home.

At the Olympia Aero Show in 1913, Vickers exhibited the prototype of a machine which was to see extensive war service, the Experimental Fighting Biplane (E.F.B.1) a two-seater 'Pusher' biplane with the engine at the rear and a Vickers machine gun mounted in the nose and operated by the observer. Eventually nicknamed the 'Gunbus' it went on to be used in extensive numbers by the Army's Royal Flying Corps throughout the coming conflict. Ironically, in the period leading up to the war, they manufactured for sale only twenty-six aircraft of the type.

The politicians were beginning to come around. CID, under the advice of such men as S F Cody and J W Dunne, two well-known aviators at their time, agreed to establish an air battalion within the Royal Engineers. Although no one took very much notice when it came into existence on 1 April 1911, the new arm had to be equipped and, in 1912, the War Office undertook a series of trials of possible machines to be used in the scouting role for which it was intended. One of those trialled was the B.E.2. It achieved a speed of 70mph with

15

a rate of climb to its ceiling of 10,000 feet at 365 feet-per-minute. Others considered included the Sopwith Tabloid. Later de Havilland offered the B.E.2c for consideration, of which 2,000 would be built and used extensively during the war.

There was to be no fighting role for these machines however. Even in their limited role as scouts they met with resistance. The Army still maintained a large cavalry arm, and having relied upon them for many years to gather information they poured scorn on any supplanting of their role. Indeed, only a month before war broke out in 1914, General Haig announced to a military gathering...

> I hope none of you gentlemen is so foolish as to think that aeroplanes will be able to be usefully employed for reconnaissance purposes in the air. There is only one way for a commander to get information by reconnaissance, and that is by the use of cavalry... .

—=≈≈0≈≈=—

Events were beginning to assume a momentum of their own, however. In a futile attempt to create some cohesion between the conflicting interests of the War Office and the Admiralty, the Royal Flying Corps (RFC) was established on 13 May 1912 to consist of a naval and military wing. But inter-service rivalry determined that the two arms drift inexorably apart from the moment they were clumsily united. Even the best efforts of Lord Seely, appointed to head a committee to unite the two parties, failed. Competition and jealousy made cooperation impossible. Finally the naval wing was withdrawn from the RFC on 1 July 1914 and became the Royal Naval Air Service (RNAS).

While the Admiralty looked to private companies to meet their needs, the War Office relied upon their Farnborough factory. As a result the Naval Wing entered the war with some of the most advanced aircraft in the world with the Army fielding a miscellany of designs and types, collected as and when they were delivered by Farnborough. This created a serious imbalance, which would further impair the ability of the two arms to cooperate effectively. So while a tacit understanding was formulated that the Admiralty was responsible for operations up to and including the UK coastline, and the War Office was to respond to enemy incursions beyond the coast, there was no mechanism in place to ensure that this could work. It was fortunate for all concerned therefore that upon this scene should enter an individual renowned for doing his own thing and relishing the taking of risks.

In October 1911, came the man who would arguably become its most famous First Sea Lord, Winston Churchill. His dynamism and imagination would give the Naval Arm the fillip it badly needed to meet the demands soon to be placed upon it.

Churchill had made his name as something of a firebrand and maverick from his earliest days in public life. He served on the Indian North-West Frontier in the cavalry, and later in the Sudan and South Africa as a journalist. He entered Parliament in 1900 and by 1910 was Home Secretary, a year later demonstrating his aptitude for drama and self publicity by attending the infamous siege of Sydney Street in London's East End, when armed police and troops fought a pitched battle with foreign anarchists. As First Lord he flew in the face of opposition with his plans to convert the Royal Navy from coal to oil power, and to upgrade the calibre of guns on battleships. It was only a matter of time before his imagination was sparked by the concept of a strong air arm for the Navy.

His interest had been aroused two year's previously when, as President of the Board of Trade, he sat on the CID and contributed his own views. He took this enthusiasm with him to the Admiralty, urging the treasury to sanction funds he would need to make the air arm effective.

He was anxious that Britain keep up with its European competitors and, in September 1913, wrote to Sir John Jellicoe on the subject. He believed that 'the number of machines must be such as to enable the war establishment to be continually maintained intact', which would constitute at least 100 machines, and he wanted airfields to be established at a number of locations such as Calshot, Grain Island, Felixstowe and Yarmouth. He had also mulled over the need to protect ports, harbours, magazines and other establishments which might be vulnerable to air attack. He even made spot checks of his own and submitted stern rebukes where he felt that insufficient measures had been taken to protect them.

He issued instructions for a small committee to be set up to look into what measures should be taken to guarantee their protection and listed his own suggestions, such as earth and concrete bunkers, decoys and anti-aircraft gun emplacements. He ordered that seaplane bases

17

be sited as close to those locations as possible which were likely to become targets in the event of war. His concerns anticipated problems which would become abundantly clear when the threat from the air became a reality in 1914. For example, on 21 December 1913, he wrote to Murray Sueter urging that all the aircraft be of uniform design, and suggested that measures be taken to make them suitable for radios to be fitted.

In January 1914, he expressed his concern that the spheres of responsibility between the Army and the Navy be clearly laid down and approved the 'proposed distribution of machines' for Cromarty, Dundee, Yarmouth, Felixstowe, Calshot, Eastchurch and Grain Island; the last of which at twenty-five was to be allocated the largest number of machines. On 5 March 1914, he wrote again to Sueter concerning the provision of landing places and 'how such places should be made available to airmen from aloft'. He suggested that signs be laid on the ground which would be used to provide instructions and directions to the air crew.

Despite his loyalty to the concept of a naval air arm, Churchill was inclined towards the belief that some form of overall coordination between the two arms was also important. On 12 December 1912 he wrote to the First Sea Lord, Prince Louis of Battenburg, stating his position that both air arms, naval and military, cooperate closely and devise a plan which would permit them to act as closely as possible in the event of war.

By contrast to the advances achieved under Churchill, the Army had barely begun to get its house in order. Diehard opposition in the higher echelons of the War Office continued to frustrate those who were determined to make the Royal Flying Corps work and comments made by men such as Haig hardly helped matters.

Not everyone on the Army side however was so contemptuous of the air arm. One man who deserves mention, more for his efforts perhaps than his achievements, was Major Herbert Musgrave of the Royal Engineers. He was one of the spectators who witnessed Blériot touch down in Kent in 1909 and he had been convinced since then that a strong air arm would be an indispensable element of any Army. In December 1911, he gave a lecture in which he told his audience:

When war comes, be assured it will come very suddenly. We shall wake up one night, find ourselves at war. Another thing is certain, this war will be no walkover. In the military sphere it will be the hardest, fiercest, and bloodiest struggle we have ever had to face and probably every one of us here tonight will take part in it. We need not be afraid of overdoing our preparations.

Major Musgrave pursued his belief in the need for a military air arm with a determination close to fanaticism. He pushed for the formation of the Royal Flying Corps, and when it was finally formed in 1912 was seconded from the Army to help organize it, as well as being placed in charge of experiments into the use by aircraft of wireless. His efforts, like others, were not helped by the almost complete lack of support from his superiors. Even at this stage, opposition to flight was bordering on the hysterical. Sir William Nicholson, British Chief of the General Staff from 1908-12, insisted that aviation had no practical role to play, stating that it was a 'useless and expensive fad advocated by a few individuals whose ideas are unworthy of attention'.

Despite this Musgrave went on to try to make the new service work, and experimented with bomb-dropping during September 1914. But lacking the muscle of men such as Churchill, his efforts were largely in vain. He eventually returned to the infantry and served with distinction on the Western Front. He was wounded in August 1916 and sent to England to recuperate. Returning to active service, he was killed in action in June 1918.

Because of the work of men like Herbert Musgrave, the Royal Flying Corps had, despite itself, managed to develop some sort of grounding in the type of work it would later routinely undertake. However, such was the opposition to it from vested interests and conservative self-servers, that it had no one at its helm, as did the RNAS, to mould it properly.

Not that its services were not exploited. Despite continuing enmity, it soon found itself with additional tasks to perform. In August 1912, the RFC Military Wing was informed that its duties would now include the protection of docks and other vital objectives but, even by June 1914, it was unable to present a plan for a home defence establishment. Its preparations assumed that in time of war, all its available squadrons would accompany their Army to France. Not until a week before war broke out did it have anything approaching a policy, when it presented a draft proposal for the establishment of six Home Defence Squadrons with two in Scotland, one in the Humber and one each at Orfordness, Dover and Gosport, some 162 aircraft in all. In the words of Seely himself... 'we are what you might call, behind...'.

CHAPTER 2

AEROPLANES MAY COME OVER THIS COUNTRY

When the tiny British Expeditionary Force (BEF) steamed to France in August 1914, this 'contemptibly small' Army as the German Kaiser called it, was accompanied by an equally diminutive air force. As anticipated, the Royal Flying Corps was expected to accompany the Army to war, and it took practically every man and machine it could muster with it – some four squadrons, totalling sixty-three aircraft of various types.

A motley collection of various aircraft was left behind, a force which, even to the less discerning, was clearly unsuited to the task of Home Defence.

Consequently Lord Kitchener, then Britain's redoubtable Minister for War, was left with the thorny problem of how to bridge the gap left in Home Defence. The Cabinet keenly eyed the Flying Wing of the Navy, an organized, competent body which offered a plausible deterrent to possible enemy attack. When the War Cabinet met on 3 September 1914, Kitchener raised the issue with Churchill who, despite his achievements in helping to create the RNAS, was lukewarm about the idea and freely admitted that he could not promise to do any more than his best with the resources at his disposal.

> I carefully stated that the Admiralty could not be responsible for Home Defence, but could only be responsible for doing the best possible with the material available.

He appreciated that Home Defence was now a pressing issue. The 'Zeppelin Mania' which swept much of the country during 1912-13 was the result of numerous alleged airship sightings. These, plus frequent reports of the developments in the performance of the machine, convinced many that an attack of some kind was perfectly feasible. Indeed, one of the first memos issued by Churchill was one which dealt with the need to take into account the behaviour of the civilian population should air raids materialize, and to ensure they knew what to do in the event of an attack. He also anticipated the need for coordination of the emergency services in order to maximize their resources.

He also appreciated that simply stationing his squadrons along the south coast to lie in wait for the enemy was inadequate. He advocated instead that a more proactive and aggressive policy be adopted against the Germans; one which would take the fight to the enemy rather than allow them the initiative. Churchill sent instructions to Commander Charles Samson RN, commander of the RNAS at Dunkirk, then still in Allied hands, to establish a forward air base from which the Zeppelins could be attacked before they set off on their flights to England. On 5 September, he wrote to the Board of the Admiralty, suggesting that:

> A strong overseas force of aeroplanes [be established] to deny the French and Belgian coasts to the enemy's aircraft, and to attack all Zeppelins and air bases or temporary air bases which it may be sought to establish, and which are in reach.

He also wrote to Prince Louis of Battenburg, the First Sea Lord, and Captain Murray Sueter, who now commanded the RNAS, with detailed plans for his forward base at Dunkirk. Such was the eccentric nature of the plan in many observers' eyes, that the entire exercise was soon dubbed the 'Dunkirk Circus'. The circus embarked upon its campaign as soon as it was organized, carrying out a number of combined reconnaissance and bombing raids on the enemy. They received their first endorsement early on in the enterprise when the British Consul at Dunkirk confirmed that the German reaction to these incursions was verging on panic.

Throughout the second half of September, Captain E L Gerrard and a squadron of four machines had been stationed at Ostend, making plans for an attack on the airship sheds at Dusseldorf and Cologne. Churchill was urging Gerrard to get on with the job, eager as ever to see one of his plans realized. Eventually, after much waiting and careful preparation, four aircraft took off on 22 September, Gerrard himself and Lieutenant Charles Collett flying to Dusseldorf, Lieutenant Commander Spencer-Grey and Flight Commander Marix to Cologne.

At first, this pioneering stab at the enemy was not regarded as wholly inspiring. Only Collett managed to locate the objective, a series of elusive sheds, which were shrouded in thick industrial smog. The young pilot dropped three bombs from a height of just 400 feet. The first fell short of the shed and exploded harmlessly, the other two hit the target but failed to explode. However, 'the surprise was complete',

Gerrard wrote to the Admiralty,

> ...and the numerous Germans in the vicinity ran in all directions. The moral effect must have been considerable. A great many people must have been disturbed by the sound of our engines close over their heads.

It seemed that indeed, the effect of this quite unexpected intrusion had been considerable. As the people of Venice had discovered over half a century earlier, the shock of being attacked from above was a chastening experience. Fisher wrote to Churchill, confirming that the raids were causing 'real panic'.

But the ever-advancing German legions were fast closing on the Channel ports and threatening continued British operations as, once the ports were seized, the forward bases would have to be abandoned and the strategy along with them. Despite this, Churchill sanctioned another attack from airfields outside Antwerp on 8 October. Suffering a two-day delay after being hampered by enemy activity and poor weather conditions, the attack did not fare well. Spencer-Grey later admitted to the Admiralty:

> On arriving at Cologne I found thick mist... I came down to 600 feet, failed to locate them... I considered the best point of attack would be in the main station in the middle of town where I saw many trains drawn, so let fall my two bombs in this...

Marix had better luck than his comrade and managed to locate the shed. He dropped his bombs from 600 feet and achieved a direct hit on the target which sent sheets of flame 500 feet into the sky.

Meanwhile, his forces were concentrating on keeping one step ahead of the advancing Germans, and operations finally ceased when Antwerp fell. The day that the British pilots opened their attacks, the Germans began a sustained bombardment of the city. Several shells hit the aerodrome, wrecking parked aircraft. Orders were issued to evacuate and the following day the Germans marched triumphantly into the city.

Arguably, such an energetic pre-emptive offensive against the airships by attacking their sheds could have achieved tremendous results had it been sustained. Although their stepping off points had been lost, the strategy could have continued from other suitable bases. But Churchill's maverick ventures had long been frowned upon both by his peers and by his superiors. The success of his operations was being jealously watched by Lord French, who disliked the fact that the Navy was succeeding so well having taken over home defence from the Army. Consequently, on 14 November, Churchill received a terse note from the Commander-in-Chief of the British Expeditionary Force, stating that he intended the RFC in France to assume responsibility for bombing airship sheds. He went on to state that he personally would decide 'the times at which attacks on Zeppelin sheds should be delivered'. Churchill was deeply disturbed by this development, not least because it indicated damaging interference in a clearly successful strategy. He warned gravely, however, that the best way of preventing an airship raid had been proven to be by bombing it in its shed. Trying to shoot it down once over the UK would prove to be a far more difficult, if not impossible, proposition.

On the day Churchill received French's note, a further raid had been planned against the German hydrogen factory and Zeppelin sheds at Friedrichshafen. He had no intention of calling it off.

It was a particularly audacious project, secretly transporting four aircraft earmarked for the task in crates to a site from whence they could set off against the target. Bad weather prevented the attack from actually taking place until 21 November, when one aircraft crashed on take-off. The three remaining aircraft reached the target and, despite intense ground fire, dropped nine bombs on and around the objective. One pilot, Commander Briggs, fell victim to machine-gun fire, crashed and was captured. But his two comrades, Flight Commander Babington and Flight Lieutenant Sippe, returned home safely, and on 22 November were awarded the *Legion d'Honneur* by their French allies.

Contemporary accounts suggested that the attack had not only taken the Germans by surprise, but caused widespread panic. A Swiss engineer had witnessed the attack from a nearby hotel. He later reported to a Swiss newspaper how '...the bombs made the town tremble, and the military officers lost their heads and gave contradictory orders to the troops...'. The Swiss Government claimed that their neutrality had been violated when the pilots flew over their air space. They also claimed that a Swiss national was killed in the attack. Churchill, far from being chastened, remained pointedly unrepentant about the entire episode and is reported to have suggested that the Swiss Government be told to 'go and milk their cows'. Nevertheless, questions were asked in Parliament and serious misgivings resurfaced about Churchill's handling of home defence responsibilities.

While Churchill was being admonished, the Germans were beginning to take advantage of the greater scope afforded them following the fall of Antwerp.

Their aircraft, limited in range and performance, had previously little hope of reaching the British coastline. The capture of the city and the surrounding airfields had greatly reduced the range between themselves and the UK and subsequently made air operations over the English Channel more practical.

Abortive attempts had been made two months earlier, but now the Germans were in earnest. Three daylight forays on 21, 24 and 25 December were staged against the UK, the first two against Dover and the third against London. The attacks, carried out by seaplanes, were of no great military consequence, but they were significant, demonstrating that the defences closer to home were far weaker than those Churchill had established nearer to the airship sheds. (Ironically, some of the machines were constructed at Friedrichshafen.) The lesson was clear; if the Germans could get as far as the English coast, it would only be a matter of time before they possessed machines capable of penetrating even further inland.

Subsequent British reports revealed what was later to be all too clear – that the aged Home Defence machines detailed to foil these attacks were quite incapable of doing so. Furthermore, the folly of letting the enemy come to them rather than the other way round, was graphically demonstrated during the night of 19-20 January 1915, when two Navy airships crossed over the Norfolk coast and the ground defences proved incapable of any effective reply.

Sorties were mounted by Captain Mansfield and Quartermaster Sergeant Chaney, and Second Lieutenant Pike and First Air Mechanic Shaw - both crews flying Vickers Gunbus aircraft. Neither managed to identify the raiders, thwarted by the darkness and thick cloud. Chaney's machine even suffered the added indignity of having come under 'friendly fire' as it made its final descent.

One airship claimed to have dropped a parachute flare and a number of explosive and incendiary bombs on Great Yarmouth, whilst the other, having got lost, reported dropping bombs on King's Lynn. In fact they only succeeded in harassing a small group of villages, but the real damage was done in revealing the woeful state of the defences and proving there was indeed little or nothing to prevent a more concerted attack being made against the UK.

Perhaps it should have come as no surprise that they were so poorly disposed. Churchill had also been saddled with organizing the anti-aircraft defences that were placed around London. He appreciated that this would be a vital element in his plans, but resources were typically lacking. Only twelve 3-inch guns, thirty-eight 1-pounder pom-poms, and 150 3-pounder and 6-pounder Hotchkiss quick-firing guns were available or in the process of being made so, for the defence of the capital. Many of these had been commandeered from reserves, and the pom-poms had been hastily converted so that they could fire vertically. The issue of whether the capital warranted defending at the expense of other possible targets was also raised. London might have been the heart of the empire, and to have it severely damaged might have affected morale, but it was strongly argued by many, Churchill among them, that there were many dockyards, oil storage depots, magazines and airship sheds which demanded their share of the available guns too.

A compromise was reached through which the vital targets outside London could be allocated guns by having London itself carefully limited to a so-called 'vital-area'. This was understandably the major political and military headquarters buildings principally taking in the area around Whitehall. Here, a relatively concentrated array of anti-aircraft guns and searchlights were stationed. As more guns became available, however, the extent of the vital area could be increased further eastwards towards the City of London and south of the Thames. The principal drawback of this plan was that attacking aircraft could only be engaged once they were actually above the target. There was no means by which they could be effectively fired upon en route to London.

Because a properly coordinated strategy was still dogged by politics and rivalry, Churchill also needed to resolve a severe manpower shortage created by his expansion plans . He knew he would get short shrift if he asked the Army for men, so in an effort to circumvent this, he formed his own corps under the command of Captain L Stanfield and manned it with volunteers drawn from City and university bodies. Furthermore, he established emergency landing fields to increase the speed of response to enemy incursions. This was known rather wordily as the Anti-Aircraft Corps, Royal Naval Volunteer Reserve, and the men drafted in to crew the guns were effectively sworn in as Special Constables 'for the duration'. A more mobile force was also established, called the Eastern Mobile Air Defence Force consisting of hastily adapted lorries, mounted with machine guns and searchlights, commissioned to speed to likely areas where airships were reported and try to either shoot them down or force them high to spoil their bombing aim.

To hamper the intruders, a limited 'blackout' was introduced, by which street lights were to be obscured or extinguished completely, specifically to confound the enemy navigators seeking to gain a fix on familiar landmarks. In addition, areas previously blacked out by virtue of being parks and open spaces were dotted with illuminations to give the impression that they contained buildings. Local authorities would have a large degree of autonomy in deciding the measures they would take; along the south coast for instance, work was done to reduce lighting and break up the familiar pattern of the coastline.

The *Kriegsmarine* meanwhile persisted in taking the war to the British homeland. 1915 brought the much vaunted 'Year of the Zeppelin', with some nineteen airship attacks being launched between April and October.

They began modestly with attacks on coastal shipping in February and March 1915. Then on the night of 14 April, Navy Zeppelin L9, under the command of *Kapitänleutnant* Heinrich Mathy, carried out an attack on the north-east of England, hitting a variety of targets including Wallsend, but with very limited results. The following night, Humberside was the target, but again the results were negligible.

On 16 April, a daylight raid by an Albatross BII was mounted against north Kent which provoked fourteen sorties from the ground. It succeeded in spreading incendiaries in the Canterbury area but caused neither casualties nor much damage. Not one of the British machines got anywhere near it. On the night of 29-30 April, Army Zeppelin LZ38 launched a raid over East Anglia, but no casualties were reported, although a very modest amount of damage was done. Southend was the target on the night of 9-10 May, when LZ38 again crossed the English coastline hoping to improve on its previous performance. On this occasion one person was killed and two others injured with some structural damage done. Disappointed once again with his airship's performance, LZ38's captain, *Hauptmann* Erich Linnarz, led another raid, this time against Kent, on the night of 16-17 May. Flight Lieutenant Bigsworth flying his Avro 504B, found fame that night as the first defender to engage in combat with an intruder. Bigsworth pursued the enemy until, 10,000 feet above Ostend, he managed to gain enough height to release four 20lb bombs into the fabric of the airship. One crewman died in the resulting fire. Although badly ruptured and with its starboard propeller out of action, the vessel nevertheless made it home.

A couple of minor attacks were followed by a bigger effort on the night of 31 May-1 June, when LZ38 reached London and thirty explosive and ninety incendiary bombs spread from Stepney to

Leytonstone, killing seven people, injuring another thirty-five and causing damage estimated at over £18,000. This attack, however, prompted some reinforcement of the gun defences, when Blackheath, West Ham and Finsbury gun stations were issued with an additional 3-inch gun apiece.

Night raids during the rest of June were shared between London and the north-east of England, again exposing the woeful inadequacies of Home Defence. There was one notable exception; on the night of 6 June Flight Sub Lieutenant R. Warneford RN became the first pilot to shoot down an enemy airship. His victim was LZ37, which he pursued all the way to Belgium before dropping six 20lb bombs onto his quarry. The explosion was so great that Warneford himself barely escaped death in the backblast. He was awarded the Victoria Cross, only the second to an airman but, ten days later, he was killed in a flying accident.

There were further raids shared between northern and southern England, a night raid on 15-16 June on Tyneside which killed eighteen people, and a small daylight raid on Harwich on 3 July, which resulted in no casualties. Fourteen sorties between them in these two raids resulted in no successes for the defenders.

Another night raid followed on 9-10 August. It was mounted by four of the German Navy's latest airships, among them L13 commanded by *Kapitänleutnant* Heinrich Mathy, and had been planned as a major attack against London. Instead, confusion and farce was the outcome, bombs scattered all over the place, even as far as the Humber, but none anywhere near the target. Only the Home Defence performance was as lamentable. Another repeat performance on the night of 12-13 August, but most of the same players, was almost as risible, mechanical problems and poor navigation reducing the raid to the level of a farce. Nevertheless, there were seven killed and twenty-three injured on the ground when people were unfortunate enough to find themselves in the path of an errant bomb.

The night of 17-18 August saw yet another concerted effort against London, but of four airships dispatched, just one got anywhere near the target. Of the others, the usual spread of bombs over a wide area, mostly unconnected with the target, was all there was to show for the night's work, along with ten fatalities and forty-eight injuries. The Home Defence performance again left much to be desired.

Three airships set off on the night of 7-8 September, hoping to improve on their comrades' record. They too would have little to boast about when they returned home, as only one machine got anywhere remotely near London, whilst her colleagues became lost. The result, eighteen deaths and twenty-eight injuries.

On 8-9 September, London and Skinningrove in the north east of England were targeted. Only the London raid was pushed home, leaving twenty-six dead. This raid was the first in which the newly developed 660lb bomb was used by the Germans. It fell in Bartholomew Close, near to the hospital. The airship, L13, commanded by Heinrich Mathy, returned home unharmed, although somewhat perturbed by the ground fire from London, as evidenced by his report after the attack in which he warned that, 'The AA fire was so extensive that in future, with a clear sky, airships will only be able to remain for a short time over the city'.

Another attempt was made against London on 11-12 September by a single Army Zeppelin, but she only managed to get lost and dropped a few bombs where her captain thought they might be able to do some harm. The following night was the same story, when the intruder became lost and only managed to drop some bombs over East Anglia. Only 13 September, a daylight raid on Dover by a float plane killed two people and injured six more, and that night three Navy Zeppelins tried their hand at the capital but were again foiled by bad weather and a chance anti-aircraft shell damaging one of the intruders.

Another month passed before the night of 13-14 October saw five Navy Zeppelins launched with London as the target and some bombs did actually find Woolwich, the Strand and Limehouse, but others fell as wide of the mark as Yarmouth and even Folkestone.

Meanwhile the raids were at least giving the defences an opportunity to hone their skills. New measures were being investigated to thwart the airships, including aerial darts and petrol bombs, designed to be dropped from aircraft and penetrate the airships' skins and ignite the gas within. Some advances were also being made with the interception of the airships' wireless transmissions, promising to provide some advance warning of their approach. Churchill's tenure as First Lord however, and consequently his measures to combat the enemy air threat, were to come to an abrupt halt.

The Dardanelles Campaign had been conceived by the Allies as the best means to open a supply route to the Russian Front through Turkish territory via the Black Sea. A few months of futile slaughter had ground the campaign into a blood-soaked halt at such beach heads as Anzac Cove, Suvla Bay and Cape Helles. Although the decision to mount the campaign was a joint one made by the War Cabinet, Churchill's particularly strong advocacy of the project made him the ideal scapegoat. Tainted by his involvement in the disaster, and harassed by many enemies in the Admiralty, War Office and Parliament, Churchill was forced to resign his post and join the back benches. Soon after he forsook the relative safety of the Commons and sailed to France with the rank of Colonel to command a battalion on the Western Front.

He was replaced as First Lord by his very antithesis, Arthur J Balfour, who was convinced that every problem, no matter how complex and how swiftly it needed resolution, could be referred to a committee for detailed analysis, during which time it would probably resolve itself. His stance should have been partly offset by the reasonably healthy bequest left to him by Churchill. His efforts and those of his staff left a system in place whereby the moment a hostile airship was sighted, the alarm would be given and aeroplanes would be sortied. Those on the coast, though not able to rise quickly enough to attack airships on their incoming flights, would be ready to meet them upon their return. A variety of anti-aircraft weapons, consisting primarily of 3-inch guns, 6-pounders and pom poms were deployed at gun stations. Subject to demands made elsewhere, their number would fluctuate between 70 and 100. In addition, the defence of London was assigned a separate Command to that of the rest of the country, and was placed under the control of Admiral Sir Percy Scott. He radically updated his armoury and increased the number of guns under his command, as well as improving coordination and cooperation between the guns and the aircraft defending London. This was no panacea, but it was a step in the right direction.

The new First Lord, however, went even further than French's earlier order restricting attacks on the airship sheds and banned them entirely. He even allowed himself to be convinced that the best way to tackle a German airship was with a British airship, and sanctioned the development of the 'R' Series of vessels which, it was argued, could perform duel anti-airship and anti-submarine duties. Churchill was virulently opposed to these experiments, later insisting that one airship cost as much as 100 aeroplanes and stood significantly less chance than an aircraft of intercepting and shooting them down. He argued for a unified command for Britain's air forces and in June he pushed harder for the creation of an Air Department. The then Prime Minister, the timid Herbert Asquith, remained unmoved, but with airship raids on the UK mainland growing steadily, Lord Kitchener was gravely concerned. The RNAS, now burdened with convoy escort duties, following a dramatic growth of the U-boat menace, was stretched to the limit. It seemed to make sense to investigate the possibility of the Army resuming the Home Defence role and the Director-General of Military Aeronautics, Major General Henderson, was asked to make the necessary arrangements as soon as possible. But, he conceded, it would be early 1916 before he could assume the task, and in the meantime the Navy would have to do the best they could. This was agreed, and on 10 February 1916, the handover was made official:

1. The War Office approve the following recommendations in regards to the allocation of responsibility for the Anti Aircraft Defence of the whole of the United Kingdom outside London which have been made by a Joint Admiralty and War Office Conference, and have for some time been in practical operations, namely:

(a) The Navy to undertake to deal with all hostile aircraft attempting to reach this country, whilst the Army undertake to deal with all such aircraft which reach these shores.

(b) All defence arrangements on land to be undertaken by the Army which will also provide the aeroplanes required to work with the Home Defence troops and protect garrisons and vulnerable areas, and the flying stations required to enable their aircraft to undertake these duties.

(c) The Navy to provide the aircraft required to cooperate with and assist their Fleets and Coast Patrol Flotillas and to watch the Coast, and to organise and maintain such Flying Stations as are required to enable their aircraft to undertake these duties. The two services to cooperate so as to prevent unnecessary duplication.

2. The responsibility for the anti aircraft defence of London, details of the transfer of which from the Admiralty to the War Office are being worked out, to rest with the War Office from Wednesday the 16 February 1916 inclusive.

3. Having regard to the great importance of the munitions work concentrated in the Woolwich district, anti aircraft defence of this area should take precedence over the rest of London, and the existing defences should be strengthened as soon as possible.

With this 'thankless task' now back in his portfolio, Lord French, who had done so much to obstruct Churchill's abilities to carry out the job, took up his post as Commander-in-Chief Home Forces after being displaced from the command of the British Expeditionary Force. An ex-cavalry officer, he exuded an image of stuffy, old-fashioned stoicism, contrasting sharply with the energy and vitality Churchill brought to the job. The main reason he had been relieved of the command of the BEF was that he lacked initiative in the face of difficult decisions. During the critical first few weeks of August 1914, his failure to grasp the nature of modern warfare almost led to his Army being totally annihilated. He not only demonstrated a lack of energy, which so shocked his French allies, he showed a tendency to cry wolf that would bode ill for him in his new role. He was apparently assigned to home defence as a consolation, allowing him to save face, speaking volumes for the low priority being given to the issue of home defence.

The New Year brought with it fresh raids, small and insignificant at first, but increasing in tempo until, on the night of 31 March 1916, both the German Navy and Army mounted separate raids. The Army chose to attack East Anglia, whilst the Navy opted for the capital. The Germans suffered from a similar lack of cooperation as the British, so both attacks set off completely independently of the other, and despite the impressive array of vessels which headed for the UK that night, ten in all, the enterprise was something of a failure. Two airships returned with engine-trouble and three due to the adverse weather conditions; of the five which proceeded, one was shot down and the others scattered their bombs all over the south-east of England. Subsequent attacks also failed to bring the raiders tangible results, although they were persevered with throughout the following months. It was a double-edged sword however. The raids were taking place, so by implication they warranted Home Defence measures to be taken, but because they were so inconclusive, they failed to convince some people that they were serious enough to deserve more than token resistance.

Meanwhile, the lack of coordination between the British services once again brought further demands for amalgamation.

The cry now was 'Independent Air Force': one free to operate outside the restrictions of either the Army or Navy. Asquith smarted at such a drastic move, but did concede the formation of an Air Committee. But the committee foundered soon after it was formed. Its chairman, Lord Derby, realizing it was a waste of time, resigned. He knew that reform, through tinkering with the existing state of affairs, was useless.

Increasingly, voices were raised against the hapless situation in which the country found itself. On 22 March the newly elected MP, Pemberton Billing, castigated the Government, roundly stating that, 'our present policy in the air is one that reflects credit neither on our government nor on those officers whose duty it has been to prepare, look forward, and to endeavour to gain for this country supremacy in the air'. He insisted that an Air Board with executive powers be formed. Instead, Harold Tennant, the Under Secretary of State for War, announced the formation of another committee, this time under Lord Curzon, with the following Terms of Reference:

(a) The Board shall be free to discuss matters of general policy in relation to the air, and in particular, combined operations of the Naval and Military Air Services, and to make recommendations to the Admiralty and War Office thereon;

(b) The Board shall be free to discuss and make recommendations upon the types of machine required for the Naval and Military Air Services;

(c) If either the Admiralty or War Office decline to act upon the recommendations of the Board, the President shall be free to refer the question to the War Committee;

(d) The Board shall be charged with the task of organising and co-ordinating the supply of material and preventing competition between the two departments;

(e) The Board shall organise a complete system for the interchange of ideas upon air problems between the Services and such related bodies as the Naval Board of Invention and Research, the Inventions Branch of the Ministry of Munitions, the Advisory Committee on Aeronautics, the National Physical Laboratory etc.

To men like Churchill and Pemberton Billing, the phrase 'free to discuss' said it all. To them this was merely another short term compromise. Churchill warned that without teeth, the board would be little more than a paper tiger, and so it proved. He also took the opportunity to remind the House of his own achievements when responsible for defending London, reminding them of his own strategy of attacking the airships in their sheds, and thus preventing them from getting to the UK in the first place, pointedly comparing his own efforts with those currently in vogue.

He insisted the only realistic way of stopping the airship raids lay with a return to his strategy of bombing them in their sheds. He insisted that under his command,

...our aeroplane defence had restricted Zeppelin attacks to a few nights in certain months, and even those attacks could only be delivered erring and almost blindfold.

His policy had been abandoned despite its success and he had been personally vindicated in his decision to undertake them. 'Why then', he demanded to know, 'has it been discontinued?'

But Churchill's personal integrity was not an issue. The pressing question was how to overcome the internecine rivalry between the Army and Navy, stop the bickering and get to grips with the task in hand. Asquith had palpably failed in this aim – perhaps someone else might galvanize the various interest groups and finally take the country out of this stalemate.

That opportunity came when Asquith finally accepted that he simply was not up to the job of wartime prime minister and resigned in December 1916. Succeeded by Lloyd George, the fiery Welshman's reputation was well-deserved and few were under any illusion that he would suffer fools gladly or tolerate power groups trying to secure their own interests before those of the common good.

He was not behind his desk at 10 Downing Street long, before he pushed through the *New Ministries and Secretaries Act*. Among its provisions it created a new Air Board, but unlike its predecessors it was to have real powers. The man appointed to run the new department was well-suited to running such an office, Weetman Dickinson Pearson , or as he was known from December 1916 after his elevation to the peerage, Lord Cowdray.

He was the founding father of S Pearson & Son Ltd which, by 1900, was employing upwards of 20,000 men all around the world including South America, China and the UK, engaged in huge civil engineering projects including dock and harbour construction as well as major domestic projects such as the Blackwall Tunnel in London. His energy and industry was just what Lloyd George needed and he was to repay the Prime Minister's confidence. He pursued his terms of reference with determination and allowed neither the Admiralty nor the War Office a veto over his intention to rationalize the design and supply of warplanes and,

>...be definitely responsible for allocating our available aerial resources between the Admiralty and War Office...

Despite Lloyd George's support there was still inevitable opposition. Lord Jellicoe made the point that:

>The policy of making the Admiralty dependant upon another

department for the design and supply of aircraft would be disastrous.

But the Prime Minister was deaf to their objections and went even further. He dictated that the Ministry of Munitions, the War Office and the Admiralty, meet to discuss how to work the arrangement to the best advantage.

It seemed that Lloyd George's firmness was having some effect for, on 19 January 1917, Lord Cowdray was able to report that,

> ...today, the four departments concerned, Admiralty, War Office, Munitions and this Board, have arrived at an agreement as to their varied functions in connection with the Air Service. I am thankful that I can thus report that the draft charter, which will shortly be submitted to you for approval, will be an agreed document.

The Controller of Aeronautical Supplies, whose portfolio was held by William Weir, proved one of the most successful. Aircraft production became the biggest beneficiary of the creation of the Air Board. He rationalized the different numbers and models of aircraft constructed, so that larger volumes could be built of the better types. By April 1917 the new system resulted in two-and-a-half-times as many aero-engines being delivered than in 1916, rising to three-and-a-half-times by July and August. On 9 June, Lord Cowdray reported that as many aircraft were being built per week than were being manufactured per month the previous year. He added that he was confident that ten times as many would be built by the end of that year, than had been built the previous year.

⸻ ◈ ⸻

While the means of production was being reorganized, so too were the Home Defence Squadrons. By January 1917 there were eleven in place, with one in reserve under the command of Lieutenant General T C R Higgins.

Higgins seemed the ideal man to thrust the new organization forward. He had seen service in the Royal Navy and then fought in the last stages of the Boer War in 1900, after transferring to the Army. He was among the first contingents of the BEF in 1914, but was wounded early on. Typical of many on both sides who were wounded, he transferred to the RFC and eventually took on his current responsibilities.

The defence of London was the responsibility of numbers 37, 39, 50 and 78 squadrons, each with a headquarters airfield linked by telephone to one of the seven Warning Control Centres and three satellite airfields. 37 Squadron was assigned the task of patrolling Essex and the approaches to London along that route. Its headquarters was at Woodham Mortimer, with satellite fields at Goldhanger, Rochford and Stow Maries; 39 Squadron had its headquarters at Woodford, with satellite fields at Hainault, North Weald and Sutton's Farm (Hornchurch). 50 Squadron was to patrol Kent, with its headquarters at Harrietsham and satellites at Bekesbourne, Detling and Throwley. 78 Squadron was to patrol the south coast, its headquarters was at Hove, with Chiddingstone Causeway, Telscombe Cliffs and Gosport serving as satellites. With the exception of 78 Squadron, which was in contact with the Portsmouth Warning Controller, all the squadrons were in communication with the London Warning Controller.

Their allocation of machines however, still left much to be desired. Despite Cowdray's best efforts to produce fine machines, few of these were seeing Home Defence duties. The squadrons on the Western Front were kept supplied with the best aircraft, whilst those at home were left with the old, slow B.E. type aircraft.

Now that the Germans were sending floatplanes and, more recently, faster fighter aircraft to harass the coast, the tired old B.E.s were to find themselves even more outperformed and outgunned. Requests by the Home Defence for faster and better machines were, however, not well received in France. Clearly, the top brass argued, the Western Front was where the real fighting was taking place, a view wholly endorsed by Major General Hugh Trenchard who assumed command of the RFC in France in July 1916.

A momentous victory on the night of 2-3 September 1916 appeared to entirely vindicate the view that the airship menace was now passed, when Lieutenant W Leefe Robinson shot down SL11 over Cuffley. Leefe Robinson's achievement occurred on a night when the enemy mounted a joint Army-Navy assault on London which could have been devastating. In all, sixteen airships were allocated to the raid, but ferocious winds and freezing rain scattered the force, with only one reaching the capital. It was a complete disaster and one compounded by the exploits of the young pilot who chanced upon the bulk of SL11 illuminated by searchlights.

He was flying above the airship, and proceeded to descend to a height from which he could get a good shot, firing a lethal mixture of Brock and Pomeroy incendiary bullets along its underside. There was no apparent result at first, so he fired another fusillade along her side, a tactic he tried a third time, positioning himself behind her, concentrating an entire drum on one spot. Several seconds passed during which it appeared still nothing had happened; then a light glow developed, growing further until the airship was a massive ball of flame. Slowly it fell earthwards, gradually collapsing in on itself until it crashed at Cuffley where it finally burnt itself out after two hours. Within forty-eight hours Leefe Robinson was awarded the Victoria Cross.

This epic triumph of a David over a Goliath served to convince many that the airship menace was indeed, over. Further activity by the Germans during the remainder of the month did little to contradict this belief.

Leefe Robinson's achievement was repeated twice, once on the night of 23-24 September, when Second Lieutenant Frederick Sowrey destroyed L32 over Billericay in Essex, and again on the night of 1-2 October, when airship L31 was picked out by searchlights over Potters Bar and observed by a number of pilots, including Second Lieutenant Wulstan Tempest. The pilot, experiencing some difficulty with his machine's fuel pump, fired two bursts above and then, positioning himself below, emptied the drum into its belly. He then saw it, 'begin to go red inside like an enormous Chinese lantern', at which moment it was engulfed in fire, and sent crashing into a field near the town. This second victory was indeed the death-knell for the airships, although it would be a while before the Germans accepted the fact. The defences had carried the day it seemed; the 'Zepps' were a spent force and this had been brought to a successful conclusion.

Trenchard had apparently been completely vindicated. Or had he? For on the morning of 28 November *Leutnant* Walter Ilges and *Deck Offizier* Paul Brandt decided it was perfect weather for a jaunt to London and back. Taking aloft a handful of 22lb bombs they set off from Marierkerke near Ostend, finding themselves over Central London shortly before noon. They dropped twenty-two bombs between the Brompton Road and Victoria Station before making their escape. They nearly got away Scott free, but their venture ended in capture when their machine developed engine trouble and they were forced to land near Boulogne at 3.15 pm.

The pair's jaunt across the English Channel once again highlighted the inadequacy of the defences. The Admiralty Air Department was not informed of the enemy until 12.34 pm and the Home Defence Wing failed to order sorties for another ten minutes. A further fifteen minutes elapsed before planes were airborne, by which time the invaders were well on their way. Hardly surprising, therefore, that harsh criticism was levelled at the authorities.

Hard-liner Pemberton Billing was livid at the humiliating slight the Government had permitted. He also warned that,

> In the next summer we shall experience raids of a much more serious character than the Zeppelin raids. Aeroplanes may come over this country... at night and at 15,000 or 20,000 feet they may drop their bombs and get back before we know where we are.

However, aerial armadas failed to appear. Indeed, the failure of the Germans to launch a massive assault gave further credence to Trenchard's argument that Home Defence resources be reallocated to him. No further raids were experienced in 1916, and in February 1917 only small-scale attacks materialized.

On the night of 16-17 March 1917, an airship appeared over London. By making weight economies, the Germans were developing airships capable of achieving heights of 20,000 feet or more. That night, five so-called 'heightfinders' were sent against London. However, one distinct disadvantage of achieving more height was identified in this attack, as the airships were more prone to strong winds. It was these, rather than the home defences which prevented the attack from developing into anything serious. For their part however, the British did succeed in jamming the raiders' radios, and they consequently became lost. The home defences managed seventeen sorties, but with no success, again mainly due to thick cloud. The improved airships performance went unnoticed by the defenders as a result of the strong winds, and the negative results of the attack further lulled them into thinking that the threat was over.

The insatiable demands of warfare over the Western Front were consuming men and machines at an alarming rate. Already on 6 February the Air Board had been persuaded by the Army that thirty-six Home Defence pilots be sent to France to crew two night-flying squadrons then in the process of being formed. Later, another three front-line squadrons were proposed (to be formed out of Home Defence establishment). Although it was agreed as only a 'temporary measure' it was clear they would stay in France unless something very drastic occurred over England.

—————⊰⊱◉⊰⊱—————

Once in France, however, the fate of the Home Defence airmen was as good as sealed.

Long since dispensed with simply as aerial platforms for reconnaissance, the aeroplane had proved its mettle and established itself as an indispensable tool. From early 1915 onwards, aeroplanes had been seen in increasingly aggressive roles, and once dog fights developed in the skies, both sides searched feverishly to gain the advantage over the enemy. Adversaries such as Baron von Richthofen, and his 'Flying Circus' were spawned, matched by British pilots like Cecil Lewis, James McCudden and Albert Ball.

Major General Hugh Trenchard brought to his command of the RFC in France the philosophy of attack, attack and attack again. Before he came to command the RFC, he demonstrated his doctrine when, at the Battle of Neuve Chapelle in March 1915 and in command of an RFC Wing, he committed his forces heavily despite sustaining crippling losses.

When he first came to command the RFC, he was instructed to support the forthcoming Somme Offensive. To perform this task he had twenty-seven squadrons, consisting of 421 machines, with 316 in reserve. Their role was manifold: scouting, to assist in the ranging of the field barrage and, during the offensive itself, to cover the infantry advance and prevent the German air force from mounting effective attacks on them as they trudged to their deaths across no man's land. They would also be needed to attack the enemy's rear logistical areas, disrupting their supply lines and the movement of reinforcements. Such operations would require a vast amount of resources, men and machines which would be used up at an alarming rate; so much so that as the fighting dragged on, a further eight squadrons would be drawn into the fray. Before he had completed his brief, many more machines were destroyed and hundreds of crewmen killed. With such an insatiable appetite, it is hardly surprising that he called upon the 'idlers' at home to pitch in and help.

These constant demands worried Field Marshal French, who had found himself with not only a distinctly unwelcome job, but one that afforded little respect by his peers. On 2 March 1917, with his Home Defence Establishment whittled down from 130 to 71 pilots, he told the Army Council angrily that whilst he appreciated the need for men overseas, his own needs also had to be met. And at the rate they were going he would not be able to carry out his own tasks.

Pointedly, he was running out of men and aircraft. But to his detractors, far from suffering a famine of resources, he was enjoying a feast in lieu of the amount of work he was having to undertake. During April in France 316 RFC pilots and observers were killed or captured and 224 aircraft destroyed. The following month another 115 were killed.

And it was not only airmen who were viewed as being under utilized in England. The men manning the anti-aircraft guns were also eyed greedily as likely replacements for the losses being sustained in France, instead of anticipating raiders that never came. A meeting was held at the War Office on 6 March in which several resource-sharing measures were considered. Their deliberations resulted in one of the most bizarre orders ever to be issued when, ultimately it was decided there would be a complete firing ban on all anti-aircraft guns except those on the coast. It was somehow believed that this measure would help to alleviate the effects of the demands of the Western Front, so the following order was subsequently issued:

> No aeroplanes or seaplanes, <u>even if recognised as hostile</u>, will be fired at, either by day or night, except by those anti aircraft guns situated near the Restricted Coast Area which are specially detailed for the purpose.

The British, now facing more sophisticated forms of attack in the shape of aircraft, saw the meagre resources assigned to confront that threat whittled to the point of almost complete impotence.

⸺⸺◦⦿◦⸺⸺

For some months now, spies had been leaking news of German work on an aircraft far larger than any seen before. Evidence of this development was actually secured when a large machine was shot down, or crash-landed, in February 1917.

The Gotha was similar in many ways to the Handley Page bomber being developed by the British which, it was hoped, would help break the stalemate and lead to the 'final push' General Haig had long hoped for.

Whatever warnings may have been forthcoming, and in spite of the fact the British were working on their own technologies for similar ends, no specific preparations were undertaken to anticipate, accommodate or thwart another form of attack upon the UK. Resources both on the ground and in the air were almost non-existent. All that stood between the Metropolis and disaster, was a thin line of young men and their flimsy machines.

CHAPTER 3

THE PRESENT FORM OF PARACHUTE IS NOT SUITABLE

With their numbers depleted by transfers to France, and their very existence placed into doubt by their superiors, the men comprising the Home Defence Squadrons could have been forgiven for feeling somewhat hard done by. Compounding this was the fact that due to enemy inactivity, they frequently found themselves idle save for socializing with the ladies from the local village, and an endless round of sport. Small wonder that compared to service over France, life in a Home Defence Squadron in England was seen as a welcome rest cure away from the carnage by the pilots, and an easy life by their detractors.

Yet pilots both in and out of the theatre of war were under tremendous pressures. Aerial combat was in its infancy and noone really knew what a man must endure thousands of feet up in the air, fighting the elements and the limits of his own physiology – not to mention the idiosyncrasies of his aeroplane, due to the fact that:

> The strain reduced all men by stages until it becomes as dangerous for the best pilots to fly a machine as for a beginner...

But bravado and youthful enthusiasm, personified by airmen like Mick Mannock, Billy Bishop and James McCudden served to conceal the pressures wartime pilots were under, helping ensure there was a steady stream of willing men volunteering for duty, many of them private aviators with some experience of flying their own machines for fun.

Some attempt was made to give as good a grounding as possible for recruits, but it was far from adequate, and the training of pilots was not high on the War Office list of priorities. Even in 1915 there were only 200 pilots in full time training at any one time, barely enough to supply skilled replacements for those lost over France. Before long the supply of gentlemen weekend fliers dried up and eventually younger men entered the service until, by 1917, the average age of a pilot was just twenty.

At first, it was a difficult clique into which one could gain admittance. Before the war, the Royal Flying Corps treated entry into its ranks rather like application to join an exclusive gentleman's club. Candidates first had to qualify for the Aero Club Certificate of Competence, footing the hefty £75 bill themselves, after which they entered a selection process followed by a course at a training establishment.

This early sedentary procedure was short-lived once the first tranche of recruits was lost. By 1916, the procedure employed for evaluating a recruit's suitability for admission relied rather more on ability to fly than ability to pay large sums of money. Full medical examinations were carried out and at least some procedures were employed as to determine a volunteer's flying competence. These rudimentary procedures included ascertaining a man's likely tolerance for high altitude by having him hold his breath for forty-five seconds, and revolving the would-be flyer in a chair ten times in twenty seconds to determine whether he had the stamina to withstand the varied physical effects of flight itself. Around twelve per cent of candidates failed these tests. Somewhat more sophisticated tests evolved as the war progressed.

The men who passed their medical were sent to a depot where they underwent basic drill and physical training. From there they went to the School of Aeronautics at Reading or Oxford.

Students were later posted to the Central Flying School at Upavon where they were taught to cope with the excessive stresses of flying, instructed in aeroplanes such as the Avro 504k, DH6 and B.E.2c. Usually an instructor sat behind the trainee, but the Bristol S.2A accommodated both side by side. To an onlooker squinting up from a field in a neighbouring farm or country lane, here was simply a jolly jape in the clouds, a heady time for these dashing young men. In reality, flying an aircraft even outside the skies of combat was hazardous and demanding on all the senses.

The forces of aeronautics and nature arrayed against the airmen were quite awesome, even in machines which, by later standards, were quite rudimentary. The engine of an aeroplane produced about 120 decibels at full revs, while propeller tips revolving at about 30,000 feet per second pushed up the cacophony by a further 125 decibels, until flying at full revs was something akin to working on a building site, with hammer drills and other machinery pounding the eardrums all day.

Little surprise therefore that in the early summer of 1917 an official RFC memorandum revealed that of 6,000 pilots undergoing training,

41

about 1,200 would not complete their course, (a pilot involved in a crash had a ten per cent chance of survival). The causes were manifold, but certainly the lack of experience of the instructors, the short training time and inefficient aircraft and maintenance contributed to the situation. A total of 8,000 trainees would be killed in total, in the course of the war. Little wonder when one learns of the exploits of some of the pilots.

—⟨ 0 ⟩—

No amount of schooling could prepare the would-be pilot for the challenges with which he would be faced on active service.

One of the worst of these was the extreme cold. At the relatively low flying altitude of 10,000 feet, wind chapped the skin and rendered breathing difficult. Ground temperature of sixty degrees Fahrenheit dropped progressively to forty-five degrees below zero at an altitude of 20,000 feet. At this freezing temperature the pilot's ability to function was drastically impaired. And the relentlessly bitter effects of a long patrol could dog pilots of all kinds, even the most experienced. Air ace James McCudden once related how he felt so cold thousands of feet up in the air that he practically switched off and lost all interest in life. He felt so frozen that he couldn't be bothered if a German dived at him or not; it would be a blessed release from the misery.

To overcome this most debilitating of phenomena, pilots and observers adopted all manner of bizarre garb, appearing sometimes like some weird phenomena. So desperate were men to keep some semblance of warmth, they even took hot baked potatoes in the cockpit with them.

From the point of view of keeping warm, pilots soon discovered that it was better to be allocated a machine with the engine in front, rather than the so-called 'Pusher' type machine, with the engine behind. In this way they benefited from some of the heat radiated by the engine, whereas anything generated by the engine set behind the pilot was simply lost in the slipstream.

Oxygen starvation became a recurring danger as aircraft were driven ever higher to avoid ground fire and gain a crucial few seconds edge over the enemy.

Instructors could not teach men how to put up with the sickening stench of burnt castor oil and gas fumes – only suggesting that they take regular deep breaths from the aircraft's slipstream and imbibe some fresh air. This alone could gradually wear a man down, his

42

senses being eroded by the fumes until he all but passed out, lost control of his machine and plunged to his death.

But it was not just the forces of nature they had to contend with. The primitive design of aircraft meant the pilot and observer were often seated above the petrol tank. An SE5a for example, carried twenty-six gallons of petrol in its main tank behind the seat, with a further three gallons in the gravity feed tank in the upper wing, enough for a two-and-a-half hour flight, and more than enough to turn the aircraft into a massive ball of flame in which the hapless pilot would not stand a remote chance of survival. As a contingency in the event of becoming a 'flamer', many pilots kept their revolver close by.

This fear was all the more acute because there was one particular item of equipment upon which they certainly could not rely – the parachute. Although there were a wide variety of models available, they were never issued to either pilots or observers. The Air Boards' reason for forbidding their adoption was outlined thus:

> It is of the opinion of the Board that the present form of parachute is not suitable for use in aeroplanes and should only be used by balloon observers. It is also the opinion of the Board that the presence of such apparatus might impair the fighting spirit of pilots and cause them to abandon machines which might otherwise be capable of returning to base for repair.

One member even suggested that in all the heat and fury of battle, a pilot might not have the time to use his parachute. It was also maintained that the aeroplane, once struck by enemy fire, would probably fall too fast for the pilot to avail himself of the contraption anyway. In effect, once a pilot took off in his aircraft, and was unfortunate enough to either be shot at, have his aircraft burst into flames or fall out of control, he was on his own.

Their scepticism was far from borne out by the facts, however. Experiments with parachutes had been taking place over many years. In 1908 a parachute opened by a ripcord had been invented in the United States and in 1913, Captain Edward Maitland of the Royal Engineers made the first jump from an aeroplane. A Frenchman, Adolphe Pegous, also made a parachute descent from an aeroplane at Hendon in 1913, and during the war balloonists were issued parachutes.

Hours and days on patrol created brutal physiological and psychological changes to the pilot's character and psyche. The air service medical laboratory reckoned that eighty per cent of groundings were due to nervous disorders and that fifty per cent of pilots developed serious neuroses during their tour of duty. Many contemporary photographs graphically illustrate this point, with some taken just a few months apart, illustrating dramatic changes for the worst in a pilot's appearance.

No great surprise therefore, that men stationed in England felt little urge to exchange that posting for the quite different demands of the Western Front.

❦

If the pilot learned to cope with all these pressures and challenges, he could at least take to the air in the comforting knowledge that he was armed with the best available machine guns manufactured by the Lewis and Vickers companies.

The Lewis Gun 'Cut Down Mark One' was originally mounted on the top wing above the cockpit so he could fire over the propeller from his seated position. This was before the advent of synchronization, later developed by the Dutch engineer Antony Fokker, who pioneered a system to enable the machine gun to fire between the propeller blades. The Lewis could also be employed as what was known as a 'free gun', which would be operated by the observer, usually seated behind the pilot.

Lewis guns were famed for their reliability. They seldom, if ever, jammed and even at great height, rarely froze. The only drawback was their drums contained a limited amount of ammunition, thus forcing the pilot to constantly reload in an engagement. Even the largest, double-capacity drum held only ninety-seven rounds – compared with the 500-round belt for the Vickers. At best, the operation required the execution of three separate movements in five seconds, during which time the machine had to be flown with hands off the controls and eyes disengaged from the foe's activity. The final stage of moving the 27lb gun up and forward under such circumstances required huge physical effort by the pilots.

The other mainstay of the pilot's arsenal was the Vickers, a modification of the famous Maxim gun, 43 inches long and 31lb in weight, firing 600 rounds per minute. To prevent it freezing at altitude, a heater of nichrome wire, wound round mica and powered from the engine's 12 volt supply, was cased in copper and placed round the breech. Despite its capacity for firing hundreds of rounds before the belt ran out, it was very prone to jamming, succumbing to

44

twenty-five possible causes in flight. Nevertheless, some reliability was evidenced by one occasion in August 1916, when ten Vickers laid down a barrage in which a total of 1,000,000 rounds were fired without a problem. The Vickers was later adapted to become the first Allied machine gun capable of firing through the propellers.

Even with such formidable weapons at his disposal, the man operating it could never be assured of much in the way of accuracy. State-of-the-art fighter planes were still technologically in their infancy, making their practicality as machine-gun platforms arguable at best. To help in this respect, crude gun sights were developed, of which there were two types.

The original ring and bead sights which looked something like a small dartboard, worked thus: at 400 yards an enemy machine overlapped the outer ring; at 300 yards it overlapped the inner ring, at 200 yards it half filled the outer ring, and at 100 yards it completely filled the inner ring. The ring however, was often knocked out of alignment and was not easy to see in poor light, so many pilots opted for the far more reliable Aldis Sight.

Introduced late in 1916, the Aldis was twenty-five inches long and two inches in diameter, with two non-magnified lenses and a ground glass screen imprinted with lines and circles. Even the more sophisticated Aldis, however, found it difficult to compete with the violent vibration of the aircraft, which shook pilot and sight alike with incredible force. This often produced a bullet cone thirty feet in diameter at 500 yards, and such dispersal, combined with the small calibre of the bullets (0.303in), coming from two machine guns meant that the pilot had to be within 200 yards of the target if he were to stand any chance at all of achieving a hit.

Being as close as 200 yards created its own problems. If the pilot should have to take evasive action or manoeuvre as he was flying, he was more likely to miss altogether than if the bullet stream had a wider angle of deflection.

The combination of vibration and deflection angles meant that pilots had to exhaust huge supplies of ammunition in the hope of achieving a hit. To be certain of a measured shot, only a gun capable of firing at least 5,000 rounds per minute could hope to be really effective. Not everything worked against him however; thanks to improved factory production techniques and committed ground crew, only one faulty round in every 35,000 slipped into either the drum or belt which fed the weapon.

As time wore on great improvements were made to gun sights. One example was a design by Sergeant A E Hutton, an armourer who worked on the development of an effective night sight, and which greatly improved the chances of a pilot achieving a 'kill'. Another development, the brainchild of Lieutenant H B Neame, and which was introduced late in 1917, produced a sight purpose built for use against the Gotha bomber.

The airship threat had given contemporary ordnance its day. It was soon clear that ordinary rounds would simply go in one side of the airship and out the other; what was required was something that could ignite the highly flammable substance and reduce the vessel to flames.

Ever since the beginning of the war, Coventry engineer J F Buckingham had been experimenting with incendiary bullets. Late in 1915 he presented the perfected idea, employing phosphorous as the main agent to ignite the gas bag of the airship. The War Office were convinced and commenced mass production.

This was followed by tracer ammunition, which had been manufactured by the Royal Laboratory at Woolwich Arsenal and christened 'Sparklet'. Further development work was pursued by Flight Lieutenant F A Brock, of the famous firework manufacturing family. This was added to by the achievements of a New Zealander, John Pomeroy, whose explosive bullet was also lethal to airships.

In order to get the best results out of this cocktail of ordnance, tracer and ignition, experience and experimentation proved that the gun should be loaded with consecutive rounds so that the Sparklet indicated the trajectory, the Brock blew a hole in the fabric and the Buckingham or Pomeroy then set alight the gas in the airship. This lethal combination was instrumental in the victories of Leefe Robinson, Sowrey, Warneford and Tempest.

However, the subject of the bravery and determination of the pilots was an academic one, if the tools they were given to do their job turned out to be below standard, and not every piece of equipment and weaponry delivered to the airfields was manufactured to exacting standards. Despite the best efforts of Cowdray's department, the needs of mass production, cost cutting and simple greed on the part of the factory owners meant that many of the aircraft constructed for the aviators proved woefully short of the mark.

But even aeroplanes fine-tuned to give their best, faced a dreadful shortcoming, namely that they were outmoded and outclassed by their adversaries. Long into the war, the British were employing old workhorses like the B.E.2. Slow, cumbersome and designed as no more than an observation platform, the B.E.2 took so long to climb to the airships' height that the enemy was long gone by the time the pilot had gained sufficient altitude, and was hopeless in a combat role.

The squadrons on the Western Front were bolstered, however, by the arrival of the newer Sopwith Camel. When performing to specification, it could boast a 130hp Le Clerget engine with a maximum speed of 104mph at 10,000 feet, and could reach that height twice as fast as the ageing B.E.2. There was also the De Havilland, equipped with a Rolls-Royce Eagle 3 250hp engine which provided a top speed of 113mph at 10,000 feet – although it took longer than the Sopwith to reach that height. The Sopwith $1^1/_2$ Strutter could manage 96mph at 10,000 feet, as could the RE8 which had an RAF 140hp engine and took twenty-one minutes to achieve 10,000 feet, at which height it managed a speed of 92mph.

The RNAS were fortunate in having a much larger complement of higher performance machines at their disposal at Manston, Westgate, Dover, Walmer, Eastchurch, Grain Island and Felixstowe which all had Sopwiths. The Pup had a 90hp Le Rhone engine which took seventeen minutes to reach 10,000 feet where it could manage a speed of 102mph. The Triplane had a 130hp Le Clerget engine and took twelve minutes to reach 10,000 feet where it managed a speed of 106mph.

Nevertheless, it was no longer the RNAS upon whose shoulders the burden of defending London rested. It was Lord French and his mixed bag of men and machines who waited on the grass airfields of the Home Counties and south-east England – demoralized by their ever decreasing ranks, having to make do with hand-me-down tools and machines and knowing they were considered second-rate and somehow dodging the real war. Some of the more experienced among them may have bloodied themselves against airships; they knew what it was like to try and coerce their slow and lethargic machines into the thinning altitudes in pursuit of a Zeppelin. The majority of their comrades however, untried in combat against German raiders, could only practice as best they could, and read and reread instruction manuals while they waited for the enemy to finally arrive.

CHAPTER 4

EAT MORE SLOWLY, YOU WILL NEED LESS FOOD

Upon the outbreak of war in 1914, the British Foreign Secretary, Sir Edward Grey, was heard to utter, 'the lamps are going out all over Europe; we shall not see them lit again in our lifetime'. For those living in wartime Britain, his prophecy quickly came to cast a very real shadow. War-weariness compounded by austerity had replaced the heady optimism of August 1914. By 1917 few thought of glorious victory, rather of achieving peace on the best possible terms.

The aura of a nation at war became manifest soon after hostilities broke out. Traffic was lighter, cars were even rarer than before the war and now the most common vehicles were Army convoys. Petrol rationing was introduced early in the war, with further economies as the conflict dragged on. By the summer of 1917, 'gas bag' propulsion had been introduced to help overcome the shortage of fuel, and heralded the bizarre sight of vehicles trundling along with huge billowing bags on their roofs. Buses too were an infrequent sight, many having been commandeered for service in France, and the general shortage both of vehicles and fuel heralded a resurgence of horse-drawn traffic. But even animals needed feeding, and where that proved too expensive, man-hauled vans and carts tended to predominate.

The Government also acted to save on light with the introduction of British Summer Time and, despite its hostile reception, the benefits proved to outweigh the disadvantages and it survives to this day.

There was little to gladden civilian spirits to offset these deprivations; by 1916 the German submarine blockade was bringing a dire shortage of food to a head, whilst the unfair distribution of supplies was beginning to cause open dissent. On the factory floor, the need to replace men lost to the Front was causing severe problems, but the solution, 'dilution', the practice of giving skilled jobs to semi-or unskilled workers, was creating just as many. Unions, desperate to defend the rights they had won for their members over many years of struggle, saw a dangerous precedent being created, and as a result strikes were becoming commonplace.

To try and contain this growing discord and its more extreme manifestations, the Government turned to a series of draconian statutory measures known as the *Defence of the Realm Acts* (DORA), which severely curtailed liberties and freedom in a way never before experienced in the country's history. On 8 August 1914 the War Cabinet produced measures designed to secure, 'the public safety and the defence of the realm'. They were initially designed for the purpose of preventing useful information falling into the hands of the enemy and to protect important bases and installations. At the heart of the acts was the measure which placed offenders under military not civil, law which meant that they could be tried by court martial. The Acts were added to and amended throughout the course of the war, and could be invoked to allow government control of food, pub opening hours and air raid measures. Press censorship also came within their scope, and all cables and foreign correspondence could be and was censored. Failure to comply with such measures laid the offender liable to prosecution under DORA.

—=≈=○=≈=—

The German submarine campaign, initiated almost from the very outset of the war, had varying degrees of success, bringing shortages to a range of staple foods and other supplies. This convinced many that those supplies which successfully broke through ought to be distributed as fairly and evenly as possible, i.e. rationed. But such ideas were condemned as playing into the enemy's hands. The Government position was outlined by Walter Runciman, President of the Board of Trade, in the House of Commons in October 1916, two years into the conflict:

> The one thing we ought to avoid in this country is, from any cause whatsoever, to put ourselves into the position of a blockaded people. Bread tickets, meat coupons, and these artificial arrangements are harmful, and they are harmful to those who have least with which to buy... we want to avoid any rationing of our people of food.

But whilst those with the money could enjoy almost as good a table as before the war broke out, the ordinary worker had to make do with whatever their limited funds could provide. In order to assuage the resentment of the working classes, the Government made every effort to look for alternatives to rationing. This resulted in the 'Cultivation of Lands Order' which was passed in December 1916. This empowered the Board of Agriculture to seize any appropriate land and turn it over to the cultivation of food. A month earlier it took the step of appointing Lord Devonport as Food Controller. His brief was to make the very best use of what foodstuffs were produced, spread them as far as possible and, even more importantly, prevent waste and the production of unnecessary goods. The Board of Trade was also given powers to restrict the uses to which raw materials could be put; for example, bread had to be made from specific grades of flour. Lord Devonport restricted meals in restaurants to three courses, between 6.00 pm and 9.30 pm a move which it was hoped would limit consumption. He even fixed maximum prices for meals which could be served to soldiers in public places.

However, these measures were hardly a vigorous answer to the U-boat menace which in 1916 alone had sent well over a million tons of Allied shipping to the bottom of the Atlantic. The meagre measures put in place were of little benefit to workers forced to spend hours at their workplace with empty stomachs. Lord Devonport went further. On 11 January 1917, he announced that the use of wheat for any purpose other than seed or flour milling was forbidden and it had to be mixed with at least ten percent barley, maize or rice. Sweets, chocolate and expensive pastries were outlawed completely, production of sweetmeats was cut to fifty percent of its pre-war level, and the use of sugar and chocolate coverings was also banned.

And still the merchant ships were sunk. By the Spring of 1917 there was only nine weeks supply of grain remaining. Persisting with his view that rationing was, 'too bad for morale', Devonport came up with a system of 'voluntary rationing', inviting senior dignitaries like Lloyd George to extol its virtues. On 3 February 1917 he addressed a meeting in Caernarfon, in which he stated that:

> I want her [the housewife] to hear what the Food Controller has got in the papers today as to what each of us is to have next week to eat, the national menu... Saving of food means the saving of tonnage, and saving tonnage is the very life of the nation at the present moment.

But by its very nature, anything voluntary would only be pursued by those with considerable reserves of willpower and sense of duty. It could not be monitored or enforced and failure to comply could not meet with any sanction.

Voluntary rationing led to hoarding by those who could afford to do so, effectively worsening the situation by denying supplies to others, and helping to feed black-marketeering, not to mention fanning the flames of resentment between the classes still further. Eventually, severe penalties of anything up to £600 fines were introduced for those found to be hoarding specified goods.

In March and April 1917, still more initiatives were introduced. Bread had to be twelve hours old before it could be sold; hotels, clubs and restaurants were subject to compulsory potato rationing and the making of muffins, crumpets and teacakes was outlawed. To make sure that flour was only used for the purposes laid down by the Government, it effectively nationalized the main mills for the duration of the war.

To give a sense of self-sufficiency to those who could manage it, Lloyd George was again asked to vouch for the benefits of adopting an allotment for growing basic vegetables. It is unlikely that exaltations from politicians would have found favour among housewives trying to sustain their (often fatherless) brood so it was decided to entreat the King himself to set an example to the masses. Consequently, in May 1917, George V issued an Appeal in the form of a Royal Proclamation.

Nevertheless, the black market was booming. Trade in prohibited or restricted foodstuffs was exacerbating shortages and pushing up the price of what little was available. Lord Devonport was forced to consider price controls, while his successor, Lord Rhondda, in June 1917, introduced sugar rationing when it was revealed that there was just ten days supplies left.

The Government's best efforts short of universal rationing would not however, make up for shortages caused by the German submarine campaign. Only after the introduction of the convoy system in June 1917, in which merchant vessels travelled in large groups protected by the Royal Navy, did the situation improve so that by the end of the war losses to the U-boats were minimal. The toll had been real enough however. Between 1914 and 1918, 11,000,000 tons of Allied shipping had been lost, 8,000,000 tons of which were British flagged.

However, growing industrial unrest would eventually compel action. An enquiry revealed that the rising cost of food, despite higher wages, was a major cause of disturbances. In April 1918 meat was rationed across the nation, followed by tea, butter and margarine. Milk rationing was not deemed necessary until after the war however, and only in March 1921 was the Ministry of Food closed down entirely.

⟨◦⟩

One commodity no country at war could afford to be without was munitions. The upheaval and the repercussions that would result from the need to satisfy the demands of a war economy would produce some of the most far-reaching side effects ever felt in this country, before or since.

An early shock came soon into the war, when it was realized that women would have to be called upon to fill the large gaps left by men called up to the services – destroying at once the long-held homily that a woman's place was in the home. Support for female participation came from both sexes, including suffragettes Emmeline and Christobel Pankhurst. Under the banner 'A Woman's Right to Serve', they sought to pressure the authorities into extending scope for women to work in factories and in other vital areas of the war effort. For many women, it meant a boom-time with their incomes rocketing and a corresponding sense of independence. The social revolution this sparked was immeasurable.

The single munitions factory at Woolwich Arsenal in London was expanded to three by July 1915, with ten more on the architect's table. The opportunity for women to work alongside men and perform tasks of equal complexity and importance had come, and women were soon lured away from other jobs in domestic service and shop-work by the comparatively high wages offered by industry. By the end of the war something approaching a million women were employed in munitions alone.

Though it required little skill, it was a dangerous job to fill shells with explosives. There were many accidents, with fuses detonating in workers' faces as they went about their task. The noxious nature of the explosive filling, TNT, produced serious side-effects after prolonged exposure to the mixture. This often proved fatal, with 181 cases reported in 1916 and 189 in 1917. Even when not fatal, the explosive would at the very least turn the workers' skin a sickly yellow, causing the sufferer to earn the nickname 'Canary'.

A greater threat lay in the very volatile nature of the factories themselves, housing thousands of tons of explosives in confined areas. One of the greatest tragedies to occur was associated with the

52

explosion of the Brunner Mond factory at Silvertown on 9 January 1917.

A small fire had started, which spread quickly until the entire complex disappeared beneath a fantastic ball of flame, completely demolishing everything within 500 yards, including the local fire station, flour mills and two schools. One eyewitness, a child at the time, remembers the noise and seeing 'a glow in the sky'. The sound of the explosion was heard fifty miles away in Cambridge and in all upwards of 70,000 surrounding properties were affected to some degree by the blast. Sixty-nine people were killed and four fatally injured; ninety-eight were seriously injured and 328 slightly and a further 600 needed attention to cuts, grazing and shock. It was half an hour before help arrived, and some fires raged on for a further two days. Over £3,000,000 damage was done. It was widely speculated to have been the work of German spies or 'invisible Zeppelins' – anything but the reality, a terrible accident all too likely in the exigencies of war.

Despite such risks the contribution of women to the war effort soon became indispensable. The shortfall caused by the loss of men would result in an extra 1,600,000 women entering civilian employment by 1918, as they took over as bus crew, in arms factories, as postmen, office clerks, milkmen, in farms and a multitude of other tasks previously the preserve of men.

Most notable of these were perhaps, engineering-based jobs. Notable because it provoked a storm of protest.

———=◦○◦=———

Trade Unions who thought the demands of war might give them the upper hand through increased demand for labour, were to be proved wrong – certainly in the long term. Labour shortages did give the unions added muscle at first, and the government and employers seemed content to give in to demands to maintain productivity. Strikes brought rich rewards and in Clydeside in February 1915 industrial action heralded another penny to the hourly rate. However, the Government anticipated possible disruption and ensured that provision was made in DORA to circumvent any manifestations of industrial unrest. These measures would however, bring only limited benefits to the authorities and the factory bosses, since it was easier to pass laws than it was to enforce them. Later in 1915, the *Munitions of War*

53

Act, made such strikes illegal.

The influx of women into many trades was far from welcomed by those men still in jobs, many of whom felt their natural role as head of household and breadwinner to be under threat. Worse however, was the need dilute the skills required to do some tasks, so that those previously only performed by skilled craftsmen after years of training, could be done by untrained workers. And these were to be almost exclusively women, bringing changes to the work patterns and practices which unions had fought hard to secure and maintain.

It was inevitable that complaints would follow and when these met with little or no response from either management or Government, strike action was threatened. The unions knew that if the bosses could find ways of recategorizing jobs previously recognized as skilled, then there would be little incentive to return to the old ways once the war was over.

In 1916, strikes broke out along the Clyde in protest at the employment of 'Dilutees'. Disruption spread quickly and that year saw millions of working hours lost through strikes. A Rochdale firm had turned dilutees to commercial work as well as to their war work, incensing union leaders who, during April and May 1917, called their men out. It was clear, however, that the Rochdale bosses had overstepped the mark, with even the Ministry of Munitions agreeing this was the case. The bosses of the firm were instructed to stop abusing the system, which they refused, saying it was for them to run the businesses as they saw fit. Some of the strikers were sacked and they threatened to close down the works entirely if the Government continued to interfere in their business. Strikes spread to other factories where workers walked out in sympathy, until some 60,000 men had withdrawn their labour in disgust over the Rochdale action and the Government's weak response to it.

Before long 200,000 men were on strike before the firm was finally brought to heel and some 1,500,000 working days had been lost.

⇒≈☘≈⇒

Discontent and anger was endemic throughout the country. The Government decided in 1917 to investigate the main causes of discontent and see what could be done to address them. They were, of course, manifold. Workers were fed up with overcrowded living conditions; they were angry about rising food prices and high rents; they were angry about the restrictions on mobility whereby

54

permission was needed to change jobs; and workers were especially angry about the way in which Conscription, when introduced in 1916, had been practised.

Here again, dilution was implicated because, it was claimed, higher paid skilled workers were called up so lower paid dilutees could take their place - serving also to fuel the belief that factory owners were profiteering on Government contracts.

Where would this discontent lead? Real fear on the part of the authorities was compounded by events in Russia, when the first of a series of revolutions broke out in April 1917. These ultimately unseated the Tsar and led to the country pulling out of the war altogether, and indeed the discontent of the revolutionaries was not entirely dissimilar to that being expressed by British workers, including inept handling of a war which was being perceived as a rich man's venture.

When a Joint Union Convention was held in Leeds in June 1917, it urged British workers,

> ...to organise the British Democracy to follow Russia... and begin a whole new era of democratic power in Great Britain... it would begin to do for this country what the Russian Revolution has accomplished for Russia...

In Glasgow, there was talk of setting up a 'Workers and Soldiers Soviet'. The local magistrates however, were having none of that and the meeting they were to hold was banned outright. One of the most vocal of the trades union leaders, John Maclean, was sentenced to five years' hard labour for sedition.

Uprising, however, failed to become a reality perhaps because it was unlikely that any orator could galvanize the naturally conservative British public into turning against 'King and Country'. Many times before in British history workers failed to demonstrate the extremism witnessed abroad, where revolution was often a regular occurrence. The ringleaders had to content themselves with the knowledge that they had aggravated the nation's war effort by losing 6,000,000 working days in disruption and strikes.

If there was hostility towards the establishment, that directed towards those members of the population known as the 'enemy within' was even more virulent. These were the Germans who lived in the country, people who increasingly found themselves the scapegoat for every perceived act of brutality carried out in Europe by their former compatriots. Citizens who had previously lived quite happily with Germans among their number, began waging campaigns of intimidation, smashing windows, violating homes, administering beatings and wrecking businesses. At Smithfield Market in London, German butchers were set upon and their premises wrecked when the liner *Lusitania* was sunk. The fact that the ship was also carrying 5,000 3-inch shells and 5,000,000 rifle cartridges was not publicized.

Sentiments ran so high, that even the loyalty of members of the aristocracy with German links going back generations was questioned. Prince Louis of Battenburg was forced to resign as First Lord of the Admiralty despite being a British citizen for fifty years. Charles Beresford, a retired naval officer explained in August 1914, how Prince Louis was 'an exceedingly able officer', but nothing could alter the fact 'that he is a German, and as such should not be occupying his present position.' He had to resign that October, and eventually changed the family name to Mountbatten.

Even the Royal Family came under suspicion. The dynastic name of the Royal House had been Saxe-Coburg-Gotha since the marriage of Victoria to Prince Albert in 1840 (before which it was the equally Germanic House of Hanover). To sever the unfortunate association, it was quietly changed, in May 1917, to Windsor, the momentous decision being quietly and discretely announced in a Royal Proclamation. Close family ties to the Hohenzollerns were also dissolved, with their Garter banners removed from St George's Chapel. The German Kaiser and the German Princes, of course, were stripped of their honorary colonelcies of British regiments and the honorary rank of Admiral of the Royal Navy. George V was said to have been greatly hurt by a suggestion by H G Wells, that the Royal House was, 'alien and uninspiring'. He announced angrily in response, 'I may be uninspiring, but I'm damned if I'm alien', but determined to redefine the role of the Monarchy in British society.

The King – invariably accompanied by his Queen, Mary – embarked upon a series of 'meet the people' tours and visits around the country and, in January 1917 visited the scene of the Silvertown explosion. In March and April he visited parts of working-class London which had been particularly affected by bombing. Royal visits went some way to improving the short-term morale of the ordinary workers too, who regarded the Royal Family with status and not a little mystique, and certainly provoked a better response than trips by politicians.

The King also went to the Western Front, where he visited troops and awarded decorations. However, even his weighty contribution did little to satisfy the more paranoid elements of the public who were obsessed with what became known as the 'Unseen Hand'. This invisible though highly potent force had been partly responsible for the Battenburg scare and the suspicions which fell upon the Royal House itself. The winter of 1916 had seen huge gatherings to demand Government action against this insidious form of corruption, which it widely held as responsible for every piece of bad luck to befall the country. It was also believed that in Berlin, the enemy had amassed a list of 50,000 people, compiled by the 'Unseen Hand', who would be called upon to turn against their fellow countrymen.

<hr/>

The introduction of the airship raids served to further compound the miserable lot of the ordinary man and woman. Confined largely to the capital, the Midlands, the north-east and the south-east, the raids nevertheless affected thousands of people all over the country. Once they had started, anxiety and anticipation of further attacks took their toll on public morale. Lives were further disrupted by the necessity to take measures to safeguard home and family should an attack come. Winifred Harris recalls how:

> When the maroons [rudimentary air raid alerts adapted from maritime distress flares] went off, my mother would rush us all to the church crypt, which must have been at least fifteen minutes away. Installed on the roof of Peak Freans biscuit factory was a light which would be green when everything was all clear, but change to red when the raiders were near. We could see this light on our way to the church crypt, but at one point the light would become obscured by a building, and someone would call out 'it's gone', making us all tear along the rest of the way.

Doris Frank, too, has distinct memories of the broken nights' sleep, being taken from her bed, still wrapped in a blanket by her father:

> I remember getting on the No. 17 tram that ran up and down the road all night, no fares, dropping off passengers at King's Cross or Caledonian Road tube stations. We all lay down on the

platforms and the trains rattled by... .

Often however, the defences could be just as disruptive to normal lives as the enemy. Phyllis Jones remembers how:

> Our house [in Fulham] faced a 'T' junction, and anti aircraft guns on lorries fired outside, making the whole house shake and on one occasion shattering the dining room window... . I often did my homework under the kitchen table aided by a torch... . At school we used to spend the mid-morning break searching the school field for shell fragments with which to adorn the mistress's desk.

— ⇒ ⊰0⊱ ⇐ —

As the pressure increased during confined times people, like air, sought release.

Cheap and easily available before the war, drugs were once an easy form of social recreation for the more avante garde. Now substances such as opium and cocaine, which could be legally purchased over the chemist's counter, were taking on a more sinister and lethal role. Smoking dens were common in dockland areas such as Poplar and Limehouse where the local Chinese communities thrived, and were frequently visited by soldiers on leave. Commandant Mary Allen of the Women's Police Reserve, took herself on a tour of the Capital where matters were worse. She related how:

> The Strand at this time was at night a veritable Devil's Playground; white slavers crowded there, drugs were bought and sold with the freedom of confectionery. Scenes of indescribable disorder prevailed.

Prostitutes had crowded into London to meet the demands of the thousands of soldiers from all over the Empire who packed its streets in search of fun. There were 60,000 call girls at one time, 40,000 of them foreign women, many refugees from Belgium. With this came contagion and widespread sexually-transmitted disease, incapacitating soldiers and rendering them unfit for service.

Eventually, VD Regulation 40D of DORA was imposed, making it illegal for any infected women to have sexual intercourse with a serviceman; those suspected of carrying the virus could be taken into custody for up to a week without charge for medical examinations to be carried out.

58

The war effort also found itself seriously threatened from another great British institution, the pub. The extra money which found its way into the pockets of workers, mainly munitions workers, inevitably found its way into the local hostelries. As early as August 1914, an Act was passed which gave local authorities the power to take limited measures to control the sale and supply of liquor. Minister of Munitions, Lloyd George, saw the 'lure of drink' as a problem as great as strikes, stemming no doubt from reports of munition workers being too intoxicated to do their job. In the Spring of 1915 he declared, 'we are fighting Germany, Austria and drink, and as far as I can see the greatest of those deadly foes is drink'. In March 1915 a deputation of shipbuilding employers urged him to impose prohibition for the duration of the war, similarly claiming that because of drink their workers were in no fit state to work. Pubs were allowed to open for up to eighteen hours a day, giving little incentive to the workers to leave so long as they had the price of another pint.

The drink scandal however, became somewhat fortuitous as far as the government was concerned because it coincided with the 'shell scandal' of March 1915. It had been revealed that the guns at the Front were being starved of ordnance, and that much of what was delivered was defective. Rather than simply concede the problem might lie in the failure of the factories, Lloyd George preferred to blame the problem on drunken workers, his action against which was promptly endorsed by the King. The King's secretary, Lord Stamfordham, wrote to him on 30 March 1915:

> The continuance of such a state of things must inevitably result in the prolongation of the horrors and burdens of this terrible war. I am told that if it is deemed advisable, the King will be prepared to set the example by giving up all alcoholic liquor himself, and issuing orders against consumption in the Royal Household, so that no difference shall be made, so far as His Majesty is concerned, between the treatment of rich and poor in this question.

This sentiment articulated itself as the 'King's Pledge'. It had however, little effect on seasoned drinkers, so on 29 April 1915 another amendment to DORA was passed to deal with drink in munitions productions areas. It gave the Government the power to control its manufacture and distribution, the opening and closing of pubs and any other measures it deemed necessary. This action was taken at Enfield Lock in London, and at Carlisle and Gretna in the north. Soon after, opening hours were severely limited to an average of five hours a day with a break in the afternoon and, in the Budget Speech on 29 April, decreases in the alcoholic content of beers to around three to four per cent was announced together with considerable increases in duty.

The amount of grain brewed and distilled was restricted, the brewing of heavy beers like stout and porter were banned altogether and in October 1915 it was made illegal to buy a round of drinks under the 'No Treating' Order. Drinkers and publicans alike could be heavily fined for any breach of the regulations – a £40 fine and loss of his licence – but it seemed to work. Consumption dropped from 89,000,000 gallons in 1914, to 37,000,000 in 1918, and cases of conviction for drunken behaviour fell from over 67,000 in 1914 to around 16,000 in 1917. One way of offsetting the increases in wages was to put up the cost of beer. Between the war years the price rose from an average 3d a pint to nearer 10d. Spirits could be no more than seventy per cent proof and restrictions were imposed as to when they could be sold. By the end of the war the price of an average bottle of whiskey rose five times.

As an alternative, canteens were set up in factories to give workers alternative places for their recreation and sustenance. Not quite the diversion that hardened shipbuilders would have welcomed, but they went some way to alleviating their withdrawal symptoms.

What effect having to drink 'Lloyd George's Beer' or paying through the nose for it had on worker productivity is difficult to evaluate. But being denied the one diversion from the rigours and demands of work they truly enjoyed could have done little for morale, and may even have contributed to some of the many strikes which broke out during this period.

For all this however, London and the rest of the United Kingdom remained the armoury of the Allied Powers. The country remained more productive than Italy, France or Russia, and even when the United States entered the war this supremacy was not seriously threatened. By the end of the war, Britain provided the Allied war effort with 4,000,000 rifles, 250,000 machine guns, 52,000 aircraft, 2,800 tanks, 25,000 artillery pieces, 170,000,000 rounds of artillery shells, 85,000 motor vehicles and 34,700 motor cycles.

CHAPTER 5

AN AIRSHIP RAID AGAINST LONDON HAS BECOME IMPOSSIBLE

Of all the technological landmarks of the First World War, few surpassed that of aircraft designed specifically for the purpose of wreaking devastation on the cities of one's enemies.

To any proud young cavalry officer, dressed in the finely tailored uniform of an elite regiment like the Hussars or the Uhlans, and surveying such a beast for the first time, it would have been both frightening and inspiring. Its sheer scale alone would have been staggering - previously the largest beast he could have expected to have to command in battle would have been his own charger. This was something altogether different – the modern equivalent of a fire-breathing dragon. For this was the Gotha.

It was for its time a creature of unparalleled proportions. At first sight one would wonder how it could ever get off the ground in the first place, with a wing-span of seventy-eight feet, almost as long as a modern basketball court, and a forty-one foot fuselage, almost the width of one. It echoed those ludicrous silent movies depicting various odd-balls attempting to get airborne, only to collapse ignominiously, their imploded multi-tiered wings scrunched into a pathetic heap. Looking at this mechanical Quasimodo – its leaden wings weighed down by their own sheer bulk, it must have been almost impossible for the young cavalryman to picture it rising further than a foot off the ground.

However, this ponderous concoction of wood and wire could fly; it would not collapse and break its back on take-off (although a good many would on landing); it could, albeit slowly, defeat gravity and the laws of nature, gaining height until, almost invisible to the naked eye, it would compete with the elements and out fly the very creatures it had sought to emulate.

Hauling himself aboard, our young Prussian would be greeted by even more wonders of the modern age.

It may have appeared heavy and cumbersome when on the ground, but once airborne the Gotha could achieve a theoretical speed from its

61

twin 260hp six cylinder Mercedes engines, of 79mph at 17,000 feet. Each voracious engine consumed up to 175 gallons of petrol plus fifteen gallons of oil per trip, assuming the bombers took the most direct route to London and back. Auxiliary petrol tanks, which would remove the need to refuel en route, could be strapped to the upper wing. About fifteen feet long, with a varnished plywood interior, the main deck was divided into three sections connected by an exposed walkway; the forward position, perched precariously out in front, was occupied by the commander and contained the Goertz bomb-sight and one of the three 7.92mm Parabellum machine guns; the middle section was the pilot's position, with the large steering wheel control column and flying instruments; the pilot's instruments consisted of a speedometer, which was an electrical voltmeter graduated in hundreds over the range 0-1600 rpm and powered by the engines. The petrol gauge was the same as that used on the Zeppelins and consisted of a float and string passing over a pulley connected to a hand moving over a graduated dial. The air speed indicator was of the aneroid barometer type, graduating from 50 to 200kph. The altimeter was also of the aneroid barometer type, graduated from 500 to 5,000 metres. The aircraft's second machine gun was also stationed here.

Beyond that to the rear, was the third machine gun. This had been installed to provide a nasty surprise for British pilots who ventured too close; a special tunnel which passed from the rear gunner's position, through the fuselage and emerging below. The gun could be fired by the 'Tail End Charlie' from ten degrees below the horizon and vertically downwards through the tunnel. This permitted a clear field of fire from just behind the propellers, the breadth of the tunnel allowing a clear traverse of about twenty degrees, thus having a duel purpose, one for the top of the fuselage against aircraft attacking from above, and one for aircraft intercepting from below. The design provided for rudimentary guard fences at this point, to ensure that the gunner did not decapitate himself should he be tempted to lean out too far and accidentally come into contact with the propellers.

The most important single piece of equipment was the Goertz bomb-sight. The commander would view the passing landscape through an eyepiece at the top of the tube, and using a fitted stopwatch was able to record the time that a landmark took to cross part of the sighting scale. He was then able to set the correct aim by correlating his height against a calibration chart. This instrument, though far from 100 per cent accurate, and rudimentary to the extreme by today's standards, would be the only thing to stand between some element of ad hoc accuracy and a completely random display of indiscriminate bombing.

The *raison d'être* of the bomber, its payload, consisted of 50kg and 12.5kg bombs. On average, seven 50kg and six 12.5kg bombs were carried; the 50kg bombs were carried nose forwards in three racks underneath the centre of gravity of the machine, under the nacelle between the pilot and observer. These racks were arranged to carry, counting from the nose of the aircraft, two, three and two bombs each. The bombs were slung from the racks by a hinged steel strap passing round them and fastened by a bolt through two fixed eyes and one long one on the strap. These bolts could be withdrawn by a wire attached to a set of seven triggers within reach of the commander. The smaller bombs were carried in a wooden funnel-shaped magazine with a sliding door which enabled the pilot to release them by means of a lever.

The 50kg bombs consisted of a mixture of forty per cent hexanitrodiphenylamine and sixty per cent TNT. The explosive detonator, otherwise known as the gaine, comprised thirty-eight per cent tetryl and sixty-two per cent TNT, painted a light sky blue with a cigar-shaped body about five feet in length and seven inches in diameter. It was fitted with a sharp steel point for penetration and a three-vaned tail. It was very effective against buildings typical of the period and could easily damage an ordinary three-storey house or similar structure - its weight alone, increased by the velocity at which it approached the earth, ensured it would smash through most roofs of the time and penetrate several floors, leaving craters twelve to fifteen feet in diameter and five to six feet deep.

The 12.5kg bomb consisted of forty-five per cent hexani-trodphenylamine and fifty per cent crude TNT and was thirty inches long and three-and-a-half inches in diameter. It was of the same overall shape as its bigger brother and it was constructed mainly of brass. It had an optional delay mechanism of about 1/50th of a second, together with an automatic safety arrangement, in addition to the usual safety pin. It was essentially an anti-personnel device and, in fact, had been employed by airships since November 1916.

Its fuse allowed for it to explode on impact before it had time to penetrate the ground, thus inflicting maximum casualties. In addition, the tail was packed with a mixture of red phosphorous and TNT to assist the bomb aimer in determining accuracy; it also served to inflict severe wounds on people. The hexanidrophenylamine was very poisonous and its yellow stain caused severe swelling and irritation, such as one might expect to suffer if accidentally exposed to battery acid.

Life aboard would also provide a great contrast to that on terra firma. The extreme temperatures experienced at high altitude meant all manner of bizarre clothing was adopted. Like the British and Allied pilots, the Germans donned a vast range of personalized garments in addition to their regulation fur-lined overalls and leggings, including padded leather flying helmets, goggles, scarves and fur-lined mittens. The challenge posed by the extreme cold at high altitude, plus that of breathing rarefied air, presented further difficulties.

Crews would anticipate similar discomforts, including headaches, relentless vibration and jolting, biting wind, chapped skin and cut lips. Operating the bomber would be like working on a rollercoaster, battered from all sides and afflicted from all quarters, bodies shaken like rag dolls as they tried to go about their duties, and all the while their unprotected ears were assaulted by a howling noise likened to that of a saw mill. The problem of coping with the merciless elements was not helped by the fact that the cockpit was large and completely open. But none of these factors could be permitted to impede the efficiency of the men. To this end, in addition to the official pick-me-ups, some crewmen, like their British counterparts, sought their own remedies such as brandy.

Should the bomber be shot down over the sea, various survival measures of somewhat dubious value were available. It had been estimated that an aircraft forced to land on water might remain afloat at best, for thirty minutes, so an air float had been developed by the Gotha company which it was hoped would extend this period to eight hours; air brakes were fitted to the machines in an attempt to slow their descent and consequently improve stability in the water. Pigeons accompanied the crew with the optimistic purpose of being released to fly back to safety and summon assistance. A further measure to reassure the crew was the supply of crude life jackets, but like nearly everything else issued to the men with the intention of increasing their chances of survival, their design was rudimentary and their value very limited.

Not only in this respect, however, were the crewmen being sold short. A bomber captured by the British in 1917 graphically betrayed the dire state of the German war economy. Deficient materials added to the delays getting the squadrons operational and, according to the official report of the GHQ Home Forces:

The workmanship and the construction of the machine does not appear to attain a very high standard. In this respect, one noticeable feature is the construction of the main spars; these were of hollow square section and were not even screwed or pinned together, being merely glued.

The quality of the propellers too, was found wanting. Although almost ten feet in diameter, with the outer edge bound with brass, they consisted of a core made of the higher quality hardwood, walnut, but, 'with laminations of other [inferior] woods,' The report also commented that 'taken as a whole, the propeller was a roughly finished and clumsily designed affair'.

It was in such conditions that men volunteered to fly to England.

Each bomber consisted of a crew of three. The aircraft's commander who was responsible for navigation, releasing the bombs and operating the forward machine gun. The pilot, was either an NCO or an officer and the third member was an *unteroffizier*, or corporal, who acted as observer and rear-gunner. The men chosen to crew the bombers came from all branches of the German military. Many officers had previously served either in the infantry or the cavalry and transferred to the air corps after being wounded, where they were assigned observation duties, later to become fully-fledged pilots. The NCOs and Other Ranks were usually conscripts.

Pilots had undergone intensive training at the flying school at Freiburg-in-Breisgan; observers and gunners were schooled at the *Flieger Kompagnie* and mechanics, fitters and bomb operators at the *Werft Kompagnie*. Acclimatization to flying for long periods over the sea and navigation by dead-reckoning was undertaken at Sylt and Heligoland using seaplanes; formation flying was taught at the *Geschwaderschule* at Paderborn in Prussia, where the 'hedgehog' formation was practised again and again, by which close cooperation of their machine guns should, in theory, have seen off any but the most determined intruder. Also, a minimum of ten night and ten day landings had to be practised to familiarize the crews with the Gotha's instability after it had shed its fuel and bombs. Once they became accustomed to their duties, it was not long before the various crews adopted their own distinctive mascots which were painted on the fuselage of their machines to give them some individuality and enhance their esprit de corps.

———— ◁═◆═▷ ————

Before our Prussian could take command of his aircraft however, the German High Command faced the vexed question of whether they would be able to reach the British capital at all. But it was an ambition which many influential German warlords dared to dream could be fulfilled. As early as August 1914, Rear Admiral Paul Von Behncke, Deputy Chief of the Naval Staff, wrote to Hugo Pohl, then commander of the High Seas Fleet, advancing the belief that London should be attacked,

> ...with aeroplanes and airships from the Belgian and French coasts... the panic in the population may possibly render it doubtful if war can be continued.

In November, despite insisting that he was not in favour of 'frightfulness', and maintaining that 'single bombs from flying machines are wrong when they hit an old woman,' Grand Admiral Tirpitz insisted,

> If one could set fire to London in thirty places, then what in a small way is odious would retire before something fine and wonderful. All that flies and creeps should be concentrated on that city.

There was little doubt that huge conflagrations ignited within the boundary of any great city would have the most disastrous consequences. In writing their thesis the advocates of bombing may have envisaged a repeat of the massive fire which broke out in the Cripplegate area of the City of London in November 1897. It was the biggest fire since that of 1666, consuming 200 premises and two-and-a-half acres entirely, and seriously damaging another fourteen acres of offices, factories and warehouses. £1,000,000 worth of damage was done, but perhaps of even greater significance was that, of fifty-nine fire appliances available to the Metropolitan Fire Brigade, no fewer than fifty-one had to be brought to bear on this one fire. It must have been more than coincidence that Behncke, in proposing 'particular attention to the dangerous zone in the heart of the City of London between Aldersgate Street and Moorgate Street [sic] the soft goods quarter crowded with inflammable warehouses...' he was referring precisely to that area devastated in 1897.

The notion of terrorizing the stubborn English into submission may have appealed to the Teutons, but admitting it was another matter. Hilmer von Bulow, wished to underline the purely strategic and military thinking behind the proposals:

> ...to disrupt war industry, disorganise the communications between coastal ports and London, attack the supply dumps of the English ports, and hinder the transport of materials across the [English] Channel.

In response to such pleas, the Kaiser gave in bit by bit, slowly increasing his captains' terms of reference and authorizing an Imperial Directive in January 1915. Although it still fell far short of what was wanted it permitted raids to take place, but expressly forbade attacks on 'residential areas, and, above all Royal palaces'. The Directive insisted that 'historic buildings and private property... be spared as much as possible'. Even their best efforts could not prevent one bomb only barely missing the Royal residence at Sandringham in Norfolk which brought the severest rebuke from an already nervous Kaiser, and another directive. On 5 May, it was forbidden that bombs be dropped west of the Tower of London.

Whatever the Kaiser's reservations, the German media was busy mesmerizing the population with the idea of bombing London. When the Zeppelins launched a raid on the night of 31 May-1 June 1915, Leipzig's *Neueste Nachrichten* responded, 'the City of London, the heart which pumps life's blood into the arteries of the brutal huckster nation, has been sown with bombs by German airships... At last, the long-yearned for punishment has fallen on England, this people of liars and hypocrites'.

From the day Belgium was invaded, the idea was that the German Army would simply occupy sufficient territory from which air raids with conventional machines could be made and, in anticipation, one Major Wilhelm Siegert was placed in command of a new force called *Fliegerkorps der OHL*, (*OberstenHeersLeitung*). Code named the *Brieftauben Abteilung* or 'Carrier Pigeon Squadron', it was supplied with thirty-six B-Type aeroplanes and divided into two Wings. Posted to the airfield at Ghistelles, a small village near Ostend in Belgium, it was, according to one of its officers, Major C C Neumann, composed of 'the best and most experienced pilots from every branch of the Air Force'. To increase their mobility they were quartered in railway sleeping carriages and carried out their first raids on Dunkirk and other objectives behind the enemy Fourth Army Front. The onus was now on the Army to capture the requisite territory from which Siegert could operate.

The man charged with this task was General Erich Von Falkenhayn. In what was to become known as 'The Race to the Sea', he attempted to penetrate the Allied lines at Ypres on 14 October 1914, using the Fourth and Sixth Armies, but nine days later they were still being held at bay and, despite horrific casualties – the Germans alone suffering 130,000 – the offensive had petered out by 11 November resulting in stalemate. With both sides digging in for the winter, Siegert's plans were looking forlorn. In the meantime the nascent squadron was employed in operations behind the enemy lines against Dunkirk, Furnes and La Panne, giving it plenty of practice whilst it anticipated being able to fulfil its actual role.

The spring of 1915 saw a reorganization of the force. The *Fliegerkorps* was divided into four units: the 'Carrier Pigeon Squadron' was transferred to Galicia to carry out operations against the Russians on the Eastern Front and a second squadron was formed at Metz near Nancy. Two reconnaissance Squadrons, A66 and A69, were also established. Neumann tells us:

> Shortly after our Army broke through to Gotlitz, the Ostend Carrier Pigeon Squadron returned to the Western Front, having been equipped in the meantime with a newly designed 150 or 160hp C-Type machine in which the pilot sat in front with the observer behind. However, even with this type of aircraft it was not possible to attack England.

Their return to the west was timely, as the airships had by late 1915 proven not to be the war-winners it had been hoped they might be. Their eventual arrival also gave the airship mechanics a new use for their skills, serving as ground crew for the bombers. On 1 January 1916, the 'Ostend Carrier Pigeon Squadron' was given a somewhat more prestigious title in line with the greater kudos now attached to its intended role. It was henceforth known as No.1 Battle Squadron, or *Kagohl 1*, and divided into six flights. They were employed once more in a support role against enemy rear areas, and Neumann reports that these *Fliegertruppes* (Aviation Troops) were,

> ...employed with excellent results in every undertaking of any importance and in various districts on the Western Front during 1916.

≈=≈○≈=≈

The prospect of capturing the necessary ground still eluded the Germans. Consequently a number of German aircraft construction companies had to be approached, and the practicality of constructing aircraft capable of reaching Britain from the territory currently held was discussed.

The firms consulted included *Flugzeugbau Fredrichshafen Gmbh*; *Allgemeine Elektrizitäts Gesellschaft* (AEG); and *Gothaer Waggonfabrik AG* (Gotha), and it was the latter which won the main contract to construct the aircraft. It called its prototype the Gotha 'Ursinus' G-I, equipped with two 160hp Mercedes engines. It first flew in 1915, and was followed by the G-II with its two 220hp engines. A number were provided to the squadron after further reorganization in September 1916. At this time one *Hauptmann Gaede* was given command of *Halbgeschwader* (Half-Squadron) No.1, which comprised *Staffeln* 1, 4 and 6. *Halbgeschwader* No.2 was allotted *Staffeln* 2, 3 and 5 and was dispatched to Bulgaria, and then to the Macedonian Front until May 1917 when it returned to duties in Belgium.

The Gotha G-IV had been developed by this stage, and large-scale production was to proceed at the Gotha, LVG and *Siemens-Schuckert* factories. On 25 November 1916 the *Kommandierender General Der Luftstreitkrafte – Kogenluft –* was established as a separate entity from the Army under the command of General Ernst Hoeppner. Upon assuming command he issued the first policy document which outlined the functions expected the squadron in its operations against the United Kingdom:

> Since an airship raid against London has become impossible, the Air Service is required to carry out a raid with aeroplanes as soon as possible. The undertaking will be carried out in accordance with two entirely different schemes:
>
> 1. Bombing squadrons equipped with G (Large) Aeroplanes...
> ...Scheme 1 will be carried out by Half-Squadron No.1 using Gotha G-IV aeroplanes. The requisite number of thirty aeroplanes will be ready by February 1 1917.
>
> By despatching eighteen aeroplanes, each carrying a load of 300kg of bombs, 5,400kg could be dropped on London, the same amount as would be carried by three airships, and so far three airships have never reached London simultaneously.
>
> Scheme 1 can only succeed provided every detail is carefully prepared, the crews are practised in long-distance overseas flight, and the squadron is made up of specially good aeroplane crews. Any negligence and undue haste will only entail heavy losses for us, and defeat our ends.

The project was code named *Turkenkreuz*, - Turks' Cross, and the squadron would be called the *Englandgeschwader*, or 'England Squadron'. It had four airfields allocated to it; Mariakerke, Melle-Gontrode, Ostacker and St Denis-Westrem, all sited around Gent about, forty miles behind German lines.

It was now that the full implications of the aircraft's change in centre of gravity after losing its bombs and fuel, was fully appreciated. None of the airfields were anything like flat and level enough to accommodate a returning bomber and land it with much chance of it not crashing. As a result, the respective airfields would have to be made as flat as possible to reduce the possibility of this happening and this meant shifting tons of earth around to smooth and level them. Melle-Gontrode and St Denis-Westrem would not be ready until April, Mariakerke and Ostacker until July, so Ghistelles was to be used until then to house the aircraft, sharing facilities with Half-Squadron No.1. The force was to consist of six *staffeln*, each of six machines, and in theory a total of thirty-six bombers were to attack London in the forthcoming operation.

One vital element which an undertaking of this scale and magnitude needed was also in short supply by this stage in the war; first rate leadership. However, luckily for the squadron, one man would enter, stage left, to fill this void in the person of thirty-four year-old *Hauptmann* Ernst Brandenburg.

He had found his way into the Air Force like many of his colleagues, after being wounded in the trenches and subsequently assigned to what were considered lighter duties as an observer in a two-seater reconnaissance aircraft. He would prove to be the perfect candidate for the demanding assignment, to mould a cohesive unit practically from scratch, capable of launching the first-ever daylight strategic bomber raid. Such were the qualities of this man, that despite the punishing regime and unremitting requirements of the endless training, he would be able to earn the respect and admiration of officers and men alike, leading by example in his quiet, unassuming way.

It would be a task completely different to that which his colleagues in the airship service would have faced. There, the mighty vessels operated largely alone, with all the component parts, namely the crews, in one place; the bombs would be dropped from a single platform; there were none of the completely new skills that Brandenburg and his men would need to master. Almost forty different machines, untested in the kind of warfare upon which they were about to embark, would have to rise and fly in formation, keep together over featureless seas, and then, above hostile territory, finally unload their bombs in a tight pattern in order to gain the maximum results. Keeping in formation they would then attempt the perilous journey back to their airfields, expecting to be harassed all the way by enemy fighters baying for their blood.

Organization, training and tactics – all completely new and untried – General Staff maps of the North Sea and Dover Straits were studied intensely, while the flight path over Ostend and then Foulness, on towards the capital from the north-east (with Epping Forest serving as their marker) had to be rehearsed again and again. Just as important for the crews was to know the way back to base, along the north side of the Thames to the Estuary.

One of his first decisions was to form *Staffeln* 16, and place it under the command of *Oberleutnant* von Seydlitz-Kurzbach, by drafting in personnel from the *Luftstreitkrafte*; *Staffeln* 17 and 18 would follow in July. There were to be seven headquarters staff, Brandenburg, Adjutant Gerlicht and five officers whose responsibilities ranged from intelligence, reconnaissance photography, motor transport and administration. Three bombers were allocated to headquarters staff. So he could be identified easily by his men in flight and his instructions conveyed, the fuselage of Brandenburg's machine was painted red.

In April 1917, *Kagohl* 3 was ready to move from Ghistelles to Melle-Gontrode and St Denis-Westrem. Despite this, things were not going well. As we have seen, examination of a wrecked German aircraft by the Allies exposed the sub-standard nature of much of the materials used in their manufacture and as a result the standard of construction of the engines left a lot to be desired and extensive modifications were required on the pipe work installed in earlier models. This rework alone took up most of the month.

By the middle of May both the aircraft and crew were as ready as they would ever be. Morale was boosted by visits from such dignitaries as Hoeppner and later by General Hindenburg, both of whom had bold words of encouragement for the crews, words which they were all too keen to justify.

CHAPTER 6

THAT'S RIGHT
IN TONTINE STREET

Hindenburg's visit left the crews buoyed up and keen to get into action. The burly old Field Marshal, as imposing a sight as the aircraft he had come to inspect, had left them in no doubt of what Germany expected. Fired with enthusiasm, all they could do now was wait for the order to go.

This order, however, was beholden to prevailing flying conditions. In this respect it was the weather watchers as much, if not more, than the commander who would have the final word. *Hauptmann* Cloessner had made his calibrations, interpreted the signals from his weather balloons and decided that for the next few days at least, the weather might prove accommodating. An anticyclone was covering France and moving towards the UK, where the south-east of the country was expected to enjoy perfect summer weather. The wind would be pleasantly light from the south-west and was not expected to exceed 25mph at 9,000 feet. However, Cloessner could not predict with any accuracy much beyond that. When Brandenburg opted to begin operations on Friday 25 May he was not to know that the weather would seriously deteriorate towards midday, becoming increasingly overcast by the afternoon.

The weather was not to prove the only upset. British intelligence had become curious about the unusual activity on the German airfields and the RNAS at Dunkirk concluded, perhaps, that heavy raids were being scheduled for Dunkirk and its environs. Taking no chances, orders were issued to pay the two airfields a visit. Consequently, DH4s attacked on 24 May and dropped bombs perilously close to the Gothas, though no serious damage was done and preparations continued undisturbed.

At approximately 2.00 pm the following day, the twenty-three Gothas, heavy with bombs, struggled into the air from St Denis-Westrem and Melle-Gontrode. Almost immediately, the engine of one machine began to give trouble. The engineer could do little to repair the fault once the aircraft was airborne, so the commander fired the signal to indicate they were aborting the mission and proceeded to land at the reserve field at Thielt.

The remainder of the force proceeded as planned to the refuelling site at Nieumunster, where they landed thirty or so minutes after take-off. Refuelling completed, the Gothas took to the air again at around 3.00 pm, climbing to a height of 10,000 feet before forming up into a diamond shaped phalanx – the three headquarters machines in front, led by Brandenburg – and followed by the rest of the force.

No sooner had they formed up than a second machine signalled engine trouble, and this time made for the emergency landing ground at Ghistelles. About an hour later, after an uneventful flight over the English Channel, the North Foreland Lightship hove into view and the Tongue Lightship was passed at 4.45 pm.

Here, the men of the Lightship were probably anticipating another boring day fending off seasickness. Instead they were to be the first to set eyes upon the German armada as it bumped and heaved its way through the sky at 15,000 feet. Eyes strained through binoculars to try and identify the aeroplanes; were they friendly or hostile? A call was put through to the Admiralty to make sure, while the Gothas passed over Tongue and on towards the Swan Middle Lightship. At this point they roughly divided into two sections, crossing the English coastline between the Rivers Crouch and Blackwater.

⎯⎯⎯◦⎯⎯⎯

Fifteen minutes or so after the Tongue Lightship sighting, the RNAS were informed and pilots were sortied at airfields throughout the south-east. One of the first airborne was Flight Sub Lieutenant H R de Wilde, who took off from Manston in his Bristol Scout. He was followed ten minutes later by Flight Sub-Lieutenants Bart, Daly and Scott, and Squadron Commander C H Butler. At 4.55 am, Flight Sub Lieutenant Drake took off from Westgate in his Sopwith Schneider, closely followed by Flight Sub-Lieutenant L G Maxton in his Sopwith Baby.

Next up from Westgate, at 5.02 pm, was Flight Sub Lieutenant F C Lander, flying another Sopwith Baby. They were to be followed at varying intervals by another four machines. At 5.00 pm Felixstowe dispatched Curtiss H-12s, followed during the next forty-five minutes by five more aircraft, mainly Sopwith Babies.

Despite the early warnings, however, all were destined to patrol too far to the east, and consequently this formidable force failed

73

completely to sight a single enemy bomber. At 5.00 pm further warnings were given to the emergency services named in the 'Special Warning Lists' for London. In keeping with current practice, no alert was to be given to the general public.

A few minutes after 5.00 pm the first enemy machines were over Southminster in Essex, flying 'very high' according to one contemporary report. Already, witnesses were assuming the raiders, obscured by cloud and haze, to be more airships owing to the loud noise being made by the engines. These kind of claims were being made as far north as Bradwell and Mersey, many of which were made by people who claimed to have seen airships escorted by aircraft. At 5.07 pm, witnesses at Burnham were certain they had seen 'high white machines making a loud noise' travelling at 9,000 feet; another observer at the same place described one of the machines more accurately, as 'silver colour, appeared like an aeroplane but [making] a noise like a Zeppelin'. As the lead planes were being spotted, the vanguard was just crossing the coast, the last of which passed at around 5.15 pm.

<hr>

Ten minutes after the RNAS sortied, the three Home Defence squadrons husbanded their meagre resources: 37 Squadron scrambling the first of nine aircraft from flights stationed at Goldhanger, Stow Maries and Rochford; 39 Squadron sortied eleven aircraft from North Weald, Sutton's Farm (Hornchurch) and Hainault; and 50 Squadron sent up thirteen from Detling, Bekesbourne and Throwley. All were fielding the elderly B.E. type machines and all were woefully ill-equipped to intercept the Gotha raiders.

In the meantime, the Gothas were passing over the mudflats of the Crouch Estuary, meeting the first resistance from the defenders and the only response from the ground until their return flight. At Highland Farm, Burnham-on-Crouch, stood a solitary 3-inch 20cwt gun of the 13th Mobile Anti-Aircraft Battery. At around 5.15 pm a Gotha came tantalizingly close; the crew leapt into action, opening fire with a single round – but it had no effect, the Gotha disappearing into the haze once again.

Police Constable Dale, drawing a typically quiet and uneventful day to a close, was one of the few witnesses to accurately identify the intruders. In his report, he wrote that he was:

...in Station Road, Burnham, when I heard the sound of aircraft. It appeared like several aeroplanes - they were very high and came from an easterly direction, and went in a westerly direction. I could not see them.

Leaving Constable Dale standing bemused on the ground, the bombers then crossed the Crouch between North Fambridge and Canewdon; groups of them were seen at 5.20 pm from Paglesham in the south to Purleigh in the north and heard as far north as Maldon and as far south as Wakering as they flew south-west in a ragged line. They were now flying close to the airfields of 37 Squadron at Stow Maries and Rochford, but the B.E. aircraft were still struggling to reach them. It would be another thirty minutes before they could even approach their height and then, flying at speeds of 70mph, the Gothas would be thirty-five miles away.

At 5.25 pm they were over Rayleigh, where twelve machines were reported. They were also heard from Leigh and Rochford, and even as far as Margaretting, but here again, the sound was assumed to be that of an airship. Their course then took them over the tiny Essex villages of South Benfleet and Pitsea, and Canvey Island, Kynochtown and Thameshaven.

RFC pilots were inching towards these dim specks. Captain C B Cooke of 'C' Flight, 37 Squadron stationed at Rochford, took off at 5.22 pm in his B.E.12a. As he left the ground he noticed:

Four hostile aircraft over the aerodrome proceeding north-west. I immediately turned my nose towards them but owing to the clouds being at 5,000 feet and the slow climbing of the machine, by the time I got through the clouds the hostile aircraft were out of sight. The hostile aircraft appeared to be at about 15,000 feet, and I consider that had I been on a fast climbing scout I would have been able to keep in touch with the hostile aircraft.

When I got to 13,000 feet my aircraft suddenly burst into flames, so that I had to tail slide to put it out. I was successful in doing this but afterwards I noticed the centre sections of the plane swaying in an alarming manner, evidently owing to the inability of the machine to withstand rough usage such as it would undergo in a fight.

Captain Cooke was forced to return to land. Frustrated, he also decided to let his superiors know that if they thought raids could be defeated by men flying obsolete machines, they were kidding nobody but themselves, and submitting a forthright report in which he said he:

> Should like to point out the unsuitability of the B.E.12a for chasing hostile aircraft... [it] will not climb above 14,000 feet and at that height it is impossible to do a sharp turn without losing about 500 feet, owing to the fact that the machine has no [power] reserve and it is only just able to keep that height. Another thing is the liability of the engine to catch fire in the air.

The same frustration was experienced by the commander of 'B' Flight at Stow Maries. Captain Claude Ridley took off after the raiders in his B.E.12a at 5.12 pm:

> It seems a pity that scouts cannot be supplied to flights for this purpose, as the B.E.12a climbs so very poorly and is so very slow at height in comparison with a good machine. It takes a long time to reach 14,000 feet and at this height there is no reserve of power, which seems absolutely useless when it comes to attacking first-class German machines. If I had been flying a fast scout I am almost certain that I should not have had the slightest difficulty of coming in contact with the hostile formation. If the Germans make a practice of coming over as they did today, it seems hardly fair to expect pilots to gain satisfactory results.

Such complaints underline how frustrated and despondent these first-rate pilots must have been, knowing they were being expected to stop an elephant with a fly-swat.

⋯⋯⋯⋯⋯

As it turned out, the Germans were to be thwarted, not by the impotent defenders, but by the British weather. Whilst the Gothas flew south-west towards the capital they were met by a developing depression shrouding London in a protective layer of strato-cumulus some 7,000 feet thick.

Perhaps cursing Cloessner for not having anticipated this, Brandenburg accepted that an attempt on London was not worth chancing. At 5.30 pm, with the formation over Tilbury, he decided to abort the mission. He reluctantly fired a flare and in response the raiders wheeled over Gravesend and the two headed south.

While London, oblivious of its close shave, continued about its business, the German commander began searching for appropriate secondary targets. He decided to track a line over the South Eastern and Chatham Railway lines, the Royal Military Canal, the naval base at Dover and, most significantly of all, the military encampments in and around the port of Folkestone in Kent.

The British pilots were oblivious of the sudden German swing southwards, and continued on their route to intercept the raiders over the capital. Owing to cloud, all attempts by ground signals to inform them of course changes were fruitless, so they were left to flounder haplessly over the metropolis.

Strung out over a front of about five miles, the Gothas were concealed by the cloud for another twenty-five minutes, but such was the confusion on the ground that still the southern England military authorities remained oblivious to what was heading their way.

Changing from line into groups for greater protection, probably expecting that by now the enemy would be on to them, the raiders were observed from Northfleet and Longfield, travelling south-east towards Meopham and Wrotham. Many reports still included the mention of airships, as one Gravesend naval unit told the local anti-aircraft commander apparently with complete confidence that 'a fleet of Zeppelins, making a great noise, overhead a stink of paraffin, Zeppelins flying very high towards Snodland'. On the left flank, some of the raiders were seen from Cobham to Malling, whilst on the right flank they were observed from as far south as Seal near Sevenoaks. A group that passed over the Hartley and Weike Searchlights, south of Fawkham at about 5.35 pm, was described by one officer of the London Electrical Engineers as consisting of two airships flying at about 14,000 feet. At Wrotham, a mile or so east of Weike Farm, the enemy were estimated to have numbered fifteen. On other occasions the machines were described as 'very large' monoplanes, painted with low visibility paint, flying very fast and high.

At 5.42 pm the first bombs were dropped in an attempt to damage the railway line; two 50kg bombs fell, one each on the villages of Harvel and Luddesdown, halfway between Meopham and Offham. In episodes which would be repeated many times over in the weeks to come, the bombs failed to perform effectively and no serious damage was done. The first authorities on the scene in the persons of Constables Carter, Dennis and Ellier and Sergeant Turner, later reported how:

> ...we found that two high explosive bombs had been dropped in cornfields, one at Swanswood in the parish of Luddesdown and one at Plum Rush, Harvel, in the parish of Meopham. One hole

caused by the bombs was six feet deep and fourteen feet across. We searched around and collected several pieces of bombs from persons who were there before we arrived. We then cleared the people from the fields.

Only the bombs landing at Luddesdown came close to the railway line. That falling at Harvel was still farther off target. However, people were still convinced that the perpetrators were Zeppelins, such as the witness at nearby Kemsing who reported seeing an 'egg-shaped' airship.

After crossing the North Downs the Gothas passed over Malling and Aylesford. They proceeded to sweep south-east of Maidstone dropping a couple of bombs as they went. It was at this critical time that the dire state of the intelligence network was exposed further by the report made by the local policeman, Constable A S Lyons:

I saw seven planes pass over Coxheath Linton. They came from a north-westerly direction and went easterly. They were flying very high and I could only just see them as they came out of one cloud and into another. They looked like a silver bird. I could hear others about half-a-mile west of me but could not see them. I tried to get the Intelligence [to] London but could not do so as the reply came they were engaged.

While Lyons was trying to get through, four smaller 12.5kg bombs were falling towards Marden on the main line of the railway. If broken, communications between London and the south coast could have been seriously disrupted, with troop movements between Folkestone, Ashford and London delayed for days or even weeks. But, despite getting so far, and being so close to a key objective, the bombs fell wide; the only casualty was a sheep in a field. Superintendent J H Cheesman reported:

A large squadron of enemy aircraft passed over Marden approaching from a northerly direction and dropped four bombs in a wheatfield at Dairy Farm, Marden... Neither of the bombs appear to have exploded and did no damage with the exception of making four small holes in the field. The aircraft made off in an easterly direction.

Reserve Police Constable Hart reported a sighting of fourteen aeroplanes (of the left wing) over the village of Pluckley, coming from the south-west. This village too, was astride the railway line but again, the bombs failed to find their mark. It must have looked to Brandenburg that the whole escapade was going to be a complete failure, as bomb after bomb either missed its mark or exploded early.

Continuing on their south-easterly course, and still no British aircraft had yet tried to engage the Gothas, neither had there been ground-fire since the incident at Burnham. The raiders reached Ashford in Kent at 6.10 pm, dropping the first of four 12.5kg bombs. Two of these would fall near Bond Road, one behind and one on Providence Street near the railway and gas works, one at Beaver Green and one in Rugby Gardens killing eighteen-year-old Gladys Sparkes of 15 Providence Street – perhaps the first fatality of the day and the first victim of a Gotha bomber. Labourer James Hook, of 26 Providence Street was seriously injured, and Thomas Brooke, another labourer of 36 Bridge Street, was slightly injured. Ernest Burden, a schoolboy who lived at 13 Providence Street was also slightly injured. Thirty-two-year-old Bessie Payne of 13 Bond Road was slightly injured in the shoulder by shrapnel.

Suddenly, in the midst of all this appeared an RFC Ferry pilot, Flight Lieutenant Baker, who was taking a Bristol Fighter from the factory over to France via Lympne. Baker was instantly fired upon from all directions by the Gothas, who must have thought that at last the enemy had decided to put up some resistance. Having no ammunition in his gun, the startled flier took what evasive action he could and was forced to find a suitable place to land.

As Baker raced for Lympne, pilots from 78 Squadron stationed at Telscombe Cliffs in Sussex were doing their best to engage the enemy. The first to get airborne was Flight Lieutenant J S Castle, who took off at 5.57 pm in his B.E.2a. He was to search in vain, finally giving up and returning home at 6.40 pm when his aeroplane developed engine trouble. He took up another machine, but was again thwarted by engine trouble, landing at Arlington at 7.45 pm.

Captain E R Pretyman took off in a B.E.12a at 6.00 pm, but was also unsuccessful. But not only were their engines failing them. Woeful communications meant they were searching for an enemy who was actually forty miles away.

Meanwhile the right flank passed Ashford at 5.15 pm, midway between Kingsnorth and Shadoxhurst and four 12.5kg bombs were dropped. The formation flew on towards Romney Marsh and Lympne, bombing the villages of Bilsington and Ruckinge, north of the Royal Military Canal.

The Gothas pressed on, passing over Ruckinge at around 6.00 pm, where more bombs were released, hitting a farm and some woods. They then proceeded towards Lympne, no doubt wondering if they could have any better luck if they found this secondary target. Thirteen minutes or so later, they were over the airfield dropping three 50kg and nineteen 12.5kg bombs. One 50kg and one 12.5kg bomb burst near a hangar but inflicted no damage; a 50kg bomb fell in a quarry east of the aerodrome and a third exploded 400 feet in mid-air. The other 12.5kg bombs peppered the centre of the airfield where several craters were blasted, but little damage of note was caused.

As the Gothas commenced their attack, who should arrive on the scene but the hapless Baker in his unarmed Bristol. Once again he had to flee. Moments later the raiders were over Saltwood, dropping more bombs and hoping to hit the Royal Military Canal.

As usual, no significant damage was done but there was a lucky escape for those working inside the Metropole Steam Laundry in Dymchurch when a bomb exploded above the building. Fragments of shell penetrated the roof of the laundry's drying room, although women working in the ironing room escaped injury.

Proceeding over Saltwood, the intruders reached Hythe. A bomb fragment struck a man in the right shoulder while he was working in his allotment but he was spared serious injury. Less fortunate was Daniel Stringer, Verger of St Leonard's Church. He was standing chatting to the vicar's wife when a bomb exploded nearby. His right thigh was ripped apart by shrapnel and despite receiving prompt medical attention, he bled to death.

In Ormonde Road a bomb sent a shower of shrapnel in all directions; a shard of metal penetrated the left breast of Amy Parker, a forty-three-year-old housewife as she was walking back home to No.50. She died within minutes.

The Hotel Imperial had a close shave when two bombs fell on the nearby beach. A third fell on the hotel's golf course eighty yards away and although it exploded, simply added another small bunker to the course. Hythe Golf Links received the next bomb which exploded 600 yards west of 'Blue Bungalow' creating another feature fourteen feet in diameter. Surprisingly perhaps, no attempt was made to bomb the RFC School of Gunnery at Hythe. Possibly the Germans were unaware of its existence, or Brandenburg may not have had it listed in his book of secondary targets. Of more surprise to the locals was the lack of warlike activity at the base. However, regulations forbade the use of training machines for operational duties unless Flights from the Home Defence Squadrons were based at the same airfield. There were no such Flights operating from Hythe and the training machines were, in any case, of an even lower standard than those trying desperately to reach the raiders. So those on the ground could only sit tight and hope for the best, much to the irritation of their neighbours who, unaware of the rules were disgusted by their lack of enthusiasm. Later they vented their anger by lobbing bricks, as well as brickbats, at the men inside.

Leaving Hythe, the raiders proceeded towards Sandgate. Here seven bombs were dropped, two of which exploded in mid-air and two in the vicinity of Shorncliffe Military Hospital. One bomb made an insignificant hole and the other landed about five yards from the Sergeants' Mess, blasting another crater some three feet deep.

⸻⸺⸺◦⸺⸺⸻

As the Gothas entered the skies over Folkestone, more lucrative targets came into the bombsights. At 6.20 pm the raiders were above the military camps of Shorncliffe and Cheriton, where hundreds of Canadian troops were stationed in preparation for embarkation to the Front.

First, a 50kg bomb fell in the north-west corner of the hospital block by the married quarters and another south-west of Martello Tower No.9. Neither exploded. Another however, fell on a tent between two huts in the 'Howitzer Lines', killing eight soldiers and wounding fifteen. A fourth bomb fell on the tailor's shop in the 8th Canadian Battalion's lines, injuring another twenty-five men. Then a 12.5kg fell in the Canadian ASC Lines, and another twenty yards south of the tailor's shop, failing to explode. One damaged a house in the married quarters, Risborough Barracks; two fell harmlessly in Risborough Field just opposite; one fell on a tent killing two soldiers, and another fell on a tent in quarantine quarters, killing a private. Three 12.5kg bombs burst in allotments close to the railway, one in a yard in Military Avenue, killing a man; another near the Cavalry Drill Ground causing another fatality. Another fell on the roof of a lavatory in the Officers' Mess of the Canadian HQ, Napier Barracks but because of the building's sturdy construction no real damage was done.

The few short moments the Gothas had been over the Canadians' barracks had brought a swift and costly toll. Civilians too, were caught in the hail of bombs; sixty-two-year-old Alfred Downage of

81

52 Military Avenue was killed; six-year-old Francis Considine was killed and his mother injured; Henry Hunt of 35 Military Avenue, John Matthews of 12 Alma Road, Rose Burgius and Mabel Ellender of 21 Oaks Road and Mrs Long and Ernest Davey of 46 Military Avenue all sustained injuries of varying degrees. These tragedies so far were, however, as nothing compared to the massacre soon to be inflicted on the town.

By the time the Gothas started bombing the camps, the sound of explosions would have been audible to those promenading along the seafront. But still no warning had been received even at this late stage. The pandemonium was probably dismissed as one of the many military live-firing exercises carried out by the Army.

Folkestone had been a legitimate target for the enemy from the very start of the war, serving as a transit point to some 7,000,000 troops and accommodating large camps where wounded soldiers recuperated before returning to France for training at the hated facility at Etaples. Once, Folkestone basked in the reputation as 'England's Riviera', but now it was awash with Belgian refugees and transitting Army personnel, who had occupied the entire seafront of Marine Parade and Lower Sandgate, while the sinister thud of artillery barrages could be heard across the Channel. As the war had progressed, so the townsfolk came to witness the true carnage in France as the daily, almost medieval, procession of maimed and blinded men made their way past the boarded up windows of this increasingly miserable town.

Today, however they were being visited by Brandenburg's squadron, whose two flanks had reunited to begin its next bombing run.

More and more people began to turn to look at the distant specks in the sky. 'People were standing in the gardens looking upwards as if knowing something had happened', recalled Mrs E Craig. Alan Salter, then just four years old, can still remember,

>...being taken for a walk up Canterbury Road... and seeing shiny objects and a lot of smoke.

The bombers were 15,000 feet up, resembling 'bright silver insects', or looking, as Edith Cole noted, 'beautiful with the sun on their wings...'. Others met their arrival with a mixture of confusion and panic. An American journalist reported how,

>...an American clergyman residing in Folkestone was alerted by cries of Zepps! Zepps! coming from the street. He dashed out of

1. German airship L31, photographed with an unidentified German warship. IWM
2. (Inset) Ernst Brandenburg. IWM
3. Early bomb damage in the City of London in 1915. Curious onlookers examine a crater in Broad Street, close by Broad Street Station. GUILDHALL LIBRARY, MUSEUM OF LONDON

4. Officers of the
England Squadron
entertaining visiting
lady friends at
Chateau Drory in the
Spring of 1917. IWM

5. Gotha crew
prepares for take-off.
IWM

6. Gosnold's
Store, Tontine
Street,
Folkestone,
following the
air raid of 25
May 1917.

KENT ARTS &
LIBRARIES

7. Stoke's shop, Tontine Street, Folkestone, following the air raid of 25 May 1917.
KENT ARTS & LIBRARIES

8. Bomb damage at Upper North Street School, London following the air raid of
13 June 1917. AUTHOR'S COLLECTION.

Metropolitan Borough of Poplar.

Telephone—No. EAST 73.

BUTEUX SKEGGS,
Town Clerk.

COUNCIL OFFICES,

POPLAR, E.,

15th June, 1917.

Dear Sir,

The funeral of the little children who lost their lives in the Air Raid on Wednesday last at the L.C.C. School, Upper North Street, Poplar, will take place on Wednesday next, the 20th inst.

A Service will be held at the Parish Church of All Saints', Poplar, at 2 o'clock p.m., and the interment will follow at the East London Cemetery, Hermit Road, Plaistow.

I enclose two tickets of admission to the Church. Members of the Council and the Board of Guardians will meet at the Town Hall, Newby Place, at 1.30.

Yours truly,

[signature]

Town Clerk.

---

an Borough of Poplar.

POPLAR PARISH CHURCH.

esday, June 20th, 1917.

At 1.30 p.m.

he Service preceding the burial of the e Upper North Street (L.C.C.) School, ring the recent Air Raid.

[signature]

Town Clerk.

9. Letter announcing details of the children's funeral. AUTHOR'S COLLECTION.

10. The funeral cortège making its way along the East India Dock Road, London.

AUTHOR'S COLLECTION.

In Sacred Memory of
THE VICTIMS
of the Hun death-dealers
in the great AIR RAID on London,
Wednesday June 13th, 1917.
IN SINCERE SYMPATHY FOR THE RELATIVES AND SUFFERERS
May God Rest Their Souls.

11. Memorial card presented to the relatives of the victims of the air raid on London 13 June.

AUTHOR'S COLLECTION

The number of Victims in this raid constitutes a new record in Air Raid casualties.

The Germans don't kill women and little children from the sky for the mere fun of the thing. It is part of their scheme of frightfulness. They believe that the murder of the little ones will cause the parents to revolt and overthrow authority, and by that means peace will come. Of course, they are wrong again.

Half the profits will be given to the Relief Fund.

IN MEMORY OF
18 CHILDREN
WHO WERE KILLED
~ BY A BOMB ~
DROPPED FROM A
GERMAN AEROPLANE
UPON THE L.C.C.
SCHOOL ~ UPPER
NORTH STREET ~
POPLAR ~ ON THE
13th OF JUNE 1917.

ALFRED H.WARREN O.B.E.
MAYOR
J.BUTEUX SKEGGS
TOWN CLERK

ERECTED BY PUBLIC SUBSCRIPTION.

AGED FIVE YEARS
WILLIAM T.H.CHALLEN
AGED FIVE YEARS
VERA M.CLAYSON
AGED FIVE YEARS
ALICE M.CROSS ~ ~
AGED FIVE YEARS
WILLIAM HOLLIS ~ ~
AGED FIVE YEARS
GEORGE A.HYDE ~ ~
AGED FIVE YEARS

12. The monument to the eighteen children killed at Upper North Street, School. AUTHOR'S COLLECTION.

13. Names of some of the child victims, immortalized on the base of the memorial. AUTHOR'S COLLECTION

14. Monument to PC Smith, who lost his life saving others on 13 June 1917.
AUTHOR'S COLLECTION

15. Bomb damage to houses in Caeser Street, Hoxton, London following the raid of 1–2 October 1916. IWM

16. The Central Telegraph
Office, Newgate Street,
London blazes following the
raid of 7 July 1917.
IWM

17. Devastation caused to the
Odhams Printing Works, Long
Acre, London following the ai
raid of 28-29 January 1918.
IWM

his seaside house to find crowds gazing upwards in the direction of the sun.

The reporter himself tried to find out what all the fuss was about but:

I could see nothing for the glare. Then I saw two aeroplanes, not Zeppelins, emerging from the disc of the sun almost overhead. Then four more, or five in a line and others, all light bright silver insects hovering against the blue of the sky... There was about a score in all, and we were charmed with the beauty of the sight. I am sure few of us thought seriously of danger.

Seconds ticked by. Captain C Russell, an RFC pilot on leave from France, was in the town when the bombers arrived. His vision too was diminished by the haze, but he could hear the engines clearly enough. As they came nearer he recognized them as German aircraft, but was further confounded by their shape. They looked nothing like the adversaries he was used to fighting over the Western Front:

Three things surprised me. They looked much bigger than I would have expected; they were coming over the land instead of the sea; and if they were returning from a raid on London I couldn't understand why they hadn't been spotted. But there wasn't any air raid warning in the town...

...about sixteen Huns. One was ahead of the rest and flying above them. Behind him were about six other machines in line abreast, and they were followed by a group of about six, with some others forming a rearguard. Then they closed to make a 'V' shape like a skein of geese.

A bomb fell in the grounds of Enbrook Manor and proved to be the first to have fallen within the Folkestone Borough area itself. The second, a 12.5kg bomb, fell west of Coolinge Lane and a third came to earth a quarter of a mile away in Turkatel Road. The fourth, a 50kg bomb, exploded in Grimstone Gardens, near the military commander's HQ, killing a woman and injuring a soldier. Around the corner, in Grimstone Avenue, R S Body, a twelve-year-old pupil in a small cottage school, remembers how:

We were all hurriedly marshalled out into the asphalt playground at the back of the school, where we waited until it quietened down.

The fifth bomb to fall was a 12.5kg, landing in Earls Avenue, but it failed to explode. Stanley Coxon was:

> ...one of the townspeople who was out for a stroll on such a perfect evening. Before I got any distance, I became interested in a very large flight of about twenty aeroplanes circling and pirouetting over my head.

He then stopped to watch their graceful antics and thought to himself, 'at least we are up and doing,' assuming like most other people that they were British aircraft exercising:

> I leisurely walked on and as I was crossing Earls Avenue, I noticed a woman coming towards me carrying a basket. I had hardly time to reach Oliver's garden gate when a bomb fell [the sixth] behind me, killing the poor woman I had just seen.

The seventh bomb fell in neighbouring Jointon Road. Mrs K Holloway was with her father at the time, helping him in his allotment when:

> German planes came out of the brilliant sunshine. My father hurried me up a bank and under some trees. I saw the church clock blown out, and at the top of Jointon Road a woman had her legs blown off.

The eighth bomb recorded in chronological order, a 50kg, fell in the grounds of the Pleasure Gardens Theatre, but failed to explode. To the north, the Gothas which had attempted to bomb the railway line, and which had contributed to the carnage in the military camps, had followed the line to Central Station. Here, at around 6.25 pm a number of bombs landed. Three 12.5kg bombs fell between the railway and Shorncliffe Road. One, which fell among a group of children playing in a field at the back of a girls' school, did not explode and narrowly missed hitting any of the children. A second landed behind another girls' school but also failed to explode; while a third exploded in a garden and claimed the life of a man. Then three 50kg bombs fell without exploding south of the station at the back of Kingsnorth Gardens. Meanwhile, for William Eastwell, it was a tense moment. His father ran a florist's shop in Central Station, and as far as he knew he could easily have been a victim of the bombs which were coming down:

> Running back from the blacksmiths' shops in Hawkins Road [I] saw high in the sky as they flew away after releasing their bombs,

84

a large number of aeroplanes. Luckily our father had gone to pick flowers at his allotment for the shop. On returning he found that the centre rod in the gate in front of his shop had been knocked out by the flying shrapnel from one of the bombs, and he probably would have been standing there.

William remembers, 'a cab driver and his horse killed after a [50kg] bomb straddled the line'. The residential area north of the line now received five 12.5kg bombs which fell in the area of Wiltie Gardens and Boscombe Road. Eddy Williams was on his way with his brother to buy a loaf of bread when:

> We crossed Dover Road from Bradstone Road, where we were living at the time, and stopped by the church on the corner to watch two Gothas approaching. We dawdled along, eyes upturned so we shouldn't miss anything, when suddenly everything was noisy – lots of noise and dust – I remember people running and screaming. It was sheer pandemonium. I was very frightened but my brother and I, scared as we were, started to walk towards the baker's. We were stopped by a man and told to run home. I have since measured the distance from where we were standing to where the bomb had dropped. Approximately ninety yards, so we were lucky.

The bombers were now beginning to get the range of the railway line, or seemed to, as bombs were falling perilously close to the track. One, probably a 50kg, exploded over Junction Station at a height of about 4,000 feet.

Meanwhile the 4.40 pm train was due to arrive from Charing Cross, London. Douglas Lidderdale saw,

> ...some Gothas in line ahead, not less than two, probably three, making their approach run flying low immediately above the Dover-Folkestone-London line.

The train was due to cross a critical and vulnerable viaduct of nineteen brick arches 100 feet high. At that time it was the only rail link between London and Folkestone Harbour since the line between Folkestone and Dover had been closed by a massive landslide. Lidderdale recalls:

> All I saw was the flight of Gothas a few hundred feet above the line of the railway, I was standing on the doorstep of my home at 4 London Street clutching my fathers' hand...

85

After the Gothas had vanished from sight, still following the railway line to Folkestone, my father went off with his doctor's bag heading for Junction Station with all speed... as the Gothas approached the station it was thought that the target for attack might well be the train from Charing Cross. It was also feared that a head-on attack by 'aerial torpedoes' launched by the Gothas would result in the engine being lifted off the track, over the side of the viaduct and, with the coaches still coupled, crash on to the gasworks below, setting fire to the gasholders and causing major explosions. This would result in wrecking the viaduct, thereby interrupting rail traffic to and from Folkestone Harbour for a long time... The railway solution was simple and effective; the train was held at Folkestone Central and did not proceed onto the viaduct.

Areas in and around Bouverie Street and Cheriton Road also found themselves in the heart of a stick of bombs. Nine-year-old Richard Pinney was on his way home from Bouverie Square when:

The house at the corner of Alexandra Gardens and Bouverie Road East got one in the basement which left the house standing on two walls. A second after this bomb exploded a man's head rolled across a path and into the gutter. I didn't stop running until I got home to my parents.

Mrs. A V Sharman, who was living at 32 Alexandra Gardens with her mother, aunt, sister and grandmother, was at the top of her house with her aunt when:

We heard explosions which we thought was some kind of practice, but the bangs came nearer and louder and we realised it was a raid. We rushed down the flights of stairs, and on going down the last flight to the basement, there was a terrific bang. The blast hit me and for a moment I could not move. All the windows had been blown out. A friend had been visiting my mother, and she went out to see what was happening. She was soon brought back with a gaping shrapnel wound in her back. Fortunately, a nurse was soon on the scene and the victim was given immediate medical attention. Our house was third or fourth from the corner into Bouverie Road where some bombs had fallen, causing the damage to our house.

The Gothas were now over the heart of the town, an area of about one square mile north and west of the harbour. Much of this constituted the main shopping district, with numerous lanes and alleys converging on Tontine Street, which ran north-west from the harbour. Being Whitsun, the streets were packed with late-evening shoppers, most of whom were concentrating on whatever meagre bargains were to be had in the quarter-mile-long street. Of the numerous commercial premises, two of the most patronized were Gosnold's Drapery Store and Stoke's Greengrocery. From these two stores in particular, queues were winding out into the street. As the bombers approached, William Mitchell's sister was standing at the top of White House Hill, where the family owned their plot of land:

> As each bomb dropped my mother said exactly where it fell. The thing I shall never forget is that I actually saw the bombs leave the Gotha. The picture of what happened will always be clear in my mind. My mother said. 'that's right in Tontine Street,' and she was right.

A 50kg bomb fell amid the queue outside Stoke's, where scores of shoppers, mainly women and children, were trapped out in the open or inside the shops themselves. The roof of Stoke's collapsed on those inside, killing both customers and staff. Surrounding properties too were shattered by the force of bomb detonating in such a confined space; lethal shards of glass, splinters and shrapnel flew in all directions, while a fractured gas main ignited and sent a bolt of flame some fifty feet into the air. Altogether, the casualty toll would amount to over sixty dead and injured.

Young Lily Hayward was supposed to be in Tontine Street with her mother shopping but, 'I asked to go home and play, so left her at the Dover Road end of Tontine Street.' When the explosion tore through the street, her mother was blown over the back of Stoke's store and killed.

Mrs Adelaide Moore was shopping in Gosnold's store at the time of the explosion, and, as a member of the St John Ambulance, immediately applied herself to helping the dead and dying. She was later awarded a Silver Medal for her act of valour. The accompanying citation recounted how:

> Mrs Moore was in the showroom at the time of the explosion; her face and head were cut in several places, severing the facial artery, and her back was slightly burnt... although bleeding

profusely from her injuries, she took no notice of them, but went to George Gosnold and rendered first-aid, applying dressings to a severe wound in his right side. She remained with him until a doctor arrived, when she assisted in getting him on a stretcher. Afterwards she remained at the shop attending to the wounded until all the cases had been removed and was then treated herself at the Royal Victoria Hospital.

The carnage in Tontine Street was frightful. Albert Taylor, who lived with his parents at the Brewery Tap pub, recalled how 'the street was a river of blood and the arms and legs of the staff and customers of the Stoke's store were blown onto the flat roof of the pub'. He remembered the head of a curly, fair-haired child on the saloon bar step. Years later, when he had taken over the pub, he would still scrub and whitewash the step every morning, and still he could 'see' the stain where the small head had lain. Memories of the tragedy scored themselves into peoples' minds. One, Stella Furnival, was able to draw upon the recollections of her mother who told how her sister, Winifred:

Had been sent to buy something from Stoke's, but seconds after leaving, returned home saying she was scared. This probably saved her life. My mother took the basket and a few minutes later began descending the steps from St. Michael's Street. As she reached the bottom of the steps she was lifted like a feather onto Tontine Street. She later described the street strewn with bodies. She was seven months' pregnant, and the horror of the scene and her fear for her children made her leave this scene of carnage and hurry home.

Although barely recovered from her own frightening experienced Mrs Sharman decided to go and see what she and her family could do to help in Tontine Street, and, 'with a friend we got a lift on a military lorry, but we were soon turned away because of the carnage in there'. Edith Cole remembers how:

...people were gathering anything they could find to take the injured to hospital. There were people piled on carts and others running up to the Royal Victoria Hospital with children in their arms. The news spread quickly; one person told the next and soon the streets were filled with people looking for their relatives.

A Canadian Army sergeant, wounded at Vimy Ridge only a month previously, recalled:

> The whole of the street seemed to explode. There was smoke and flames all over, but worst of all were the screams of the wounded and dying, and mothers looking frantically for their kids. A couple of minutes before, those of us who were in the street were like innocent kids ourselves, as we watched those swine in the sky.

One of those searching for their relatives was Lily Hayward, who ran to find her mother but when she got to the scene was turned back by a policeman. She sneaked a look round him and all she could see was, 'bodies, dead horses and blood. It was terrible'. Chief Constable Reeve of the Kent Constabulary told the subsequent enquiry how:

> I saw an appalling sight which I shall never forget to my dying day. Dead and injured persons were lying about; several horses were lying dead and a fire had broken out in front of premises which had been demolished. Several of the business premises were very seriously damaged; others had their plate glass windows blown out.

Douglas Lidderdale's father too, did his best to help:

> As Tontine Street was within a quarter of a mile from my father's surgery in London Street. I don't doubt that he made his way there to attend to the more seriously wounded as they lay in the street and then went back to his surgery to those who had been able to make their way there. It was likely too, that he responded to an emergency call by the Royal Victoria Hospital to help cope with the operating programmes for the casualties.

<hr/>

The bombers left the shattered town to clear up, their course now set for Dover, which had been alerted of their impending arrival. As they approached Western Heights the sirens sounded and all six Army guns engaged them, firing some 358 rounds during the course of the next few minutes. Naval vessels in the harbour opened fire with a variety of weapons, but their efforts were fruitless and, as one witness sourly reported, 'they might just as well have been using pea-shooters'.

The pea-shooters, though, were enough to convince Brandenburg that he would be wise to quit while he was ahead, and at about 6.35

89

pm the squadron veered out across the sea towards home.

Only now were the defences beginning to consolidate, hoping to intercept the raiders as they made good their escape. Vice-Admiral Dover Patrol signalled the 4th (Naval) Wing HQ at La Panne with the news that the German squadron would soon be within range. Subsequently, three Triplanes and a Pup from 9 (Naval) Squadron at Furnes, and one of five Pups from 4 (Naval) Squadron at Bray Dunes headed for the skies.

While the navy pilots started climbing, the Home Defence pilots on the other side of the Channel were fast on the heels of the intruders. One of these was Flight Lieutenant GW Gathergood, a ferry pilot stationed at Lympne who:

> Left the ground at 6.40 pm and climbed out towards Dover, following the AA bursts in the sky... flew a little north of east and about five miles out I saw a Sopwith Scout which came quite close and then turned away to the south. About five miles further out I caught a sight of the HA [Hostile Aircraft] about 1,000 feet above me and well in front. Just at that time a Sopwith Triplane came up beneath me and so close that I was able to wave and point to the HA. The Triplane also turned away south.

Gathergood then:

> ...followed the HA, climbing up to him. After some time I got close under his tail at point-blank range, stalled, and pressed the firing lever. The gun refused to fire. This was at 14,500 feet, having sighted the HA first at 11,000 feet; the DH5 being 10,000 feet. The HA then apparently saw me for the first time and turning his tail, opened fire on me. I manoeuvred to keep underneath him, and tried to get my gun working. The HA then put his nose down, and I steered an erratic course with my feet, fiddling with the gun with my hands. When at last I got it working the HA was some distance ahead, and I fired at him at fairly long range without apparent result. The DH5 had only just arrived from Hendon and had not yet been filled up, and as I was some distance out of sight of land, and the compass swinging owing to engine vibration, I was unable to pursue the HA up to point-blank range again. Having used up all my ammunition, I returned to Lympne, landing at 6.50 pm.

Another ferry pilot, Flight Sub Lieutenant Reginald Leslie, was waiting at Dover to deliver a DH4 to an airfield in France, when the warning siren howled. His machine was unarmed so, eager to get airborne he climbed aboard the nearest aircraft he could find. This was a Sopwith Pup, in which he approached the enemy formation at around 6.25 pm, midway between Dover and Gravelines.

He pursued his foe until he came upon a Gotha at 11,000 feet. Urging his rattling Pup to greater effort, he eventually closed to within 150 yards of the quarry and opened fire. His shots were wide, so he closed to within fifty yards to expend a further 150 rounds. The German machine then seemed to issue smoke and dive, soon spewing more smoke and steam from its fuselage. However, any thoughts Leslie may have harboured of finishing his prey were dashed when he came under fire himself from two other German machines. He banked to avoid them, took his machine into a steep dive, and spun earthwards for several thousands of feet before he brought his machine back under control. By the time he did so, the enemy machine had put too much distance between them to make further pursuit worthwhile.

Next it was the turn of Flight Lieutenant W Humphreys, a Canadian pilot from Ontario, serving with 37 Squadron to take on the invaders:

I left the ground at 17.13... and climbed to 10,500 [feet] over a heavy cloud bank, but, my throttle refusing to work, I was compelled to land at Stow Maries at 1750. Acting under instructions, I went to Goldhanger and left the ground at 1825 and proceeded to Chatham on a course of 120, allowing for the north wind. I crossed the Thames and reached Chatham at 18.55...

At 1905 I saw a machine going east about 16,000 [feet] and about a mile away from me. I climbed to 15,000 feet but he had a great deal of pace on me, and at 1925 I left him over the sea ten miles out. So I turned back, crossed the land at about 1945 and not knowing where I was, proceeded to look for a landing ground. Seeing a suitable landing field I came down to 2,000 feet, circled it and landed.

Humphreys' landing turned out to be something of a disaster. He failed to notice that the hill finished in a ditch, and he crashed into it, severely damaging his aircraft, wrecking the undercarriage, engine and wings.

Thirty other B.E.12, B.E.12a and B.E.2s were scouring the skies that evening for a sight of the enemy, but only machines from 37

Squadron managed as much as a glimpse of the raiders. Flight Lieutenant L P Watkins, flying his B.E.12a, and Flight Lieutenant L F Hutcheon in his B.E.12, took off from their airfield at Goldhanger at 5.13 pm and 5.14 pm respectively. A third pilot, Flight Lieutenant Orr-Ewing, taking off from Rochford at 5.15 pm in his B.E.12a, also joined in the hunt for the elusive German quarry. Suffering the same fate as his colleagues, sighting the enemy was just about all he could manage in his clapped-out aircraft. Faster machines were also thwarted in their efforts to intercept the intruders; Captain A J Capel took up his Vickers ES1 from 50 Squadron's airfield at Bekesbourne at 5.35 pm, and he landed an hour and five minutes later empty-handed.

By 8.45 pm Nos. 4 and 9 (Naval) Squadrons were coming into contact with the returning German formation. Thirty miles out from Dunkirk amid a gathering sea mist, at least one Gotha was shot down and another seen to fall out of control. A third enemy machine crash-landed at Beernem, near Bruges, killing all three crewmen. It could not be confirmed for certain whether or not it crashed as a result of British fire or a mechanical fault, but there is little doubt that another raider was raked by gunfire of a 9 Squadron aircraft. This one, however, succeeded in landing safely.

The only British achievement therefore, occurred over the Continent, and throughout the raid the single factor which in any way compensated for the dire state of the defences was the stoic determination of individual pilots to get to grips with the foe. One, Flight Lieutenant Leslie, earned himself a Distinguished Service Cross for his efforts. As for the Germans, they claimed to have brought down three of the defenders; probably accounted for by Leslie's spin, Gathergood's erratic flying to clear his jam and Cooke's engine blaze.

In recognition of their participation in the attack, *Leutnants* Reulner and Elsner, and *Feldwebel* Helger were decorated.

———※○※———

Back in Folkestone the initial sense of shock and disbelief slowly gave way to one of outrage, both at the Germans, but also the Government for failing to protect against sneak attack, in broad daylight. The town's newspaper, the *Folkestone Herald*, commented grimly:

> ...for nearly three years immune from the immediate horrors of war, Folkestone has eventually passed through a terrible

ordeal. The material damage, however is as nothing compared with the appalling casualty list, upwards of seventy having been killed at the time or succumbing since to their injuries...To those who have lost kith and kin the heartfelt sympathy of the community goes out.

On Tuesday, 29 May the people of the town attended an 'Indignation Meeting', presided over by Councillor R Forsyth. He reflected the views of the community when he referred to the 'awful calamity' suffered by the town in an 'abominable attack in which women and children have been the major sufferers.' He further pointed out that the town was to send a delegation to see Lord French in London, to demand that in future the town receive adequate warning of an impending raid. The meeting then passed the following resolution:

...the residents of the Borough of Folkestone demand that the Government be asked immediately to hold an enquiry into the air raid of Friday last, May 25th... We ask why no warning was given, so people could return home and take cover. We urge that the Government take such steps as will prevent further attacks of a similar nature and the wholesale murder of the women and children of the town...

In Parliament, Noel Pemberton Billing was at his usual outspoken best, attacking Lord French outright, demanding his dismissal in favour of someone better equipped to undertake the tasks entrusted to his post. He said that:

We are told that Lord French is in command in England. I would like to know what he did on the night of the Folkestone raid, or whether he knew anything about it until all the people were dead.

Meanwhile, Folkestone's deputation, accompanied by councillors and aldermen from neighbouring Hythe, were met by Lord French at Horse Guards on Wednesday, 30 May, and received their resolution. He told them confidently, the *Herald* reported, that:

The matter has been reconsidered in the light of experience gained in this latest raid, and he hopes the measures which have been taken will make any future raid a very risky operation and will ensure heavy loss for the enemy.

National newspapers too, took up the cry. On 31 May, the *Daily*

Express reported Government proposals to respond to the threat:

The tragedy of Folkestone will not be repeated anywhere if timely warnings can avert it... it is certain that hereafter an entirely new and thorough system of notification will be introduced and we shall lose no time in applying it. The details are not yet fixed, but it will ensure that the whole of the coast towns, possibly as far inland as London, shall be notified as soon as hostile aircraft are sighted over land... certain alarms and lights may be used at night, and other means will be adopted in the daytime. One system strongly favoured is the ringing of all telephones, public and private, by an arrangement now under consideration. People with telephones in their houses would be expected to communicate with neighbours not on the telephone... previously to the Folkestone raid the inhabitants of towns might have complained of being unnecessarily alarmed if a warning were not succeeded by an attack. They will be less likely to complain now. The warnings will enable them to take cover. Undoubtedly, the death-toll at Folkestone must have been much lower if the streets had been empty.

Although the paper undoubtedly voiced views which were generally shared by the general public, the idea of ringing every telephone in the event of a warning was never adopted. However, it was not only the conduct of the Government prior to the raid that was criticized. The Home Forces communiqué issued after the raid was so vague as to create more concern and anxiety than it was designed to allay. Issued the day after the attack it ran:

A large squadron of enemy aircraft, about sixteen in number, attacked the south-east of England between 5.15 and 6.30 pm last night. Bombs were dropped at a number of places, but nearly all the damage occurred in one town, where a number of the bombs fell into the streets causing considerable casualties among the civilian population. Some shops and houses were also seriously damaged.

Obviously, the Government's intention was to deny the enemy knowledge or intelligence of the target they had bombed, but it was not the shrewdest piece of propaganda to come out of Whitehall. The inadequately worded note merely served to incite panic among thousands of friends and relatives along the length and breadth of southern England. When people demanded to know where the attack took place, *The Times* newspaper was grudgingly permitted to expand on the available news by reproducing a German communiqué which stated that, 'During the course of a successful raid one of our air squadrons dropped bombs on Dover and Folkestone on the south coast of England'. At least now the victims knew almost as much as the perpetrators of their tragedies.

⸻⸺◦⸺⸻

The uproar caused by the raid, and vitriolic criticism levied at the authorities, convinced the Cabinet that they needed to decide how to handle the inevitable repeat performance – possibly on the capital itself.

A meeting was convened at the War Office on 31 May to thrash out what best could be done. It was attended by Lieutenant General Sir David Henderson as chairman; Major General F B Maurice on behalf of the War Office; Rear-Admiral G Hope, and Commodore G Paine for the Admiralty; Major General Sir F C Shaw and Colonel T Higgins for the Home Forces.

The agenda was dominated by the need to take measures which could avert another Folkestone; better inter-service cooperation, improvements to communications, distribution of information and the allocation of available aircraft. Henderson began by telling the meeting that the policy laid down by the War Committee in February 1916, namely that the Navy dealt with all intruders as far as the coast, and the Army to those inland had, with very minor variations, been adhered to. The Navy still had the task of giving information about impending raids and of intercepting raiders on their return journey. The meeting went on to discuss the areas most exposed to attack and assuming that with four hours fuel capacity, the range of the raiders could be assumed to be something in the region of around 125 miles. Therefore the most vulnerable areas were those bounded by the coastline from Southwold to Rottingdean, and a line through Bury St Edmunds and Brentwood to Rottingdean.

The meeting was told that training squadrons were being transferred to the area as an immediate measure, and that Orfordness and Martlesham Heath Experimental stations were being organized for the protection of Essex, north of the Blackwater River. When these changes were completed it was believed that there would then be forty machines available to patrol around London; seventeen for

95

the patrol from Goldhanger to Detling, eight from Chiddingstone to Marden, Hastings and Romney and six aircraft for the patrol from Dover to Broadstairs. There would also be ten machines between Throwley and Bekesbourne – a total reinforcement of fifty-nine aircraft of 'a better type'.

Word was out that the rickety old B.E. type aircraft needed to be upgraded as a matter of urgency. Because they would be used largely for training purposes, only half would be operational at any one time! The total number, however, had increased from twenty-two at the time of the raid to fifty-one, still a noticeable improvement.

The meeting concentrated on the resources available for the key Goldhangar/Detling patrol. Not only were there just seventeen serviceable aircraft available, they were not even modern, being mostly B.E.s. Sir David undertook to remedy the situation.

On the question of warnings, the meeting discussed the length of time it took the Tongue Lightship to send notice of the enemy bombers to GHQ Home Forces via four transmitting stations. The Admiralty and Home Forces representatives agreed to investigate the delay and decide upon the best way, 'to ensure more rapid communication in the future'. Shaw also agreed to confer with the Admiralty over the question of employing more trained military observers on the lightships. A total of some twenty-five would be stationed on the Tongue, Kentish Knock, Sunk, Shipwash, Edinburgh Channel, Nore and Maplin. Furthermore, the Admiralty:

> ...undertook to instruct the Royal Naval Air Service at Dunkirk to keep a careful watch on the enemy's aerodromes at Ghistelles and St Denis Westrem for any unusual movement of enemy aircraft.

This measure should, it was hoped, pre-empt any further forays by the enemy by allowing raids to be mounted against the airfields before the bombers took off. It was also agreed that Tongue should be named the principal observation post, and Admiral Hope undertook to arrange for a direct line from Foreness to the Admiralty, and for another from GHQ Home Forces to DCAS Chatham, 'which should materially speed up outgoing information to the naval stations'. Hope also agreed to a suggestion that a look-out vessel be placed on station south of Kentish Knock, but the idea of stationing lookout patrol ships was discarded because it was likely the vessels' noise would drown out that of the incoming raiders.

To achieve some uniformity between the RFC and RNAS, it was

agreed that the Navy would adopt the Ingram system of ground signals, but they were unpopular enough with the RFC, taking too long to lay out, and being prone to obscuring by inclement or hazy weather. The idea would prove to be of little practical use. An idea by Henderson to investigate, 'using wireless to communicate with machines in the air' was foiled by Hope who claimed that fleet communications might be jammed. Thus was this excellent means of communication dismissed. It was one incidentally, which Churchill had advocated in his earliest days as First Lord in 1913.

The question was also raised as to the assistance the Admiralty might be able to give over England, rather than just as far as the coast. It was agreed that there were about six assorted machines each at Manston, Walmer and Dover, and they could be made available to assist the Army.

The practicality of using RNAS seaplanes in an interceptor role was also raised. Hope commented that:

Seaplane patrols could be and were sent out at various times during the day, but they were too slow both in rising and on the flat to be effective as sentries and so they would be easy to avoid.

The meeting concluded that at least at that time it was not possible to allot any more aircraft to Home Defence, without prejudicing, 'the requirements of other theatres', and that, 'it was considered that no measures which could be taken would prevent bombs being dropped on towns'. It did agree that, 'there would be no likelihood that the enemy aeroplanes would be able to avoid an engagement with our own fighting machines'.

Thus, all the meeting could decide was that a few minor points could be accepted. The idea of re-adopting Churchill's initial plans to attack the bases and the aircraft before they took off was not grasped with any enthusiasm.

The whole episode suggested an air of resignation that nothing significant could really be done without detriment to the Western Front's resources. The people of Folkestone for one, would just have to hope that some other town was selected next time.

———✦———

The meeting left as many questions unanswered as it addressed. Higgins was worried about what would happen if the daylight raids were supplemented by night-time operations, especially as the Home

Defence establishment had been so severely depleted. The day after the raid he had written to the GHQ Home Forces and the Air Board, reminding them that since February 1917, seventy-seven trained night pilots had been withdrawn from Home Defence Group, leaving 107 against the agreed establishment of 198. He also pointed out that too many men needed to keep the aircraft serviceable had been sent to France. He urged that the planned formation of 101 and 102 Bomber Squadrons for France, which threatened further calls on his resources, should be deferred. He expressed his belief that the enemy would not content themselves with daylight attacks; when they got the taste for this new form of warfare they would want to supplement them with attacks at night. French endorsed Higgins' views with some of his own:

> I cannot too strongly impress on the Army Council my opinion that the means placed at my disposal for aeroplane defence are now inadequate and that a continuance of the present policy may have disastrous results.

However, some action was generated by the meeting. The day after the conference, a Home Defence Guidance Letter was issued to all units. It stated that the use of Ingram Signals in conjunction with pre-arranged patrol areas should make it possible for large numbers of machines to consolidate an attack or pursue enemy aircraft. The Home Defence pilot was expected to do his best to break up the bomber formation to divert it from its target, and was told that:

> Any delay a home defence pilot can cause by compelling an enemy to defend himself, or compel him to decrease his height by forcing combat upon him will be of the greatest value to the defence organisation as a whole.

These of course could not have been considered to have been anything short of stopgap measures – the War Office was not completely blind to the urgency of the situation. Three days before the conference, twelve Armstrong Whitworth FK8s and eight Sopwith 1½ Strutters were hastily handed over to the Home Defence Group. They were certainly an improvement on the B.E. machines, but still fell far short of what was really needed. The FK8 was essentially an artillery spotter, taking thirty minutes to reach 10,000 feet where it could maintain a speed of 85mph. The Sopwith however, could reach 10,000 feet in twenty minutes, and had a speed of 90mph, whereas the B.E.12s rarely managed more than 70mph.

On 29 May, 50 Squadron received four FK8s and 39 Squadron two, while 37 Squadron received five Sopwiths. Training (T) units were also converted to operational duties. As a result, 35(T) Squadron Northolt came up with six Bristol fighters; 40(T) Squadron Croydon, twelve Sopwith Pups; 56(T) Squadron London Colney, six Spads; 62(T) Squadron Dover, six Pups; 63(T) Squadron Joyce Green, six Pups and 65 Squadron, working up for the Western Front at Wye, provided six DH5s.

Training aircraft not ready for combat were to be made available as soon as possible, whilst in addition, No. 2 Aircraft Acceptance Park, Hendon was required to provide DH5 aircraft. The airfield at Lympne, still perhaps smarting from the outrage of its neighbours, was declared operational.

It would be only a week before resolutions, aircraft and pilots were to be put to the test.

CHAPTER 7

THE GUNS WERE WELL FOUGHT

Having lost the laurels at the last moment over London, Brandenburg could at least console himself with the fact that he had given the British a run for their money over Folkestone. He had also blooded his squadron and sent shock waves through Britain and the world.

The bombing of the Canadian encampments in particular, demonstrated the potential for creating chaos behind enemy lines, while the near misses on the railway line and military canal suggested how, with better luck and better ordnance, he might isolate parts of the south coast for days, even weeks. How wonderful it would be if the flow of reinforcements to France could be held up? What results could be achieved if the country's capital could be struck down in a similar manner?

After giving his men a few days' rest, Brandenburg was determined to resume the campaign as soon as possible and instructed Cloessner to prepare another weather report.

The meteorological team advised that around 5 June, the weather conditions should be similar to 25 May without, hopefully, the huge cloud bank over the capital. Brandenburg decided to wait no longer, and ordered his men to make ready for take-off at 4.00 pm on 5 June.

Plans were nearly scuppered before they got off the ground however, when the British decided, as agreed at the meeting in Whitehall, to have another crack at St Denis Westrem. On the day before the Germans were due to set forth on their own raid, 27 Squadron of the RFC was ordered to divert its energies from attacking German front-line positions and accompany 5 (Naval) Squadron in an attack upon the German airfields. Nine Martinsyde bombers from 27 Squadron went into action alongside machines from 5 Squadron, scattering bombs across the airfields. The outcome was much the same as before; enemy preparations were only marginally disrupted and plans were to proceed as arranged.

Thus on the morning of 5 June 1917 the twenty-two Gothas assigned to the raid rose from their airfields. This time there would be no need for a refuelling stop at Nieumunster since the long awaited extra fuel tanks had arrived and been fitted to the bombers, enabling them to make the trip non-stop. To avoid detection by the RNAS at Dunkirk, Brandenburg also considered it prudent to follow a more northerly route than that of 25 May.

His tactic did not, however, avoid a chance sighting by a routine patrol of three Pups under the command of Flight Commander J D Newberry of 4 (Naval) Squadron. They pursued the Gothas until they ran dangerously low on petrol over the Thames Estuary, diverting to Manston to refuel. In this chance encounter, only Newberry got close enough to the enemy squadron to try and engage them, but at the crucial moment suffered a gun stoppage. To make the best of a bad job the subsequent British communiqué attempted to claim that in these, 'indecisive engagements', the raiders were, 'chased to England'.

Having rid themselves of their erstwhile pursuers, the Germans passed Kentish Knock at 5.55 pm and GHQ Home Forces were alerted at 6.00 pm, although the RNAS, probably thanks to Newberry, had been alerted some five minutes previously. In another strange coincidence, a practice 'Aircraft Concentration' – or exercise – had been scheduled to test the defences as a result of the reorganization carried out following the Whitehall Conference. At 3.00 pm about thirty aircraft set off skywards. Little did they anticipate they would meet the real thing later on.

Meanwhile the Gothas made their landfall at around 6.05 pm, once again between the rivers Blackwater and Crouch. At the same time, the first UK-based aircraft were airborne, and Home Defence squadrons were at 'Readiness' between 6.04 pm and 6.08 pm and at 'Patrol' eight minutes or so later. While this was going on, the Gothas were getting their usual sightings – from as far north as Mersea Island, Bradwell-Juxta-Mere and Goldhanger. But when over the River Crouch, the raiders changed their direction south-west towards Shoeburyness, more southwards than on the previous attempt on London, flying at a height of about 10,000 feet.

At 6.17 pm the 13th Mobile Battery at Highlands, two miles north-west of Southminster, observed the intruders and fired off two rounds before they disappeared. They must have felt more than a little irritated to have been frustrated twice in a row; this had been the battery which tried its arm against the Gothas only a few days earlier.

Three minutes later and the formation was over Shoeburyness. Superintendent Scott of the Essex Constabulary was on hand to witness their arrival, and noted afterwards how he heard:

...a rumbling noise in the air in a north-easterly direction from

Rochford. After watching for a few seconds, I saw hostile aeroplanes emerging from the clouds. In all I counted eighteen. They were steering south... .

As he watched, the Gothas began to drop their first bombs, two 50kgs, at Great Wakering, one fell by the gasworks at North Shoebury and the other not much farther away. As unreliable as those dropped on the last raid, none caused any damage, and neither did the subsequent twenty-four bombs – twenty 50kg and four 12.5kg – of which nine exploded in the air and seven failed to detonate on contact with the ground. Scott reported that three 50kg bombs fell on the artillery gun park, 'killing one soldier and severely injuring another,' who died later of his injuries.

The ground forces began to respond to the enemy incursion at 6.23 pm, when two guns at the School of Instruction opened up, calculating the enemy to be at a height of between 12,000 and 14,000 feet. They were joined shortly afterwards by a third gun at the Experimental Ranges. The enemy formation began to break up, according to contemporary reports and go off, 'in scattered array', across the estuary towards Sheerness. More wishful thinking than anything.

What they perhaps saw however, was the results of Brandenburg once again deciding to allow common sense to be the better part of valour when he realized the weather was to thwart his plans yet again. He decided that the nearest alternative target would be the vital port of Sheerness, on the Island of Sheppey in Kent. He fired off the necessary flares and the squadron wheeled. At this point two machines signalled that they were experiencing engine trouble and broke away to proceed independently to their bases. This inadvertently served to give the illusion to observers on the ground that the whole formation was losing cohesion in its haste to flee.

Nevertheless, because Sheerness was an important military objective it was now being served with warnings of the Germans' impending arrival, and as they were received, telephones rang and air raid sirens began their morbid wail, calling for people to take shelter.

<hr/>

As sirens sounded throughout the town and the immediate vicinity, the Gothas closed in, seven being seen flying from the north-east in a right-handed circle over the town and neighbourhood and then away in an easterly direction. Others appeared to have circled the town to the west, going north-east over the town from the Medway. With the raiders two miles from the town, the Whitehouse Farm Gun opened fire at 6.23 pm, followed by the gun at Barton's Point which would continue firing until 6.37 pm loosing off ninety-three rounds at the enemy as it swung feverishly, 'to all points of the compass' as the Gothas circled the town. The raid was to last only five minutes or so, but caused significant damage, with the pandemonium rising to furore as more guns joined in; Port Victoria opened up from 6.30 pm to 6.35 pm; Queenborough from 6.29 pm to 6.35 pm; Eastchurch engaged the enemy from 6.30 pm – firing at two of them as they took off eastwards. The gun at High Point joined in at 6.29 pm, but only managed to let off a single round before the enemy disappeared into the vastness of the sky. Meanwhile, the Gothas went to their task.

The first bomb to fall was probably a 50kg which landed in the canal west of the naval gun range buildings, and was closely followed by a 12.5kg bomb which fell perilously close to Barton's Point. Two more fell in the sea east of the naval gun range targets. All four seemed to have been aimed at the Barton's Point gun, which perhaps explains its zealousness. Further west, bombs fell near the canal bank at Botany Camp; one 50kg did not explode, but two 12.5kg bombs killed three men and wounded eleven of the 5th Labour Company as they were working. More bombs were dropped nearby, one near the station company store tent, blasting a crater four feet deep and wounding one man.

Sheerness New Town received a number of bombs which exacted a toll of varying degrees. A 12.5kg bomb in Invicta Road demolished the back of a house, and another killed two men, one civilian and one naval rating. Again the reliability of the bombs was letting Brandenburg down badly. A 50kg fell in the yard of the pumping station in Trinity Road but did not detonate, leaving a potentially important target unscathed. A 12.5kg bomb fell in a field near Cheyney Rock, doing no damage.

In Sheerness itself, two bombs were dropped on the Ravelin Battery; one 50kg bomb on the inner side of the sea wall, which blew down a portion of the wall and railing; the other, a 12.5kg bomb, fell on the right flank of the battery on waste ground wounding a sentry. A 50kg bomb which fell in the moat 400 yards south-west of Ravelin Bridge killed three men and injured fourteen more. Two 50kg bombs burst in the air over the King's Royal Rifles' camp in Well Marsh. A

50kg bomb knocked down part of the Crown and Anchor and Pier Hotel in High Street, its piano crashing into the street. Another hit the neighbouring premises of Messrs Gieves, a gentlemen's outfitters. The building was demolished and two men were killed, the manager of the shop and a Chief Warrant Officer visiting the premises.

On the dockyard itself, five 50kg bombs were dropped. One fell on the Grand Store, a huge and important warehouse building, setting fire to the top storey. It was packed with highly flammable naval stores including lifebelts and fenders and was completely gutted in the fire which blazed for more than two hours; for Brandenburg, his first serious military victory so far.

The rest of the raid would continue to be small beer by comparison. Another bomb burst on a quay opposite No. 3 Dry Dock, narrowly missing a ship and killing a man in a neighbouring shop. Two bombs again failed to explode when they could have wreaked havoc, one east of the police section house and one south of the Officers' Mess. One exploded in the air behind Dockyard House; unreliable ordnance sparing the target time and time again.

South of Sheerness, a single Gotha attempted to bomb the power station and the airship sheds at Minster Marshes. None of the five 50kg and three 12.5kg bombs dropped achieved significant results.

Throughout the mayhem and despite the spirited response from the ground, the raiders seemed to have been able to bomb with impunity, as they did when they attacked Folkestone. One bomber however, was to become the defence's first success over the UK itself.

For the Gotha crew of 660/16 everything had been going to plan; the pilot, *Vizefeldwebel* Erich Kluck was satisfied his machine was responding well to his commands as the mighty and ponderous beast glided over the town; *Leutnant der Reserve* Hans Francke was experiencing no great problems directing the release of bombs, untroubled by the harmless flak being thrown up towards them, whilst *Unteroffizier* George Schumacher, the third member of the crew was having little to do as there were no adversaries for him to fight with his machine gun. And as they watched the fall of each bomb, occasionally perhaps cursing as they failed to explode or missed the target, the three crewmen were undoubtedly exhilarated.

The bomber was some 3,000 yards north of Barton's Point, heading for a point from where they could begin their long journey home, when suddenly the aircraft shuddered and stalled. The starboard engine had stopped. All the men could do was to look at it and then at one another as it quickly dawned upon them what fate lay in store. Faces paled as Kluck struggled with the steering wheel and tried desperately to maintain the Gotha's lost equilibrium as it spiralled towards the water. It took four-and-a-half minutes for them to plunge into the icy sea. Time perhaps, even above the screaming, shredding fuselage, to make peace with their God.

A single lucky shell had found its target, or maybe one of a thousand shards of shrapnel produced by an explosion, had crippled the right-hand magneto and shorn off the teeth, rendering the machine helpless. Jubilant onlookers below as well as the gunners – probably every one of them in action since they would nearly all claim the credit – cheered and whooped with joy as the hated Hun dropped like crumpled carrion. The first Gotha had been shot down over England, and at last it looked as if the bogey-men of the skies were not, after all, invulnerable. Watching as the bomber finally hit the sea the observers were indifferent to the grisly fate of the three Germans on board. Pilot Erich Kluck would die when the bomber dragged him beneath the freezing, lapping waves. *Leutnant* Franck would survive both air and water, only to die soon after being rescued; while *Unteroffizier* Schumacher miraculously escaped, unscathed, except for a broken leg. After interrogation, he was destined to spend the rest of the war in a prisoner of war camp.

Immediately, boats were hauled into the water as men were ordered to seize whatever was left of the crew, whilst measures were taken to retrieve as much of the wreck of the bomber as possible.

The 'kill' was claimed by Barton's Point gun as it was the nearest, although other guns, including Shoeburyness, Whitehouse Farm and Neats Farm also claimed the credit. One eyewitness to the drama was Rifleman Bourne, serving in the 7th Company of the 5th Battalion, King's Royal Rifles:

...I saw an aeroplane hit, which dropped in the sea. While going to the sea wall another was hit. The first dropped very slowly into the sea, but the second, which seemed in great difficulties, drifted towards and over the sea at a height of roughly 1,200 feet... it was hit again and a lot of smoke came from it. Firstly I thought it was the exhaust of the plane, which I thought went into the clouds, but on the second glance, I saw smoke descending, yet when the smoke grew thinner the pieces of the plane could not be sighted because the distance away was too great for the naked eye; but in my mind the way the smoke drifted down to the sea the plane must have been completely smashed.

The introduction of a second aircraft serves to confuse matters. Port Victoria Gun also claims to have destroyed the enemy machine over the Medway between Grain and Sheerness. The confusion was understandable under the circumstances. Much speculation surrounded the possibility that two more Gothas were shot down; one may have been hit but then recovered sufficiently to continue, another may have been shot down but there was only the evidence of the Port Victoria Gun to substantiate this. Or it may have been the manner in which the two bombers which broke off with engine trouble wheeled away, perhaps appearing to be in difficulties or in distress. Further investigation proved inconclusive.

As the remainder of the squadron headed homewards, the guns of HMS *Blazer*, moored in the mouth of the Swale, joined in the chorus of ground fire, assisted by the anti-aircraft gun at RNAS Eastchurch. To add even more to the confusion surrounding the fates of various bombers, this gun too, claimed to have achieved a hit.

———————

Undoubtedly, Brandenburg and his squadron executed a purely military operation in their attack on Sheerness. There were few who could claim this was simply a terror attack. This was clearly a target of military significance and an attempt to put it out of commission, however unsuccessful, was legitimate. Civilian casualties would have been an inevitability.

One survivor of the Sheerness raid was Stephen Keen, then a typically adventurous boy of nine years, who lived near the railway station where his father worked in the signal box. Stephen:

> ...was playing cricket with other youngsters in a field a short way from the railway line and about fifty yards from the signal box... a beautiful day with no cloud. The AA guns started firing and my friends scuttled home, but being the clever one I stayed and watched the planes, with my father, almost frantic, calling for me to go home. I had not seen anything so fascinating as this in my life before, and was really absorbed, the planes were not a great height and I could plainly see the

way they delivered the bombs, by hand, over the side. Most of them dropped in the water and from where I was standing I suppose the angle was about forty-five degrees. I don't know the number of planes which took part but I counted six or seven when it happened – it was the last I knew of the raid until a long time afterwards, for as I was looking up I caught a shell splinter in my right eye.

Stephen was thrown to the ground, unconscious. His father rushed to him, and then went to get help as he lay on the ground with streams of blood pouring from the gaping wound. Eventually he was rescued and,

> ...taken to Canterbury Hospital, but very little was done apart from bandaging etc. as the place was full of wounded soldiers and no time and attention could be spared for me.

Stephen was blinded in one eye and had poor hearing ever since.

Henry Marley also recalls the raid vividly. He was eleven-years-old and had just come home from school when his eldest sister asked him to go to the Co-operative store. He duly obliged:

> Whilst waiting to be served, the lights went out. Immediately the conversation turned to the air raid warning. That was sufficient for me and out of the shop I went. On getting outside, many people seemed to be going in one direction and of course I followed. However, I finished up by following some soldiers. At that time hundreds of bell tents formed the camp; to enter the camp one had to cross a small footbridge which spanned the ditch. Some soldiers and myself stayed on the bridge, and after a while a whistling noise was heard, followed by a splash in the ditch. An object thought to be a bomb could be seen and some soldiers touched it with their canes.

The curious soldiers continued to tamper with the bomb until they were pleaded with to stop by less inquisitive bystanders. Mrs Valerie Simmons grandfather:

> ...George Friar, was one of two people killed by the bombs; he was the father of six children, the youngest of whom was my father, then aged ten. He worked in Sheerness dockyard as a rigger, and went outside his workplace with friends to see what was going on, whereupon he was hit by shrapnel and killed. The other person killed was a man who lived in Cavour Road, who

was hit in or near a walkway called 'Dutchell's Opening', where, I believe, the marks of the shrapnel are still visible.

<hr />

This further incursion by the German squadron did not reflect well upon the actions of the home defence squadrons. However, for one Dover-based squadron at least, (49) there was a perfectly good reason for their lack of activity on the day. As the commander, Captain Erskine Bolst explained, 'on receipt of telephonic communication 'Readiness' at 3.06 pm I notified the various flight commanders and also the OC 62 Squadron on this station. 'Patrol' was received at 3.08 pm 'All Clear' received at 3.57 pm' All this was, however, purely academic, as Captain Erskine explained, somewhat oblivious to the absurdity, 'in view of the fact that this squadron is not yet equipped with any machines, no action was taken'.

Those units possessing aircraft were still trying to locate and engage the enemy, most of them wasting their time searching over London. First to get airborne was a formation of two Bristol Scouts and Sopwith Pups from Manston. They took off at 6.05 pm with Flight Lieutenants Scott and Daly, and Burt taking to the air. Their colleague, Flight Sub Lieutenant de Wilde took off at 6.10 pm in his Bristol Scout, but he had to return when he discovered his gun sight was broken. Over Southend, Scott found the Gothas flying at 15,000 feet, and realizing the Bristols were nearing their ceiling, left them and climbed alone to 17,000 feet. Typically, by the time he reached a height at which the enemy could be engaged, they had proceeded beyond effective range. Daly crawled to 16,000 feet to attack one Gotha without result before coming under fire himself from other enemy machines.

Squadron Commander Butler followed his comrades up from Manston at 6.40 pm in his Sopwith Triplane. Despite a painful case of water-on-the-knee, he pursued them beyond Kentish Knock and attacked one aircraft which subsequently disappeared in the haze. He proceeded to Ostend, his engine running badly all the way, and fired 150 rounds at another bomber. This too, was lost from sight. He eventually landed at Dunkirk at 8.15 pm.

The only British-based RNAS pilot to intercept the enemy was Flight Commander J C P Wood, who took off from Eastchurch at 6.30 pm in his Bristol Scout. He tried to tangle with a Gotha over the Thames Estuary at 11,000 feet, spurring his struggling charge to ever greater efforts and hoping all the while his engine neither blew up nor stalled. The black crosses adorning the enemy machine beckoned his aim as he slowly closed in, but all the while the enemy machine remained tantalizingly out of reach.

Much better luck was had by RNAS squadrons based on the other side of the Channel. Three Sopwiths from 4 (Naval) Squadron, and seven Pups and Triplanes from 9 (Naval) Squadron at Bray Dunes were sortied after the first alert was received from Dover, and waited for the bombers, now escorted by fighters, to return. Equipped with excellent fighting machines like the Sopwith Camel, there could have been none doubting their ability to make mincemeat of the bombers; they could reach speeds of 104mph at 10,000 feet and were the most manoeuvrable fighters then in service. To have these at hand to meet the lumbering Gothas as they tried to sneak back home was a great benefit. After the signal of the Gothas impending arrival, the pilots climbed into their aeroplanes and waited.

They finally intercepted their quarry between Nieuport and Ostend. One Sopwith pilot, possibly attracted by the Serpent motif, dived to the attack, coming within fifty yards before peppering the bomber with a fusillade of gunfire, splattering the wings and fuselage. The Gotha's gunner tried to return fire with the lower gun, but the fast fighter was soon out of range before an effective response could be brought to bear – this was not the slow-moving B.E. they had been used to contemptuously seeing-off. Before veering away, the British pilot had managed to seriously maim the bomber, puncturing its main fuel tank with several rounds. With gallons of fuel disgorging, the bomber staggered and reeled back to base, only spared further because the Belgian coastline was coming into view.

As the Gotha's pilot, Aschoff, and his comrads looked to heaven, the pilots of the RNAS were looking to their gun sights. Dogfights broke out between the British fighters and the German aircraft sent to cover the bombers. Weaving in the skies, thousands of rounds were exchanged as the knights of the air drew feint, wispy patchwork patterns. Chapped lips were pressed together behind flapping scarves while Lewis and Parabellum barked at each other. It was a truly classic dogfight: swirling, looping fighters breaking through cloud to gain advantage, a few more feet, an angle that would give them that edge over their foe. The combat continued until the Gothas were safely out of danger and then, one by one the German fighters broke off the action and joined their stately charges in returning to base - mission accomplished.

Among the fleeing Gothas who had managed to shrug off their pursuers, and which now faced the demanding challenge of landing in one piece, Aschoff's machine was fast running out of fuel. The crew was approaching Melle Gontrode with trepidation. At least they had crossed the coast more or less in one piece, and the prospect of a long swim in the murky Channel was no longer on the cards. But the engines were beginning to splutter ominously now, and there was a definite prospect of a rather premature and unscheduled landing – face down in the no man's land of the Western Front. So Aschoff fired off a flare to indicate that he was going to have to make an emergency landing. Two aircraft had already crash-landed, and the three crewmen gripped tight and gritted their teeth as the pilot wrestled with the machine and the ground moved up to meet them. But the Serpent Machine glided down and came to a successful stop.

Relieved and disbelieving, the crewmen spent a few minutes taking stock before climbing down from their bomber. Upon inspecting their aeroplane, the crewmen finally realized just how lucky they were to have escaped with their lives; they found it peppered with bullet holes, one of the phosphorus variety which had wedged in the tail but failed to ignite. In addition, one of the propellers had been nicked, almost certainly by one of the thousands of rounds of machine-gun ammunition expended by the furious British pilots. As they strode away from their bomber, congratulating one another on a job well done as much as on their own good fortune, the ground crewmen appeared and proceeded to paint coloured circles and date, each bullet hole, proudly treating it as one great war trophy in itself.

Apart from Aschoff's machine, none of the bombers sustained any serious damage, but Flight Commander A Shook, commanding the three aircraft of 4 (Naval) Squadron, later claimed two German fighters destroyed, whilst Flight Sub Lieutenant Enstone, also from 4, claimed another kill. Two bombers were also claimed by the British fighters in the confused mêlée of dogfights which were fought in the skies above Belgium. The Germans, on the other hand, denied having lost any aircraft.

Apart from the energetic performance of the Dunkirk squadrons, there was little to commend the actions of the air defences, in fact scant improvement on the response to the Folkestone raid. A B.E.2c flown by Flight Sub Lieutenant R J M Leger and observer G R Trewin, specially equipped to communicate by wireless, had taken off from Eastchurch at 6.32 pm. Unfortunately, it appears that it lost its bearings and had to land at Orfordness, thus taking no constructive part in the action.

In all, some forty-four RFC and twenty-one RNAS pilots scrambled after the bombers, but their handful of 1½ Strutters and Armstrong Whitworths were only a little better than the B.E.s. Adding to that the flawed Ingram Signals, the erratic communications and coordination, it was clear that there was still a yawning gap between what was needed and what the British had to offer in the way of defence. What makes the whole episode all the more pitiful is that only the day before, Lord French had ordered the practice alert for the Home Defence squadrons. That drill actually proved genuine, and the consequences spoke for themselves.

⸺ ⸙ ⸺

Lieutenant Colonel C. Hankey, Brigade Commander of the Thames and Medway Garrisons, by contrast appeared a little more than pleased with the performance of his men:

> I think the guns were well fought, and that the rate of fire throughout, especially Port Victoria Gun, was good... Neats' Court and Port Victoria guns, being in Zone 'Y', were only given an order to open fire after the raid had developed, and were therefore at some considerable disadvantage as they had no full detachments, and only one fire observer was able to reach his post in time to be of service... The experience of this raid shows that when several guns are engaging a number of aeroplanes or seaplanes and constantly changing their target, height finders and fire observers are presented with an almost impossible task in identifying the target which their gun is engaging at the moment.

Hankey's views on the accuracy of his guns was supported in a report by Brigadier General R D F Oldman, who commended the Sheppey Section in particular. He stated that:

> The shooting of the anti-aircraft batteries appeared to be accurate, especially those shooting at detachments which had passed over Barton's Point. They appeared to have the range in a very short time. The number of duds reported appears to be negligible... .

Some of the damage attributed to the bombers was found to have been the result of 'friendly fire', however. Brigadier General North,

111

commander of Shoeburyness, reported that, 'several shells, evidently fired from Sheerness or its vicinity, fell in the barracks, and two houses were slightly damaged'. North also passed on the erroneous information given to him by Captain Nelson VC, a gunnery instructor, who witnessed the raid when out with a class of cadets. He told North that he was convinced he saw two Zeppelins some way above the aeroplanes.

The Major General commanding the Thames and Medway Garrison, concurred with Hankey in his commendation of the good work put in by the gun crews, and went on to say:

> The experience of this raid clearly demonstrates that hostile enemy aeroplanes or seaplanes can be successfully engaged when flying within range of 3-inch QF [Quick Firing] 20cwt guns, which thus afford material protection against such hostile aircraft by breaking up their formations and disturbing their attack on definite objectives. I consider that it is due to the AA guns having been in action that the material damage was so small and that the loss of life was not so much greater.

He qualified this by adding that he felt the number of guns allocated to his command was woefully inadequate to deal with the large squadrons of hostile aircraft which could be expected in the future. He urged that more guns be provided and also emphasised, 'the importance of the general public taking cover during hostile air raids'. A useful piece of advice young Stephen Keen had the rest of his life to regret not having heeded.

In England, the reaction to the raid was mixed. Apparently it was generally considered that the defenders had given a good account of themselves and delivered the enemy a bloody nose – based no doubt on the single bomber shot down. There was certainly much euphoria over the destruction of Gotha 660, *The Daily Telegraph* announcing that '...so effective were the defences that they only succeeded in penetrating the coastal districts for a few miles', whilst another worthy organ urged the enemy to return as soon as they liked, because in that way more Gothas could be shot down and the war won all the sooner!

One effect of the raid however was significant, the ridiculous gun firing ban issued on 7 March was lifted. Now, should the enemy return, they could be faced with the full weight of the ground defences, not just those exempt from the original ban. Two days after the raid, Lord French released the shackles from the anti-aircraft guns, and ahead of the official channels, urgent telephone calls gave out news of the fresh instructions. It was also clear that the Germans were bound to return, and on 9 June, GHQ Home Forces held another aircraft concentration in anticipation of hitting them from the skies as well as from the ground.

This time, thirty-two machines were airborne within twenty minutes of receiving the warning. It was certainly an improvement upon their previous showing, but there still remained the fact that far too many of the aircraft were simply not up to the demands to be made of them, and one demand in particular, that of defending the Empire's capital city.

CHAPTER 8

THAT'S ONE OF OURS

The magnitude of the Gotha crews' achievement could not shroud the fact that they had been deprived of their one true prize. Twice now they had fallen tantalizingly short of their objective, and to make matters worse the last two operations had lost them the benefit of surprise. It was fortunate indeed for the Germans that their adversaries were, as yet, too disorganized to take advantage of the fact.

But both Brandenburg and his men were still eager to go aloft again just as soon as the aircraft could be made ready and the conditions were favourable. Meteorologist *Leutnant* Cloessner alone could sanction another operation, and in the meantime the crews were left to make the best use they could of their time, kicking their heels and awaiting his decision.

As the days passed, the men rehearsed their roles and checked and double-checked their machines. Then, on 10 June, Cloessner, armed with his findings, gave Brandenburg the results of his deliberations. A long-range weather pattern was as usual beyond his gift, but he calculated, the next few days offered the best chance. Cloessner assured the operation of favourable weather for the outward flight, with an advantageous tail wind on their way to England. If they timed their raid well, then the elements may similarly assist their home flight.

However, the raid would need to commence before midday in order to take advantage of these conditions; by noon, cloud was expected to begin sweeping over the capital, bringing rain and even hailstones to most of Western Europe by early afternoon. Heavy storms could batter his crews, but time it correctly and the combination of tail wind, cloud and storms could speed them on their way and further foil the British pilots. It was a tight window to work within, but it was a chance well worth taking. Brandenburg decided the squadron would head for the skies once again on Wednesday, 13 June.

Attacking on a weekday also had its advantages. The great metropolis, with its massive industrial and commercial occupations, was at full throttle. One of its biggest industries – shipping – provided especially rich targets, like the Victoria and Albert and King George V docks, lying east of Bow Creek on the Plaistow Marshes; the Victoria was opened in 1855, followed by the Royal Albert – three-quarters-of-a-mile mile long with three miles of quays. The King George V, begun in 1912, covered sixty-four acres by the time it was completed. In the very heart of the City lay the Pool of London, a vast honeycomb of docks, wharves and quays on the banks of the Thames. Cranes hung from Queenhithe Dock and Hays Wharf, hauling great nets containing the food and material needs not only of London, but much of southern England. Vital supplies essential for feeding, clothing and keeping the nation in good health – wool and lamb from Australia and New Zealand, cotton from India, timber from Canada, raw materials from the United States. Well-aimed bombs could ignite the thousands of tons of combustible materials packed into the storehouses, creating ferocious fires along the riverbanks and causing extensive damage.

As well as the docks, London then contained huge industries, which had developed since the Industrial Revolution. Not merely the arsenal at Woolwich and the shell-filling plant at Silvertown, but hundreds of smaller firms; factories which produced small-arms, ammunition, mess tins, sleeping bags, bandages and rations; others making webbing, rifle straps, jackets, trousers, caps and boots, and numerous other peripherals needed to support the men at the war fronts.

Here lay the very nerve-centre of the war effort of the British Empire; the War Office and the Admiralty, coordinating and directing the resources and operations in theatres of war from the Somme to Salonika. The movement of Britain's lifeline – the merchant marine; the supply and reinforcement of Haig's armies on the Western Front; decisions as to the number, type and distribution of air, ground and naval forces, were decided here. In London resided the Prime Minister, at 10 Downing Street, and a few hundred yards down the street sat the 670 members of the House of Commons, where the progress of the war was examined almost daily in heated debates and in numerous committee rooms.

Beneath them, the bulky Gothas would find a communications network linking London to the rest of the nation; essential to the fast movement of troops and supplies; the railway stations at Liverpool Street, Euston, Waterloo, St Pancras and others. Below the ground ran the world's oldest underground railway, ferrying thousands of people each day to their employment all over the capital, where they toiled in office and factory. Trains, speeding daily along the Central, Circle and District Lines, brought bowler-hatted clerks and office girls from the sprawling suburbs into the famous Square Mile.

A mere 700 acres, the City of London was arguably the mightiest and most powerful piece of real estate in the world. Within the walls of its tiny offices and great banking halls it wielded a power and influence far out of proportion to its size. Finance houses, brokerages, insurers, shipping and business headquarters great and small, governed and co-ordinated the economic lives of hundreds of millions of people around the world.

Across the capital, tens of thousands of weary Londoners were rising from their beds to face another long day. People like thirty-seven-year-old Special Police Constable Alfred Smith, off to begin his beat despite a bad cold, verging on flu; and Mary Chinnerly, off to her new job as a clerk with British & Bennington's wholesale tea warehouse. For fifty-five-year-old Walter Golder and forty-two-year-old Thomas Parfitt, today was earmarked to do some repair work on the roof of Pink's Jam Factory in Bermondsey. Fireman Albert Vide was looking forward to his watch at his fire station in Commercial Road, and for professional boxer Charles O'Brien, Wednesday, 13 June was the day he was due to take his baby boy for a ride out in his pram. Reverend Alfred Headley in Poplar was gearing himself up for another round of soul-searching and moral support for his parishioners, whilst for working-class mothers everywhere it was another day of drudgery; getting father's breakfast ready and seeing him off to his job at the docks or in one of the hundreds of factories which, at least, meant a regular income. For many there would have been no man to send to work. Most were squatting in trenches, or had been slaughtered in one of the offensives the year before. For the ragged, undernourished and scruffy children, school meant a day out of their mum's way whilst she finished the chores before going to her own job, maybe as a cleaner or in a factory as a dilutee. Tots like young George Hyde, a typically cheeky five-year-old, who lived a last minute's rush away from school at 89 Upper North Street. He would gulp down his breakfast of porridge made by his mum Lillian, without milk, and maybe some toast made from stale bread. This was followed by a brief rub down in the sink – a bath was strictly a once a week ritual – then probably back into the rags he wore the day before. The poorest children even had to manage without underpants, but the fortunate ones might be wearing a pair of boots, even if they were well past their best. George was lucky in another way too; a club foot meant that his dad had failed his medical examination when conscripted into the Army, so at least he was at home. Instead of suffering in the Front Line, George senior was able to bring home some money each week working as a casual labourer in the docks. Just as well, as he liked his ale, albeit the grossly diluted variety then available.

George was lucky in a different way too. His father was a placid and gentle character who would have given his first-born a hug before he went off to work. Little did they know that, like nearly 170 other Londoners, they were to embrace that day for the very last time.

It was to this, the wealthiest city in the world, and to these and thousands of other Londoners, Brandenburg was again to rally his forces and inflict one of the most destructive experiences in its long history.

⸻ ⸺◦⸻ ⸺

As the day dawned, the sun began to burn away the last wispy traces of mist which clung stubbornly to the Gotha airfields. The bombers began to emerge from their concealment like sleeping juggernauts; in tents and huts around the aprons, crews woke from fitful nights of slumber as the chill morning air was replaced by the first draughts of sunshine.

Donning their cumbersome flying gear, they rushed their breakfast of black bread, sausage and coffee. A laboured trudge across the airfields brought them to their flying machines, where ground crews were making their last-minute checks, and after a slow walk around the bombers the crews satisfied themselves that all was well. Once aboard, machine guns, instruments and payload were examined for the last time before take-off. Standing high above the ground in their respective positions – commander in the 'pulpit', pilot in his cockpit and rear gunner in his compartment – the crews craned around to look at each other. Then the pilot fired the engines into life, each in turn choking and spluttering, eventually shrouding the airfield in noise. One by one they slowly moved towards their take-off position, before gradually gathering speed and lurching skywards. It was 9.00 am on Wednesday, 13 June 1917.

Climbing into the stratosphere, the biting wind again struck at the men's faces and burned their nostrils; the first sensations of giddiness manifested themselves as the air thinned, and they fought off the growing nausea with the roaring engines drowning out all other sounds. Speech was impossible; eyes welled up with tears in the alien environment. All they could do was to go about their duties as best they could, jostled and jolted by the wind and the howling engines.

Higher they climbed, until at last they began to meet in formation in the skies above Belgium as the broad expanse of the North Sea appeared before them. Their diamond formation was slowly taking shape when two machines indicated that they had to abandon the operation. Their

117

unreliable Maybach engines had failed, probably labouring and spluttering ominously in the increasingly rarefied atmosphere; rev counters dropping alarmingly.

Signal flares illuminated the sky and then trailed away as the two machines lost height and broke off; their comrades closed up and reached their cruising height of 14,000 feet. What could have been going through the minds of the crewmen as they inched closer to the British coastline? Certainly fear and anticipation, not least as they anxiously scanned the sky for enemy aeroplanes. They could only take comfort from the mutual protection offered by the aerial armada moving westwards. But no attack came. Surprise, as before would be almost complete.

⚊⚊⚊ ⚬ ⚊⚊⚊

After ninety minutes of uneventful flight over the featureless North Sea, the first indistinct glimpses of the island target came into view. As the formation approached to within about ten miles to the north of North Foreland, Brandenburg fired off a signal flare. The first diversion was to take place against Margate by a single bomber. As the flare was caught by the wind and died away, one machine broke off and headed towards Thanet, crossing the coastline and holding course as it followed the railway line towards the objective.

The last thing the people of this small coastal town expected as they went about their business, looking forward to the promise of a warm, sunny day soothed by the gentle sea breeze and salt-sea air, was the arrival of an unfamiliar Gotha bomber. Cloessner's forecast was to prove its worth; it was 10.43 am when the aircraft attracted the attention of the ground defences. Almost simultaneously, the guns at St Peter's and Hengrove opened fire. Round after futile round pounded the bright hazy sky as eyes strained to fix a position on the intruder. Later reports from the gun commanders complained that the Gotha was, 'obscured by cloud almost immediately...' and its sudden changes of course made an accurate fix impossible. The Hengrove Station was only able to fire off five rounds before admitting defeat and St Peters, nineteen, before it too fell silent.

People watched as the bomber passed south of the town, releasing five 50kg bombs between Margate East and Margate West railway stations. The damage, though relatively light, was widespread. The bombs accounted for three casualties; a twelve-month-old infant, a police officer who had been sheltering under Tivoli Arch and a young boy.

The raider had managed to avoid both ground fire and the Home Defence pilots before striking out to sea in a north-easterly direction, dropping a single 50kg bomb as it went. The Westgate Church of England School was taking its regular classes when the sound of bombs could be heard; the headmaster however, succinctly recorded the unscheduled addition to the school curriculum as the raider passed overhead:

German aircraft over Westgate at about 10.43 am this morning. Let children lie down under desks for a few minutes till danger was over. Everybody quite sensible and no panic.

A few brief moments of drama and the raider was gone.

The British Home Defence however, had fallen for the clumsy ruse, scrambling aircraft to intercept one raider whilst nineteen fully laden bombers headed for London. Pilots from Manston again included Flight Sub Lieutenant de Wilde in his Bristol Scout, which was airborne at about 10.45 am only to spend a fruitless forty-five minutes attempting to locate the decoy. Flight Sub Lieutenants Burt and Daly, and Squadron Commander Butler joined him. The only pilot to have even partial success was Daly, who pursued the rest of the squadron all the way to Southend. He attacked one machine but became lost in developing cloud. The rest of the pilots in the Manston Flight returned empty handed. Some however, would refuel and rearm their machines so that they were ready to intercept the raiders as they returned to base later in the day.

With the aim of the Margate feint achieved, Brandenburg and the remainder of the squadron continued on their way to the primary objective. They steered north-west across the Thames Estuary and approached Foulness Island at 10.50 am where three more machines broke away in response to signal flares. Two were to undertake diversionary attacks against Shoeburyness while the third reconnoitred the Thames Estuary towards Medway before making for home. After dropping a 50kg bomb on the village of Barling, north of the town, the two decoys found themselves on the receiving end of sporadic and uncoordinated ground fire. Shoeburyness, as an important military centre, had been warned of possible enemy activity after the Margate attack, and at around 10.59 am, a gun station in the town fired the first of thirty-eight shells. The Gothas responded by releasing five bombs on the town; one fell in the sea and another four were widely scattered, doing little more than shatter a few windows and slightly injuring one civilian.

119

The main force was now passing over the River Crouch, and at 11.15 am was over the small market town of Wickford in Essex. Five minutes later they were reported passing over the village of Great Burstead. Numerous eyewitness reports, most unreliable and vague, included the sound of loud engines, causing many to assume again that the aircraft flying overhead were airships, and the combined noises produced by so many engines could be heard from as far as twenty miles away.

One who did detect their passing was Reverend Andrew Clarke, who was outside his rectory in Great Leighs, on the main road between Chelmsford and Braintree in Essex. Helped by his daughter, he was engrossed in repair jobs to the rectory, when:

> We heard an unusual drumming noise in the east and southeast. It went on for some considerable time. My daughter heard it about 11.15 am. I thought it was drums in Terling Camp, or a regiment on a route march on the road beyond that. My daughter thought it was an aeroplane but out of order. It now appears as if had been a squadron of German aeroplanes.

As Reverend Clarke went on with his day, the squadron pushed on. At 11.23 am another sighting was made from the vicinity of Thorndon Park Camp, south of Brentwood. A minute later they were heard above Mar Dyke near Grays, and at 11.30 am were fired upon almost simultaneously by gun stations at Rainham and North Ockendon.

At Romford, Lieutenant Stretton, although his gun fired fifteen shells, had to concede that, 'targets disappeared before corrections could be made...'. At North Ockendon, Lieutenant O'Brien had an equally frustrating time of it. His observation post reported the sound of aeroplanes, but could not hear from the gun station itself for several crucial minutes. At last vague glimpses could be detected, and O'Brien ordered the gun to open fire. Fourteen rounds were expended during the six minutes that aeroplanes were 'visible', but none of them had the remotest chance of achieving a hit.

━━━◦◦◦━━━

Brandenburg must have been expecting the clouds to loom again out of nowhere, scotching his plans for a third time; but it was not to be.

The force had now split into two crude wings, with Romford firing on the right and North Ockendon on the left. Brandenburg maintained this formation as they closed in on their objective. No doubt imagining the hero's welcome they would all receive upon their return to Germany, it was all they could do to concentrate on their duties as, one by one, the capital revealed itself; the London docks, St Paul's Cathedral, the Central Criminal Court, the honeycombed lanes and alleys of the financial quarter, and beyond those the Strand, Whitehall and the parks surrounding Buckingham Palace and the Mall.

As Brandenburg and his comrades flew with impunity through the impotent 'cotton wool' (as it was described by one crewman) being thrown up from the ground, the three Home Defence Squadrons were scrambled. Thirty-five aircraft took to the air from 11.00 am onwards (two B.E.12s from 37 Squadron were already up, as they had been exercising that morning and been alerted by Ingram Signals). Once the scramble was ordered, machines from Croydon, Dover, Hendon, Lympne, Northolt, Orfordness and Wye took to the air.

Captain S R Stammers of 39 Squadron was in the air over Joyce Green in his B.E.12 when the Ingram showed 'Readiness'. At around 10,000 feet he saw shells from the Romford and North Ockendon guns exploding over the capital. He flew towards them and at 11.20 am saw more intense anti-aircraft fire slightly north of the last burst; about 1,000 feet above the explosions he sighted the raiders:

> I was about 11,500 feet at this time but by getting speed I sacrificed height. I estimated the height of the hostile aircraft at 12,500 to 13,000 feet. At 10,500 feet I pulled my stick back, pushing the nose up into the centre of the formation and used my Vickers Gun. This was not satisfactory so I followed the formation, firing bursts from my Lewis Gun over the centre section of the formation. After having fired three drums of ammunition away, I noticed my engine revs were only 1,500 and that I was out of range. I proceeded, following the direction of the formation, climbing all the time.

Meanwhile another 39 Squadron pilot, Norwegian Tryggve Gran suffered equal frustration. Airborne from North Weald at 10.32 am, he was flying when the Ingram showed 'Patrol'. Sensibly perhaps, he decided to make sure his guns were firing before joining the fray. After clearing a fault, he flew on towards Maidstone, where he saw 'a Gotha, flying at a height of 10,000 feet. I had the sun in my eyes and tried to get a better position'. He then sighted another British pilot attempting to engage the enemy. The Gotha was seen to turn and make off towards the east. Gran tried to cut him off, and then saw yet another Briton, this time in a Triplane. 'I completely lost sight of the Hun and then made off in an easterly direction,' proceeding to Southend where he would meet some more of the enemy upon their return from London.

121

The ground defences, their efforts increasingly hampered by the combination of slowly developing cloud and increasing haziness as midday approached, tried their best to disrupt the raiders. Lieutenant Milton was in command of Shooters Hill gun station in Greenwich and reported hearing the sound of engines at 11.32 am, and five minutes later five enemy aircraft were sighted flying in formation. Two minutes more and he opened fire, but the heat and haze again prevented the bursts from being identified and corrections made. Different fuses were tried but to no avail, and the targets were lost with none of the twenty-six rounds fired having any discernible effect. Dulwich, Abbey Wood and Grove Park guns came into action at about this time, but they too wasted their ammunition; not only were they foxed by the weather, their positions were simply too far out of range. The crew of Becton Gun Station sighted a target at 11.34 am, and the commander, Second Lieutenant Griffiths, ordered his men to open fire. Indistinct and at an oblique angle, the gunners were thwarted. At Tower Bridge Lieutenant Wontner-Smith RNVR had been visiting Central Sub-Command when the 'Red' warning was received at 10.54 am. He rushed to his post in ten minutes to find his colleague Lieutenant Bedford already in the forward observation post. Wontner-Smith had the gun cleared away for action, extra ammunition brought out, and waited for a target to present itself. At 11.16 am he received a message from Dulwich of an explosion of gunfire to the north-east followed by another report of gunfire, this time from the Tower Searchlight. Further reports came in, endorsed by the Meath Gardens Searchlight and shortly afterwards, at 11.39 am two aircraft were reported overhead. Anxiety grew as explosions were heard and at 11.40 am. Wontner-Smith and his men saw their first Gotha. He immediately gave the order to open fire but typically, the machine disappeared again. Three minutes later three more targets came into view, but two of them became lost within seconds. He ordered his men to open up on the third. Two rounds were fired, and then they lost the target for thirty seconds. It reappeared and five more rounds were fired before it was again lost. Another Gotha was then sighted and the crew tried its luck with that, but after four rounds it was lost. Another target appeared, travelling south-west, but it disappeared after the first shot.

At Blackwall, the commander, Lieutenant Buller RNVR, was called to the phone at 10.56 am and received the 'Red' warning. From 11.15 am onwards, he and his men could hear intermittent sounds of aircraft from the north-west, although he could not locate their direction accurately owing to, 'a considerable amount of local noise from the river traffic, gasworks, shipbuilding etc'. At 11.35 am he could clearly hear the sounds of engines from a north-easterly direction, and sixty seconds later half a dozen enemy machines could be seen. Buller ordered his crew to open fire but after the third shot the breech jammed:

> I took my eyes off the target and found that the breech was 3/4 closed, with a piece of leather from the loading glove jammed between the breech and the cartridge case. I endeavoured to open the breech with a 95 wrench but was unsuccessful. I tried to get the clutch activating lever round to hand, but could not manage it, eventually clearing the jam by working the 96 wrench BM lever, and Clutch Activation Lever.

Having cleared the jam, he took aim at fresh targets. The first shots burst high and to the left until the target became obscured. Buller received no flank observer's report, as the target was invisible from there too. A second group of bombers appeared at 11.46 am, and was fired upon. The targets changed course; the shots were too high. More followed as Buller reported that the Gothas came dead on the line of sight. The forward observer now reported that they were falling short, but before the sights could be adjusted, the target was lost in the haze. In all, seventeen rounds were fired, and the time actually spent in action was only ninety seconds. After so much frenetic activity the crew could only stand by helplessly as the raiders went about their business.

Meanwhile one Gotha pilot, von Seydlitz-Kurzbach waited for the signal flare, which would herald the beginning of the bombing run. Finally, the order came:

> I give the order, and in less time than it takes to tell I have pushed the lever. I anxiously follow the flight of the released bombs. With a tremendous crash they strike the heart of England. It is a magnificently terrific spectacle, seen from mid-air.

Flying high, reliant upon the fickle Goertz bombsights to guide them, the Gotha's bombs fell in their usual random fashion. The residential areas, especially those of Barking and East Ham fared badly. Instead of hitting Barking Station, a crucial transportation and communications centre, controlling routes to the docks and Essex, Cowbridge Lane and Park Avenue were hit, killing four and injuring eleven people caught out in the open.

Further to the south, the other side of The Newham Way straddling the Thames, were the sprawling docks. To have severely curtailed operations here alone would have made the raid worthwhile, disrupting work and holding up vital food and other supplies. Nevertheless, only one 50kg bomb was reported to have struck the Royal Albert Dock, where a shed, several vans, a railway truck and some railway tracks were damaged. Eight people were killed and nine injured. Other bombs, which might have created more havoc, fell instead on Goosely Lane, to the north and in Alexandra Road way back over the other side of The Newham Way. Beyond, the huge expanse of the Victoria Dock presented itself to the bombers, but their bombs spiralled tantalizingly close to the north instead.

Perhaps seeing how much of his efforts were being wasted, Brandenburg decided to draw the two wings closer together in the hope of concentrating his effort. They now approached the City of London itself. The German newspaper, *Frankfurter Zeitung*, reported another participant's account of the attack:

> Our first greetings dropped in rapid succession; gave them more and still more. Then we proceeded coolly and calmly over the suburbs as we wanted to hit the centre...We gave them plenty – blow after blow from bursting bombs in the heart of England. The sight over central London was wonderfully impressive.

The German airmen watched with pride as their loads spiralled towards the Square Mile. For the sedentary workers below, their routine Wednesday morning was about to be rudely shattered.

———◦———

It was fast approaching that time of day when office workers were thinking about lunch. Executives from Lloyds, the Royal and Baltic Exchanges and any of the numerous institutions would be preparing to go to their club or favourite restaurant for lunch. Manual labourers, working on the roads or in building sites, would be preparing to knock-off, to eat their packed lunches or nip out for a quick pint. Only the distant thud of explosions coming from the distance aroused suspicion. Slowly, one by one, people paused, sought windows and strained to see through the glare of the sun, searching out the source of the alien sounds.

Young Bill Goble was labouring away in a shipping office where he was employed as a messenger, and looking forward to lunch time. Struggling through yet another morning of ennui, he was readily and easily distracted by the sounds of gunfire and explosions which drifted across the City from the east. As the commotion increased outside, 'we should have had the good sense to stay under cover and in fact, as the youngest present this is what I was told. But being a typical teenager I rushed out into the street behind the others'. Bill was stunned by what had happened in surrounding streets which, only moments before, had been hives of productive activity:

A cloud of dust or smoke drifted down Fenchurch Street, the whole glass frontage of the Albion Clothing Store, which then stood between Jewry and Minories, had been blown out. A bus conductress lay on the pavement – her leg appeared to be severed from the knee. A policeman sat on a chair, his trouser legs ripped away and one leg covered in blood. To add to the horror of the occasion, a number of [shop] window dummies had fallen out onto the pavement amongst the bodies of the dead and the injured. A No. 25 bus stood silently by the kerb, every window shattered; a solitary figure of a man was hunched up in the seat immediately behind the driver's seat. He sat motionless, a piece of glass was said to have pierced his neck and we were told he was already dead. I crossed the road to the corner of Houndsditch. Opposite St Botolphs' Church a crowd was milling around, some hysterical, some very calm. I saw another policeman taken away on a stretcher and then the rumours went round that there had been bombs on Fenchurch Street Station, St Mary Axe, Billiter Street and Liverpool Street Station.

The hero of the hour at the Albion Clothing Store was the driver of the bus, J T Wise. Despite his vehicle practically disintegrating around him, and sustaining serious injuries after being blown out of his cab, he returned to the wreckage to help extricate his hapless passengers from the smouldering hulk.

Within a matter of a few moments, the City had erupted into mayhem as the tightly packed streets reverberated to the explosions of the Gothas' bombs. Those caught out in the open were helpless as debris, glass and street furniture flew through the air, impaling office boys and company chairmen alike. Someone out walking would suddenly find himself cut down without warning; a young secretary sipping tea in a sandwich bar would find herself immersed in glass, dust and blood; another would be bringing a cup to her lips and then have the arm blown off. At once, the simple act of running an errand would mean instead running a fatal gauntlet as explosions racked the streets and blasts made every step a gamble. Gables cracked and cornices split under the weight of the bombs. Among those which shook Bill and his colleagues from their mundane morning, was an incident which occurred at 65 Fenchurch Street, City chambers which stood on the corner of Fenchurch Street and London Street, less than a hundred yards from the railway terminus. One minute its occupants were going about their everyday work, the next a 12.5kg bomb had crashed through the top of the building and exploded when it had completed its descent through the various floors and penetrated the basement. It was 11.41 am and nineteen men and women had been blasted by the rending explosion and annihilated in its wake. Another five men and women workers were injured; only a young office boy called Stevens, and three others, escaped unharmed.

Those unfortunate enough to have been going about their business when the bomb struck were helpless. Debris crashed through the shaking edifice and onto the street itself, killing and maiming those watching the spectacle in the skies. Young Tom Burk smarted as he watched the developing mayhem; never in his life could he ever have contemplated such scenes of panic unfolding before his eyes:

> I remember seeing a man lying dead against a wall of the ABC Shop... a Certified Accountant who had an office nearby was also lying dead with his daughter... There was also a number of dead who had presumably taken refuge in 65 [Fenchurch Street].

Neighbouring 109 Fenchurch Street was hit by a 12.5kg bomb, which exploded upon impacting the roof, immediately sending shards of glass and tiles scything down onto those below. The caretaker's wife, who was working on the top floor, had her head severed from her body. As fire broke out, it swept through the building, creating one of the many palls of smoke which were starting to lift over the spires of London.

The bombs came crashing down. At 11 Billiter Square, a high explosive bomb killed two workers as it smashed through the building. Bombs crashed onto Paternoster Row, which ran alongside St Paul's Cathedral, housing a number of prominent publishing houses such as Scott, Wells Gardner, Durton and Hutchinsons. Some of these were burnt out, though no bombs hit the cathedral itself.

In Beech Court off Beech Street, nine workers were repairing the roof of R Barnett & Son, a brass foundry, when suddenly an HE bomb fell in their midst blasting them to pieces, only one of them surviving to tell the tale.

The Royal Mint, close to the Tower of London and the tracks leading into Fenchurch Street Station, was busy producing not only the currency of Empire, but also many of the medals being earned throughout the many theatres of war. Here too, curiosity was aroused by the vague thuds coming from the distance and the erratic pounding of the anti-aircraft defences. The checking of bank notes and the stamping of pennies would have to wait while the workers made their way outside – only to be met by a bomb which struck the thirty-foot curtain wall around the building, exploding in the mechanics' workshop seconds later. The clock, which had previously stood there, lay mangled and crazily distorted, registering the precise moment when the explosion occurred: 11.39 am.

Further north, in Central Street, Islington, Police Constable Alfred Smith was now on his beat, fighting off his nagging cold. But this was wartime and with London critically short of bobbies he had agreed to swap his beat as a favour to a colleague. Smith started his turn on duty at 8.30 am, and had been pounding the streets for some three hours when he was reaching the entrance to a warehouse. Inside, the 156 workers were producing goods for the Debenhams department store, but had become increasingly unsettled by the sounds of gunfire and explosions. Among them was Mrs Tripp:

> I and all the others were happily working when all of a sudden, we felt the building shake. Someone came rushing in shouting 'Air Raid - Quick !'. At the first sound of exploding bombs, a man made a beeline for the street only to be cut down by shrapnel, fatally injured. A second followed but was chopped down as shrapnel cut into one of his feet. This left only the manager to try to hold back the rush of women storming down the stairs to get outside. I was the first to run down the stairs and into the street, when a constable rushed up and pushed me and all the others back.

PC Smith had arrived at a critical moment; the manager was fighting a losing battle against the panic-stricken women, but the sight of a policeman restored some calm and discipline and PC Smith succeeded in getting them all back inside. Seconds after the last woman was squeezed back into the building, another explosion took PC Smith's life.

The Times reported the incident next day:

> One policeman, a member of the Police Reserve since the war, was killed whilst caring for the safety of others... A number of girls employed in a warehouse ran into the street on the first alarm, and he had just induced them to go back under cover when a bomb fell yards away and killed him instantly.

Similar incidents were taking place all over the City. In Grosvenor Street

Stepney, a bomb killed a woman and a child as they walked along the road, and injured two men and four other women. A bomb, which fell between High Street and High Moon Passage Whitechapel, killed a young child. More fatalities followed when a bomb damaged 52-65 Plumber's Row, killing a woman and injuring a man.

While these were tragic incidents to those concerned, they were irritating distractions to the Germans who had bigger fish to fry. They needed a substantial target to hit and, if not destroy it completely, at least have the satisfaction of knowing that they had caused widespread disruption. That opportunity lent itself to a Gotha above Liverpool Street Station.

This vast transport hub, opened in 1874 and extended in 1891, covered several acres, with eighteen tracks taking out essential military supplies as well as personnel and civilians. This graceful, glass-roofed edifice dominated its surroundings completely and could not possibly be missed by an enemy bomber searching for a prime target.

Beneath the cathedral-like expanse of this glass and iron monolith, the normal buzz of activity carried on among the steam and smoke-choked platforms. Porters, ticket collectors and passengers went about their business under the fatherly eye of the top-hatted stationmaster.

Being wartime, the trains were more crowded than normal at this time of day, with so many locomotives and stock either de-commissioned for war use or unavailable because of staff-shortages. At the 'Country' end of Platform No. 9 the midday service to Hunstanton was waiting to depart. In a little bay facing this train stood a horsebox and some special coaches in which two Army officers, Captain Bruce Payne and Lieutenant Corner, were holding a medical board. A number of railway employees, eligible for military service were stripped to the waist and undergoing examination.

On the Hunstanton train was a Mrs W Pawney:

...My companions were two men and a girlfriend... first we heard an explosion in the distance. The men exchanged a scared look; they lived at Stratford-by-Bow and had many sleepless nights due to [airship] raids. My friend and I lived at Hammersmith, so we laughed at them saying 'Don't worry, we shall be alright'. At that moment another bang, louder than the first, made them insist on us leaving the train to seek shelter. We condescendingly gave in. A porter was taking luggage down in a lift. We asked him to take us. 'Of course,' he said as we stepped in. One of the men hung behind. 'Wait for our friend', I said. But the liftman said, 'No time to wait for anyone'. Then two terrific bangs! We were all thrown up in the air and then down in a heap. My friend and I were very badly injured and the man we left behind we never saw again... the carriage we had just left was completely flattened to the rails...

A scene of terrible confusion ensued. Lieutenant Siegfried Sassoon was in the station waiting to catch the train to Cambridge, having been granted convalescent leave after being wounded in France:

Bombs had been dropped on the station and one of them had hit the front carriage of the noon express to Cambridge. Horrified travellers were hurrying away... while I stood wondering what to do, a luggage trolley trundled past me; on it lay an elderly man, shabbily dressed, and apparently dead...wounded women lay in the station groaning.

A goods' clerk, two railway fitters, a restaurant car attendant, a labourer, a hammerman and two soldiers were among the sixteen killed and thirteen injured in and around the twisted carriages and debris-covered platform. Two bombs fell close together, one just clear of the north end of the station roof, destroying some superstructure and hitting the Hunstanton coach. The second completely burnt out the coaches being used for the medical examinations; a third fell 100 yards north of those which hit No. 9 Platform, blasting a crater out of the ground but causing no casualties. However, despite the serious nature of the damage, no major disruption was caused to train services. The fire brigade reported that it took only thirty minutes to get the fire in the Hunstanton coach and the medical inspection coaches under control. Yet again, the Germans failed to exploit an opportunity and inflict a devastating blow.

The factories, warehouses and wharves which lined the south side of the River Thames did not escape the scrutiny of the Goertz bomb-sights. Here were potentially rich pickings. At British & Bennington's, a wholesale tea warehouse, word was getting round that enemy aeroplanes could be heard almost overhead. When the alarm was given, many of the workers opted to remain in the building, but around thirty, mostly women and girls, chose to shelter in the company strong room. It was a large structure with a concrete roof, and it was lined with huge shelves and massive iron safes where the firm's records were kept – on the face of it, the most logical place to go. One of those who chose to do so was office girl Mary Chinnerly, newly out of school and training as a clerk. She and her pals were working away in their office when:

We heard a terrible sound described by one of the staff as an 'aerial torpedo'. We saw it coming down and rushed inside to the basement where we were all trapped – the time was 11.49 am – our clocks had stopped! The majority got out safely and were taken to hospital; I went to Barts [St Bartholomew's Hospital] for cuts in the face. Seven were killed.

The room in which the girls had sought shelter was transformed into a charnel house; the heavy safes, iron shelves and tons of concrete were sent crashing down onto them in the wake of the explosion. After a short, deadly silence, dust and the shrill cries of the injured began to rise through the rubble. Those above scratched and grabbed at the debris in a frantic effort to reach their friends and colleagues below. A local newspaper ran the following account of the tragedy:

The father of Winifred Churchill, aged fourteen, stated that he was told that her place of business had been badly hit, 'I raced there as hard as I could' said [the] witness pathetically, 'but there was nobody there who could tell me anything about it. In the evening we heard of the death of my girl's little friend, and I knew that they were always together. Soon we found that my girl was in the hospital, dead'. A fireman said that there were five or six injured in the street. A bomb had dropped on the back of the two-storey building and it was demolished. They heard screams from underneath the debris whilst they were putting out the flames.

The paper concluded:

We got one girl out, and she was unconscious... she came round and said, 'never mind me, go back and get the other girls underneath'. We got back and discovered the girl was right. There were nine, and everyone was more or less badly injured. Later, near the same spot, we found nine more girls imprisoned underneath the wrecked building. One was dead, having been badly mutilated, but the others were alive but injured... a police officer said that when the bombs dropped on the building the ambulances were almost immediately outside.

Even though the emergency services had rarely been confronted by such large-scale incidents as these, they were quick to respond. According to one police officer on the scene:

If the whole thing had been rehearsed it could not have been done better. Within a short time of the girls receiving their injuries they were in hospital.

In all, eighteen girls and six men were killed in the explosion which completely demolished the ground floor and strong room, where all the fatalities took place. Elsewhere in the district, casualties were mounting.

A 12.5kg bomb exploded on the roof of Pink's Jam Factory in Staple Street, Bermondsey where Walter Golder, Thomas Parfitt and two other men were working. Walter's widow recounted how:

> I knew that, once a year, certain work had to be done on the factory roof... I saw the bomb drop and I somehow realised what had happened... soon afterwards I was told that my husband had been fatally injured... .

North of the River, a bomb which exploded at 18 Gibraltar Walk in Bethnal Green was witnessed by a soldier, R Lynch, on leave from France, and due to go back the following day. He was saying farewell to his friend when:

> We saw aeroplanes overhead. No thought of their being German entered our heads. It was not thought possible for them to raid London in daylight... suddenly bombs began to fall... one poor women in her terror had left her baby in its pushchair standing all alone in the roadway... I saw a cloud of smoke in Gibraltar Walk... I saw an arm sticking out of the debris... I uncovered a woman's face... some others had brought a saw and other tools and quickly got them out. The mother and the twin babies were recovered but others in the house had been killed.

In Rochelle Street, six men and six women, plus ten children were injured; the London County Council School at the junction of Rochelle Street and Arnold Circus escaped when two 12.5kg bombs burst on impact with the roof, but the sturdy six-inch breeze block construction, with steel joists covered with an inch thick asphalt carpet absorbed the force of the explosion.

Another school to escape was the Cowper Street Foundation School off the City Road. Here, a single 50kg bomb smashed through the roof and penetrated five floors before burying itself in the basement, without exploding. The pupils and staff were spared a horrifying fate because the bomb had turned on its side after reaching the third floor and continued on its passage at this angle, with its fuse put out of action. Equally ineffective was a 12.5kg bomb which exploded on impact with the roof of a building in Ducal Street, although the upper room of the building was wrecked by the sheer force of the impact.

Many parts of Limehouse were peppered with bombs, one of which damaged the Town Hall and a church in Commercial Road, killing one man and injuring eight others. Two boilers were wrecked at the Union Oil and Cake Mills, where two died and two more were injured. T J Reader was a seven-year-old pupil of St Anne's School in Dixon Street, Limehouse, where it would seem emergency drill had been rehearsed many times before:

> As far as I can remember it was about 11.00 am and we were marched out of our upstairs classrooms and taken to the cloakrooms in the basement where we had to lie face down on the floor... Salmon Lane Market was approximately twenty yards from my school, and when the raid was over I went there and saw that several bombs had been dropped on some shops.

The bomb fell near 164 Salmon Lane where it injured five men, two women and a child. Nos. 191-213 were also damaged and a man injured.

The fire service, too, found themselves at the receiving end of bombs when two crashed through the roof of the fire station in Commercial Road. One failed to detonate, the other crashed through the nine-inch concrete floor and injured one man and fatally wounded another. A young woman was also injured by the explosion. Thomas Summers was passing by the station when he saw:

> Fireman Albert Vide, who was at the wheel of a fire engine, killed when the vehicle was part way out of the station... I also saw a pram with a baby near [a] shop vanish and there was a hole where it had stood... .

The wife of Charles O'Brien had even more tragic reasons to recall the incident:

> I was walking out with my husband, and he had taken the baby across the road to buy sweets when the bomb dropped... my husband was killed... I picked up the baby and rushed it to Dr O'Brians' surgery... my baby died in the nurse's arms... my sister, who was with me, was wounded in the throat.

In Morant Street, Poplar, several houses were damaged by a bomb which fell in the roadway. A man, woman and a child were killed, and another man and four women were injured in the same few seconds. Another man died when a 12.5kg bomb fell onto 17 Woodstock Road, and St John's Church in Carpenters Road, Stratford-by-Bow, had a close shave when a bomb fell in the churchyard killing one man and

132

injuring several others.

Reverend Alfred Headley was minister of the Primary Methodist Church in Poplar, and recalls it was a:

> ...singularly fine Wednesday morning. I, in Poplar, was comforting a soldier by writing it was better to be fed up than blown up, when an unusual sound came upon us. Imagine someone drawing his elbow sharply across the strings of a harp, and fancy the musical hum swirling and growing with a horrible crescendo from piano to fortissimo... .

The Reverend had been disturbed in his letter-writing by the aircraft attempting to bomb the docks; but instead were hitting nearly everything else. Reverend Headley then:

> Ran upstairs to the bedroom window facing east. Two or three gardens away an old man was assisting his wife back into the house. Two doors away a girl with a sprained ankle who had been reading on the lawn was calling in alarm to her mother, I strained my eyes to the sky but saw nothing. Guns had begun to speak and as the pace was getting very hot I withdrew from the window and had just reached the foot of the bed when Crash !! went a bomb. The window was out: the bedroom was filled with smoke and a handful of shrapnel-like iron pellets landed in the bed. 'For Gods' sake come and help me !' It was a man from next door. His brother, attracted by the noise, had walked out at the French Window right at the spot where the bomb had fallen. Though it was clear he was past help, I ran to telephone the council offices, but all the ambulances were out, they told me. I met his mother returning home, and should have prepared her. But she had already suffered cruelly through the war; I simply could not tell her that another son had fallen.

Suddenly, for the British at any rate, the war had now been brought, quite literally into the households of ordinary men and women far from the fighting Fronts, soon to be underlined in one single, tragic incident.

The tight-knit East End community, especially those areas immediately around the docks and the Commercial and East India Dock Roads, was totally unprepared for the assault. The serried rows of jerry-built slums, in which they struggled day by day to live their lives, disintegrated under the bombs. Some were luckier than others. George Miles was a pupil at Woolmore Street School just a few hundred yards from the East India and Millwall Docks and recalled being in the classroom when a bomb came down:

Our caretaker at the time was a Mr Whitbread, and he was in the playground as the plane was over the area and he said 'please don't drop it here'. We were all told to get under our desks, when the next minute the bomb went off. We had a serviceman in our class. He was a relation to one of our staff and had some sweets to give us. When the raid was over we were allowed to go home. I remember crying all the way, and as I was running I lost all my sweets. When I got home my mother was standing at the door of our house, very relieved when one of us got home.

Young Stanley Pickering's family had been accustomed to and prepared for, the night-time airship raids on the capital, and had their drill well rehearsed; but daytime attack by a squadron of aircraft was a different kettle of fish altogether:

I lived with my parents and grandfather, and during the raids took refuge in Lustys, Nestles or the Bromley Sunflower Mills. During the summer months when there were continued raids we went prepared to stay the night before the raids began... I attended St Leonard Road's School, Bromley-by-Bow... we children were ordered to take shelter in the cellar of the school, where we watched the German planes circle overhead... .

Another schoolboy at the time was twelve-year-old H J Shepherd who attended Russell Road School in Custom House, near the Royal Victoria Docks. He and his class of fifty boys were in the playground doing PE when suddenly:

...we heard the gun go off which was near Becton Gas Works and as we looked to the sky we saw some planes come out of the clouds. They had a cross on them and we knew they were Germans. We all ran under a tin shed.

For the children of a neighbouring school, there would be no such lucky escape.

——=≈:◦:≈=——

The school day at Upper North Street School, Poplar had started as usual for parents, teachers and pupils alike. Breakfasted, washed and dressed, George Hyde joined the other children heading for the school. They came from all directions. John Brennan, also aged five-years, who lived in neighbouring Nankin Street at number 4, and William Challen, also five, who was coming to school from his house at 39 Pekin Street.

134

Also with only a few minutes to walk was five-year-old Louisa Acampora who lived at 30 Grundy Street. No. 22 Swale Street was the home of Leonard Barford, whilst older children like twelve-year-old Edwin Powell had to trek from 31 Castor Street. These and many others, were making their way to school, unaware that it was for the last time.

The regime at Upper North Street School was, like their neighbouring schools, typically strict. Not however, as draconian as we might be led to believe today. One pupil, George Cook had very fond memories of life under headmaster Mr Denner:

> We assembled in the playground each morning and afternoon, in class formation, and then marched into our classrooms. School time was 9.00 am, out at noon for dinner, back at 2.00 pm; then home or out at 4.40 pm. Mondays during winter my class walked to a piece of ground to play soccer. Some afternoons, those of us who wanted to go swimming and/or do carpentry did so. We were not forced. The curriculum was detailed on a sheet for each day's teaching. Each morning, as soon as we were assembled, we said the Lord's Prayer, and in addition to the familiar subjects we have today we were tested for voice and diction, and were also taught etiquette.

George Cook was in Form 7X, taught by Mr Knapp. He has happy memories of his teacher and recalled how, 'I cannot remember [him] ever caning a boy, although other teachers did frequently'. Mr Knapp gave his class marks each day which he would keep in a book, and at the end of the week he would award the boy with the best marks 2d.

> Since he had all our names in shorthand we had no way of finding out – when we got the chance of glancing at this book – who was winning.

Perhaps George was especially fortunate, because he also recalls an incident once when:

> I fell off a fence in my garden and landed on an iron rake. A prong went through my foot and being on crutches for many weeks I was unable to attend school. Evidently, one of the boys saw me and told the teacher. He kindly sent me half a crown.

As the clock approached 11.40 am, the school was preparing to break up for lunch. The Caretaker, Mr Batt, was out in the playground attending as usual to his duties. Then he heard the sound of explosions as the Gothas passed over the area. Realizing that the raiders were too close to his school for comfort, he ushered those children who were in the playground back inside the school and told them to take shelter. Seconds later he threw himself flat on the ground just as bombs began to fall onto houses opposite; first one, then another and then a third, destined for the school itself.

Eight-year-old Esther Levy and her class were having a singing lesson on the top floor of the school where the girls' class was situated. Suddenly the calm of the school was shattered as a single 50kg bomb crashed through the south-east corner of the Girls' Department, killing thirteen-year-old Rose Martin immediately, and slicing off the leg of another girl. Esther and her classmates were suddenly plunged into terrifying chaos:

> Of course, everyone was panic stricken. I got knocked on the floor because everyone was rushing to get out, screaming. A big fat girl called Kitty Chalmers fell on top of me, but I picked myself up... I had a few grazes on my legs...

Ivy Edwards was blasted across the room:

> The screams of the injured were terrible... I managed to grip the door handle when another horrible vibration shook the whole building as the bomb exploded. I ran as I had never run before, making a bee-line for home... .

As it continued on its crazy passage the bomb had broken in two, with one half crashing through the ceiling of the Boys' Department and the other coming to rest somewhere between the roof and the classroom. Here Mr Denner was taking his class when all of a sudden he found himself flung across the room and onto the floor, dazed and covered in dust and debris. One of his pupils, twelve-year-old Edwin Powell, was killed after being struck by lumps of rubble. Another boy remembered that:

> We were doing our sums, about fifty of us in the room, when we heard a whirring in the air. We looked up and all of a sudden there was a big noise. Something came right through the ceiling. It was the bomb. Such a lot of stuff came down with it. My pockets were filled with brick dust. When I picked myself up I saw the headmaster all covered with ink. Tables and desks and things had been knocked over, and there were two large holes where the bomb had come and gone. We were all frightened but the teachers helped us to get away, and we soon ran off home.

Stanley Lambert was also in Mr Denner's class. After the dust had cleared he saw Edwin Powell, one of his friends, lying dead with his leg hanging off, and his teacher with his head cut by the flying inkwell, whilst a desk that had been blown from the floor above was hanging crazily from the ceiling of the classroom. James Cook was working in Class Three, and had been writing the word 'cupboard' when the bomb fell. The next thing he knew he was flat on his back. He was luckier than four of his classmates, who were sent with their desks along with the bomb onto Classroom E below, where the Infants' Department was situated. The room, divided by a partition into two sections, had fifty-four children under the instruction of two teachers, Miss Watkins and Miss Middleton, assisted by Miss Moore. The strength of the partition would save the children in Miss Watkins' class.

Ivy Inch was one of the children on the ground floor when:

Suddenly I sailed through the air to land in a crater with seats on top of me... I remember calling to my teacher who was getting other children out. I had most of my clothes blown off, but somehow I managed to climb out. As I went out of the classroom I stepped over a little boy who was dead... .

Jeanette Levy was making paper lanterns with other children in her class when the explosion shook the building like an earthquake, sending debris and plaster all over the children. Somewhat bizarrely however, Jeanette, 'was more interested in getting my lantern stuck'. Ivy Major was among the children being told to sing as loudly as they could as the teachers realized that there were enemy bombers almost directly overhead:

Soon however, the noise of the anti aircraft guns and the detonation of the enemy bombs became audible even above our shrill voices. The eleven other children in my row of twelve were killed while myself, although I managed to run home somehow, [collapsed and] was unconscious for weeks... .

Bill Church was seated in the front row of Miss Moore's class, furthest from the door:

We were sitting there [and] had five sums to do. When we had finished the sum the idea was to stand on your seat so the teacher could see how quick you'd done the job. Well, I was on my fifth sum, and heard the planes coming over. The teacher saw everyone's eyes light up and said 'That's one of ours'. I thought to myself that was just what my brother said the German plane sounds like with the throb in it. I'm still thinking this as I finished my sum and put my foot onto the seat, when the crash came.

Jenny Saunders was in the same classroom, going there after playtime for a music lesson. She remembers that the two rows of desks were at the end where the piano was:

> We heard the droning of those German planes and then that [bomb] came down in the corner of the piano side and exploded. I can recall that we were all covered in yellow powder... it was TNT from the bomb. After it was all over the screams began and I saw some awful sights. My friend, Grace Jones, who lived in Crisp Street corner shop was blown out onto the street.

Fellow pupil Arthur Longworth was four-years-old and recalls the enormous bang as the bomb smashed through the ceiling. His elder brother tried to calm him down by saying that it was just the bang of a table in the Girls' Department.

Thus the little room in which the infants had been quietly learning their lessons only a few moments before had been transformed, their little desks reduced to match wood; pencils, rulers and other implements becoming flying weapons that maimed, crippled and blinded. Pictures hung at grotesque angles, pieces of clothing torn and ripped, an odd shoe here, a burnt and bloodied piece of shirt there. The force of the explosion had been so great it had blasted a deep crater in the floor of the room some six feet in diameter. Hardly anything of the concrete floor was left intact. A yawning gap was blown where there was once a ceiling. The tiny, crumpled body of five-year-old Florence Wood was found, covered in blood and dust inside the crater itself. Two of her friends had been so fearsomely propelled by the force of the blast that they had been driven like stakes into the earth. The school attendance register had been blown out of the window by the rush of air and was later found on the roof of a neighbouring shed. Miss Watkins told the inquest held after the tragedy that:

> We had not the slightest warning of the raid. We knew nothing until we heard the explosion. I was collecting things on my side of the room. Another class was on the other side. There was a terrific noise, semi darkness and a fearsome smell. I was simply covered with plaster and cement... I called to the children and made a way to a glimmer of light I could see in the corridor. I got all my children

out without injury, except for a few scratches. I carried out four small children.

Another teacher, Miss Ely, was standing in the corridor on the ground floor when the bomb exploded. She went to the sound of the blast and found children marching out covered in soot and powder. She rushed to Classroom E where, 'I helped to get some children out, and then went for assistance. I attempted to account for everybody in the room'.

Local GP, Dr O'Brian, was quickly on the scene. He already had his hands full, giving first aid to casualties being brought to his surgery. But the news of an explosion involving a school compelled him to race to the scene where he was taken inside the smoke and dust-filled building, along dark and eerie corridors to the room where the monstrous crater lay.

Miss Middleton pointed out places where the children may be, and with help, he gently removed the rubble, some of it so heavy that he needed the help of several volunteers to heave it aside. Some of the children extricated were still alive, but only just, and were taken to the local hospital. Florence Wood and two other girls were less fortunate, their lifeless bodies were gently removed and laid on stretchers to be taken away to the local mortuary.

Not far from the scene was local MP Will Crooks, who was talking with a policeman when the sounds of explosions became more and more distracting:

Suddenly there was a crash, then another and third. Three bombs had fallen within thirty yards of us. Flat on my face on the floor I went. It was the safest thing to do, there was no time to reach any shelter for I didn't know when another bomb might come, or when shrapnel from one of our own guns might hit me. When I rose I looked round for my detective friend.

Will Crooks' detective friend had made straight for the school and when he got there found that the gate had been locked. He climbed the nearest lamp-post and leapt over the railings into the playground where dozens of children were wandering around, some in a daze, some crying frantically for their parents, nearly all covered in TNT and dust. He saw the school was a shambles, and tried to restore some semblance of order among the terrified children. After husbanding them as best he could until assistance arrived, he went into the school to help out. Will Crooks reached the school where he saw that the detective:

...had his coat and waistcoat off, and was busy helping to carry something... when I recovered from my own shock, I mingled with the mothers who had rushed to the school to see how their children had fared. There were some ghastly sights. Portions of nine boys and girls were carried out. All that was left of one was covered by the card which tells of the school routine for the day.

In a nearby street, a soldier was chatting to another policeman, when they too felt the shock of the explosions. The soldier:

> ...dashed round to the school as the policeman advised, and there I found the school mistress, who had got the uninjured children into a passage. We both went into the classroom where the bomb had sunk into the earth when it exploded... many of the little ones were lying across their desks apparently dead and with terrible wounds on heads and limbs, and scores of others were writhing with pain and moaning pitifully... many of the bodies were mutilated, but our first thought was to get the injured... we packed the little souls in the lorries and gently as we could... and so at last we got them to the hospital.

Meanwhile, the survivors of the bomb were pulling themselves together after the initial trauma and shock had subsided:

> Thinking only of my little sister, aged five, I rushed down the stairs with another pupil. I forced my way along the corridor which was filled with men and women frantically searching for their children, and all were screaming and shouting... I could not find my little sister anywhere and it was two hours later when my father found her dead in the mortuary...

Esther Levy ran down the stairs to try and get out of the school. She was close to hysterics, but:

> The teachers were marvellous. They told the children not to panic and go on their way quietly. One teacher was carrying a small girl called Pittard who had been severely injured by the blast; her shattered leg dangling like a rag doll's as her protector was issuing instructions to the other children. What really frightened me so much was seeing all those little children being carried out. They were all black and their hair ginger from the TNT as their bodies were loaded onto a traction engine...

Jeanette Levy recalls that a sailor picked her up after the explosion, put her on his shoulders and carried her home to Gough Street. Her mother told her later that she went to the headmaster and asked him if she could have a look at the dead children but, 'he said that she wouldn't be able to recognise them', but she told him, 'I can tell'. Some of the children, many despite terrible injuries did not wait for an adult to take care of them. Ivy Inch had managed to get to the playground, and, after an effort, leave through the school gates into the street, now heaving with frantic, distraught parents:

> We lived in Pekin Street nearby, opposite the school and I made my way home. I had terrible pains in my side and was covered in blood; I had broken ribs and five pieces of shrapnel in my head. My father took me by tram to hospital. He brought me home and I was unconscious for six weeks.

James Cook too, worked to put as much distance between himself and the school as possible, though he remembers one boy asking if there would be any lessons that afternoon!

The explosion left four-year-old E R Herrington badly traumatized. It was his first year at school and the blast sent him scurrying for cover under the piano, shocked and disorientated. He eventually emerged from his makeshift shelter, covered in TNT powder, unable to tell anyone who he was or where he lived. A well-meaning adult took him down to Chinatown to see if anyone could identify him. In the meantime 'my family were frantically looking for me, fearing the worst...'.

Martha Stimson emerged stunned from the school building, only to find scores of adults milling around and outside the building:

> My mother picked me up and gave me to my grandmother who rushed me home while mum waited for my brother to be carried out from the school. Then Grandmother and mum went and stayed with my brother until he passed away... everyone seemed very shocked down our street; people were crying... the Salvation Army were very good. They gave me a drink and something to eat.

Bill Church recalls little of getting out of the classroom door, but only that the teacher was holding it to stop the children running out in panic. His father meanwhile had heard what had happened and rushed to get his son out of the place:

> He found that the school gate had jammed and could only be opened from the inside. He stood on a bicycle and climbed over the wall, opened up the gate and let the parents into the school. As he

141

approached the door of my classroom there was a kiddy on the floor, dressed the same as myself in those days, blue jersey and shorts, he thought it was me until he turned it over, and then he heard me from behind my classroom door, picked me up and brought me home. Coming out of the school, it wasn't a case of having ambulances and carts in those days, there was just a horse and cart there. They were putting bodies on it and there was blood running down the gutter. When we got home – my dad had given me a piggyback – I opened the palm of my hand and saw that I was still clutching the sum paper, chewed up like a lot of chaff, where I had been gripping on the handle of the classroom door.

Bill Crooks recorded the effect of the tragedy on those who waited outside the school and watched as the bodies were carried out:

[There] was quiet weeping. Men, women and children sobbed. There was not much talking. A man near me groaned, 'awful isn't it? Fair fighting, man to man, one doesn't mind. But slaughtering babies is the work of devils...'.

Mrs Thirkell's mother was coming home from work, when she heard that Upper North Street School had been bombed. She rushed there expecting the worst; her five-year-old son was a pupil. But he was safe. He told her he walked out when the piano fell over.

George Perrott lived at 54 Upper North Street. He attended the school with his elder brother, and he ran to see if he was safe. His brother had been caught in the blast and been poisoned by the noxious TNT, from which he was ill for some time.

As well as the eighteen children killed outright, or who later died from their wounds, there were as many again with shattered limbs and other serious injuries. James Cook could never forget the smell that hung around the school for a long time after the incident – the kind of smell he was to experience years later when he worked in a hospital mortuary.

CHAPTER 9

GOOD OLD JERRY!
GOOD OLD LLOYD GEORGE!

The Gotha crews turned, and made for the safety of their Belgian bases, conscious of the need to make good their escape before the weather turned against them. But their sense of achievement more than compensated for any feelings of foreboding for their trip back. The *Frankfurter Zeitung* expressed the joy felt aboard the Gothas as they headed for home:

> The squadron turned. We took a last look at the City - 'Goodbye 'til next time'. We had attained the object which not long ago was the unfulfilled dream of German airmen... .

As the formation flew eastwards, many Londoners' eyes turned skywards. Others, like young Arthur Parsons and his sister in Emerson Park, were playing quite contentedly in their house, indifferent to the dramas which had unfolded. Barely concerned by the distant plopping noise that they could hear, they were irritated by their mother's anxiety that they should not miss the flight of the disappearing bombers:

> She then made what in retrospect must rank as the understatement of the century, 'look up there, you will never see anything like this again,' and there in the sky to the south were a few dots, the planes chasing each other about like flies, and firing their machine guns intermittently. The episode probably lasted only a minute or two, during which time the planes drifted eastwards from London.

As young Arthur and his sister returned to their games, the Home Defence Squadrons scurried about in the clouding sky. After bombing the capital, the two sections of the German squadron had wheeled, one to the south, the other to the north. By chance or design, the *East End News* had a reporter in a village which lay roughly under the flight path of the returning Gothas and in the customary colourful tabloid language of the times, observed:

> At one moment a German machine, caught in the rays of the sun,

143

was seen to dive and immediately shrapnel began to burst all around, leaving little spots of white smoke suspended in the air, marking the explosion of the charge. At first it seemed as if the enemy had been hit and was crashing to earth, and a cheer went up from those who had been watching. But a moment later the real reason was apparent. The enemy had dived to avoid battle with a British machine, which had manoeuvred into a position above it, and was swooping down, its machine guns rattling their death dealing charge all the while.

The incident the reporter described may have been an encounter between Home Defence pilots around Southend, whilst the guns at Bowers Gifford and Hawkesbury Bush, as well as those at Southend Barracks, engaged the enemy. What could very loosely be termed dogfights involving Captain Cooke, Lieutenant Keddie, Captain Gran and Second Lieutenant Young of 37 Squadron were beginning to develop. Gran was crossing the River Crouch when:

> I sighted four Hun aeroplanes in formation about 500 feet above me steering eastwards. They were travelling at a speed of about 70mph and I could easily catch them up. They were probably not aware of my presence as the sun was dead behind me. I opened fire on the last of the formation. They immediately answered but did not hit me. At the same time they increased their height and I was not able to follow.

Gran continued to stalk his prey but, now unburdened by bombs, the Gothas were able to enjoy an even greater speed advantage over their adversaries in their flight from England, helped of course by the generous tail wind. Gran decided to return towards Shoeburyness, but here came under intense ground fire, shrapnel shattering the left side of his exhaust pipe and forcing him to land.

Lieutenant Young was also thwarted. As soon as he got close to the enemy, his gun jammed, and he had to rely on his observer, Lieutenant Bennett's gun. He claimed to have seen the fuselage of one Gotha hit, and a German crewman appeared to have been shot. He pursued the machine a little way further until all his ammunition was exhausted and then went back to base.

Keddie's report serves to demonstrate that even the better aircraft could not guarantee results. He was flying a Sopwith Pup when:

> Hostile aircraft were sighted near Stow Maries flying in formation at least 2,000 feet above me, my course SE. My observer

immediately opened fire, firing three drums but without visible result. The Hostile Aircraft opened fire on us, but my machine was not hit. I then chased them, trying to cut off a Hostile Aircraft that was straggling from the rest of the formation. My observer firing over the top plane, fired six drums of ammunition at this machine, but owing to the long range without result. My machine was not fast enough to gain on the formation and, after chasing them for about one hour they were all out of sight. After another five minutes I gave up the pursuit.

It was the same sorry tale for Captain Sowrey, trying to urge his RE7 until he was below the enemy, and then:

Opened fire with the Lewis Gun at one machine which appeared to be lower than the remainder. That machine appeared to me to be at 13,500 [feet]. The drum was nearly empty when it flew off, and I immediately replaced it with another, and emptied that into the formation. By this time the formation of seven had drawn away from me, but I noticed two more hostile aircraft coming behind which I followed about one mile out to sea. The difficulty I experienced was in keeping height and level with the hostile aircraft at the same time.

Sowrey used up all his ammunition and landed at 12.45 pm.

Captain Cooke was over North Benfleet when he chanced upon six enemy aircraft flying at about 15,000 feet and:

...the observer fired five drums at close range and the pilot fired about 200 rounds from the Vickers Gun. One hostile aircraft was seen to be hit many times and seemed to be nearly out of control.

However, any chance they might have had of capitalizing on the Gotha's apparent predicament was scotched when Cooke accidentally let all the fuel out of the petrol tanks and they had to return to their airfield.

Captain C W E Cole-Hamilton was with his observer, Captain C H Keevil when they took off at 11.19 am from Northolt, where 35 Training Squadron, recently mobilized as interceptors, was based. When flying east in the direction of Joyce Green they sighted fourteen Gothas over Hackney. Four minutes later they saw the white flare explode which signalled the formation to divide. They could hope to do nothing however, until the enemy squadron was on its way back, where they would be lying in wait. Cole-Hamilton later attacked three targets which were straggling over Ilford; a furious exchange ensued as the

145

Gothas returned fire. The British machine maintained a steady rate of fire but the Germans were to have the better of the duel. A lucky shot, just one of the thousands exchanged between the two antagonists in the vast expanse of sky, found Captain Keevil. The observer's gun fell suddenly silent as he slumped forward, blood gushing from his fatal wound. A glance over his shoulder told Cole-Hamilton why they had ceased combat, but he determined to carry on, turning his pilot's gun on the enemy until that too jammed. Disarmed, and with a mortally wounded man behind him, he banked away.

Other spirited efforts came from Captain Lloyd of 98 Depot Squadron. He had been in the air since 11.10 am, and observed the reconnaissance Gotha taking photographs above Erith:

> I headed him off and at Greenwich he turned SW and disappeared in cloud. An observer in the middle of the fuselage fired tracer ammunition at me the whole time from Maidstone to Greenwich. After that I turned north of the River and met four hostile aircraft NW of Rayleigh being attacked by a Sopwith [probably Second Lieutenant Young's]. I was then about 13,000 feet and I endeavoured to get in amongst them but they were too fast for me. At this point my engine started missing badly, and I had to come down.

Also from 98 Squadron, Captain B F Moore set out in his B.E.2e but in his haste to get airborne, completely forgot his flying kit. The consequences of this oversight soon began to take effect: operating an aeroplane with frost-bitten hands was becoming impossible and he finally gave up the challenge.

An RNAS pilot from Grain, Flight Lieutenant Frederick Fox, had also been scrambled. He was flying his Sopwith Pup at 17,000 feet above the Thames and spotted Gothas over Southend. He went to the attack, firing on the rearmost machine at very close range, and later reported that he could clearly see tracer entering the machine's fuselage. His target was disappearing in cloud when three more enemy bombers were observed. These welcomed his attentions with sustained fire, forcing him to take evasive action, diving 500 feet while he attempted to replace his drum and reload. But this proved impossible because the clips holding the drum onto the gun were stuck fast and he wasted five minutes trying to get the drum changed – time enough for the Gothas to make good their escape. Having overcome the problem of his ammo drum, he fired at a straggler. When the gun jammed again, he accepted defeat and now twenty-five miles out to sea, abandoned the chase, only to land at Manston where he crash landed, wrecking both undercarriage and wings.

Yet another pilot to find himself foiled by the Gothas was up and coming air ace, Captain James McCudden, who had been posted to the UK in order to serve as an instructor, in the hope that some of his acquired knowledge and experience would rub off on the trainee pilots learning their craft in England. He later recalled how:

On the morning of the 13th I left Joyce Green on my Pup, to fly to Croydon to give a lecture. I arrived at Croydon after fifteen minutes' flying and taxied up to the sheds, and noticed that everyone seemed rather excited. I got out of my machine just as the CO came and told me that a hostile formation of aeroplanes had crossed the coast and were making for London. I was much annoyed, for my Lewis gun and ammunition were at Joyce Green, and to get them meant wasting valuable time. However, I got off the ground again and made an average of 105 miles per hour from Croydon to Joyce Green. In fifteen minutes time I landed there, and while taxiing in I noticed that some German prisoners who were employed on the aerodrome seemed to be very pleased with life, and were all looking aloft. I got out of my Pup, yelled to my mechanics to bring my gun and ammunition and, while we were putting the gun on, I could plainly hear the roar of the many engines of the Hun formation which had just passed over.

Towards Woolwich I could hear the occasional bang of an English Archie, but I could not see the Huns at all as there was an irregular layer of woolly clouds at about 5,000 feet which blocked one's view. The overlap of the exhaust of the many powerful engines sounded very formidable and, judging by the noise, I was certain that there were well over a dozen machines. In a minute my machine was ready, and I took off in an easterly direction, towards the south of the Thames. At 5,000 feet I climbed into the woolly clouds, and not until I had reached 10,000 feet did I see the ground again through the small gaps between the clouds. It was an ideal day for a bombing formation to get to their objective unobserved. When I again was able to note my position I found myself over Chatham. I still flew east and arrived over Sheerness at 13,000 feet. My mind was now divided as to exactly which way the Huns would return, and I conjectured that they would fly SE from Chatham over Kent, so I still climbed, and when I had got to 15,000 feet, still over Sheppey, I caught the flash of a gun from Southend, and looking upwards saw a characteristic black and white British Archie bursting over Shoeburyness at about my own height. I increased my speed at once and flew in a direction east of the Archie and, after a few minutes, could distinguish a lot of machines in good formation going towards the south-east. I caught up to them at the expense of some height, and by the time I had got under the rear machine I was 1,000 feet below. I now found that there were over twenty machines, all with two 'pusher' engines. To my dismay I found that I could not lessen the range to any appreciable extent. By the time I had got to 500 feet under the rear machine we were twenty miles east of the Essex coast, and visions of a very long swim entered my mind, so I decided to fire all my ammunition and then depart. I fired my first drum, of which the Hun did not take the slightest notice. I now perceived another Sopwith Pup just behind this rear Hun at quite close range, but after a while he turned away as though he was experiencing some trouble with his gun. How insolent these damned Boches did look, absolutely lording the sky above England ! I replaced my first drum with another and had another try, after which the Huns swerved ever so slightly, and then that welcome sound of machine guns smote my ears and I caught the smell of the Huns' incendiary bullets as they passed me. I now put on my third and last single Lewis drum and fired again and, to my intense chagrin, the last Huns did not take the slightest notice. I now turned west and the coast of Kent looked only a blur, for although I was over 14,000 feet the visibility was very poor. On my way back to Joyce Green, I was absolutely furious to think that the Huns should come over and bomb London and have it practically all their own way. I simply hated the Hun more than ever. I landed at Joyce Green after having been in the air for over two hours, and I was very dispirited, cold and bad-tempered, but after I had had lunch and a glass of port, I thought that life after all wasn't so bad.

Equally galled were the men manning the gun stations on the ground. Lieutenant Griffith's crew sighted one Gotha and opened fire to no effect. Then five more were sighted, but no attempt was made to fire at them while the first plane was engaged again until it flew out of sight. Two more machines were engaged, again there were no positive results. Within a few minutes they had all but disappeared.

On the German side, Brandenburg and his crews felt that the prospect of encounters with British pilots posed only a slight cause for concern. Their bombers had demonstrated the potency of strategic air power. The absence of any effective response from the ground or in the air justified their confidence and sense of impregnability.

— ⬤ —

Thunderstorms made the task of intercepting the enemy as difficult from Dunkirk as it had been over England, so the fighter escort requested by Brandenburg proved unnecessary in the end.

Consequently, unhampered by the British either side of the Channel, the Germans spent a practically undisturbed return journey to their bases, arriving just before the weather turned especially foul. Fate had truly smiled upon them this day; half an hour after they arrived at their respective airfields, the storm broke bombarding them with hailstones 'as large as pigeon's eggs'. According to von Bulow:

> Had this weather developed earlier, it easily would have led to the destruction of the entire squadron. Brandenburg observed in his report that thanks to Cloessner, that did not happen in this instance.

But no storm could have overshadowed the enormity of the achievement or dampen the jubilation of the men who participated. The squadron commander was more than satisfied with the outcome; General von Hoeppner wrote:

> Brandenburg judged that the effect must have been great. The raiders had reached London under conditions of exceptionally good visibility. The gunfire over London was not particularly strong and was badly directed. Bombing had been conducted with no hurry or trouble... the majority of the bombs fell among the docks, and among the city warehouses. Brandenburg was certain that a station in the City [Liverpool Street], and a Thames bridge, probably Tower Bridge, were hit. The new Gothas had flown well and all had landed safely on their aerodrome.

Von Hoeppner then recorded for posterity the unfettered elation felt by the bomber crews at the successful conclusion of the enterprise:

> For years a squadron attack on London has been the unfulfilled dream of our airmen and our technology. By carrying out this raid, Kampgeschwader 3 has provided a new basis for air attacks... Good luck for further success under the slogan – Brandenburg over London...!

The German press was quick to champion the attack. No airship raid

149

(even those whose results were grossly exaggerated) had ever inflicted damage or loss of life on the scale of the Gothas. It seemed incredible that the capital of the British Empire, so long spared bombardment of any significant scale, could show such paltry resistance to such a raid. In order to launch the attack, the Germans had to take off from airfields well behind the front line, fly over enemy-held territory and arrive virtually unchallenged over the homeland of the hated foe. They were able to drop their bombs at will and then more or less turn round and go back home again. One newspaper wrote that:

> Even from the tearful and distorted English reports it can be recognised that this attack on London was one of the heaviest which ever took place and that, consequently, also the military damage, which the English naturally keep quiet, must have been tremendous.

Other German newspapers pursued the theme: The *Lokalanzeiger* announced that:

> The bloodthirsty rage produced in England by the success of the attack on 'fortified London', is only one more proof of its success. The British and French attacks on German unfortified towns are revolting and murderous, but the German attacks on fortified towns like London are completely permissible as military undertakings. If the British wish to return the Germans' visit in a fair and honourable way, they must attack German fortresses and fortified places. They know quite well they do not.

A more measured announcement of the operation was released by the German Government in an official *communique* the following day, informing the world that:

> A fleet of our large aeroplanes yesterday afternoon reached London and dropped bombs over the fort, and during clear weather observed the effects of good hits. In spite of strong defensive fire and numerous engagements, during which an English airman fell [shot down – possibly Cole-Hamilton] over the Thames, all aeroplanes returned unharmed.

In Britain, shock at the London attack had been supplanted by outrage. Conflicting casualty figures were posted at this time, but it was eventually decided that the total casualty list consisted of 170 dead and 432 wounded. It was later to transpire however, that many of the injuries were as a result of anti-aircraft shells exploding prematurely, or the same defending shells returning to ground only to detonate among civilians.

The Times reflected the feelings of the general public towards Germany in its issue published the day after the attack:

> It slew women and children as well as men. It wrecked buildings of no greater military value than a warehouse here, a tobacconists' shop there, and a school not far away. If it were possible at this time of day to increase the utter and most universal detestation with which he is held by the people of this country, he did it today.

In the working-class districts of the East End, where some of the worst incidents occurred, crowds gathered outside in the streets, seething with anger and frustration. Anti-German sentiment grew to unprecedented levels; shattered glass greeted anyone with a German sounding name, while individuals were jostled in the street or assaulted. Perhaps conscious now of the public feeling, and sensing that a gesture might be appropriate at this time of general grief, King George agreed it would be appropriate to take the step of visiting the areas affected and displaying empathy for their sorrow.

Not everyone was so well received. Sightseers from other parts of London and outside the metropolis were given short shrift when they turned up to view the damage. Meanwhile, the wider world began to appreciate the full details of the attack – the devastation in Fenchurch Street, the near massacre at British and Bennington's, the sacrifice of PC Smith – one grim tale after another. However, at this time, one incident came to embody the horror of what occurred that day – the tragedy at Upper North Street, Poplar which had killed eighteen. An inquest at St Bartholomew's Hospital revealed pathetic tales of agony and tragedy as parents gave evidence to the coroner, Whynne E Baxter, and described their experiences:

> A soldier's wife said that she had lost a daughter aged five. She identified the child by an Egyptian medal which was hanging round her neck. An engineer's labourer told how a long search for his little son, aged five, ended in the mortuary. Coroner – 'Have you seen what remains?' Witness – 'I have'. Coroner – 'There is no head and only half the body. How do you identify it?' Witness – 'By a particular button which his mother sewed on the wristband of his

151

shirt the previous evening.' I am told that certain limbs are still being found. A pair of boots have been found, and although the boots have been identified the body of the child wearing them cannot be found. There must be some [more] bodies somewhere.

Doctor O'Brian, who had worked so hard during the raid, told the coroner that the child may simply have been blown completely to pieces, so severe was the force of the blast. Another bereaved parent to give evidence was Mrs Jane Brennan, whose adopted son John, aged five, was among the dead. Mrs Brennan was the widow of a sergeant in the Metropolitan Police, and, the *East End News* reported, '[she] said that she took the baby from the midwife when it was ten days old, not knowing its parentage, as she was feeling lonely, her husband having been taken.'

The miserable litany continued until finally the long, painful task of hearing the evidence was complete. Coroner Baxter summed it all up by saying how,

> It is a lamentable state of affairs that this war should be so largely affecting women and children. In all countries there is a considerable amount of trouble which women and children have to suffer. The Germans claimed to have bombed the Fort of London. That is the only explanation they have to give, and there are 120 little children who have suffered from the bombing of a fort. How little children could have been in a fort passes understanding.

In all, Wynne Baxter carried out fifty-one inquests at the hospital, the staff of which were themselves recognized for their hard work during the attack. About 207 patients were treated there, of whom seventy-five were kept in overnight. Forty-four died, many on arrival, but the unstinting nature of their work was noted by the jury which stated that in:

> ...their opinion the conduct of the staff of the London Hospital under trying circumstances of the recent air raid is deserving of the highest commendation.

Others too, made their contribution. A considerable amount of vitriol came from the Mayor of Poplar, whose rhetoric perhaps accurately reflected the general feeling prevailing:

> I shall not waste epithets upon the inhumanity of the Germans... any more than to say that these boys and girls have died as truly for their country and for everything worth dying for as any of our men

at the Front or on the High Seas... .

Perhaps many of the parents of the children who died may have felt comforted by those words – many too would have preferred to have their children alive and well rather than war heroes.

The teachers and staff at Upper North Street too, came in for praise. Within seconds of the explosion, they had to regain their senses and marshal the children from the smoke-filled school. Mr Batt, endured the harrowing experience of finding his own son in the rubble, but nonetheless continued to carry out his duties and help others. On 19 June, a meeting of the Council Sub-Committee was convened with the teachers present (except for Mrs Allum who was ill). The Chairwoman, the Marchioness of Crewe, opened the meeting with the following address:

> Our business now is one none of us would willingly forgo today, but which we trust will never again appear in our proceedings. We desire to testify our unanimous sympathy with the teachers and school keeper of one of our schools in Poplar in the intrepidity and self-command so conspicuously displayed by all. There must have been ample scope for more than one variety of courage – that which confronts a sudden and unforeseen emergency with energetic determination, and another, not less praiseworthy which, after the first catastrophe is over, waits collectedly for instructions and succours the injured... You [the teachers] bore yourselves in that crisis as British men and women ought, and as our fellow countrymen and countrywomen have borne themselves in many fields in the last three years; and, speaking on behalf of the Council, and on behalf of thousands of your fellow citizens in London who would wish to do you the honour, I tender to you our full-hearted thanks for what you have done.

The Marchioness went on to say that she did not want to dwell at length on the 'crime' itself, but expressed that the Council's thoughts were with the parents, 'whose homes have been made desolate, and those who are still undergoing the torments of anxiety and dread'. She referred to the, 'massacre of the little ones' as being the almost inevitable outcome of Germany's 'greed of conquest'. In a measured but nonetheless emotive tirade, she summed up what most people thought about their foe, when she claimed that Germany, 'has attacked unoffending neighbours, she had torn up treaties and broken her plighted word', admitting that sadly, such actions had been witnessed in

153

the past, and would be seen again in the future. The biggest tragedy of all was, she went on, that for centuries mankind had progressed slowly, 'to make the horrors of war less horrible,' but in the one act of bombing the school, the Gotha crews had served only to reverse such trends. She went on to intimate that indeed, they had managed to put the clock back a hundred years, provoking decent British citizens to demand reply in kind. She concluded by saying that, 'only before the bar of history will Germany be arraigned and judged'.

Another member of the committee, Mr Norman, seconded by Reverend J Scott Lidgett, forwarded the following motion which was carried unanimously:

> That the council, having heard of the circumstances concerned with the lamentable loss of life among the young children owing to the dropping by aircraft on 13th June 1917, of a bomb on a London County Council school in Poplar, desires to express its appreciation of the courage and devotion to duty displayed on the occasion by the teaching staff and the school keeper.

Two years later, on 19 June 1918, OBEs were awarded to Mrs Allum, Mrs Middleton, Miss Watkins and Mr Denner. Mr Batt had died and could not, under the rules then receive a posthumous award. Some of the victims however, do not appear to have been quite so well recognized for their suffering. One, Ivy Inch, was to recall bitterly how:

> The only people who visited my mother were the Salvation Army; after several months my mother asked for me to convalesce and was asked for 15/-, quite impossible in those days. She worked at Nestles the chocolate factory, and took me there in a push-chair, where they gave me the old blue bag they put sugar in and I could fill it with chocolate of my choice. Also I was given a teddy bear measuring two-and-a-half-feet with a huge pink bow. Unfortunately, being bombed out in the Second World War it went astray. That was the full extent of anything we received for my appalling injuries. To this day I suffer from the raid. When I got older I had blackouts, and after some years I went to Kings College Hospital and they did several tests and X-Rays and could still see the scars on my brain. I have been on phenobarbital twice a day and will be for the rest of my life. I did get a letter from the LCC the following year and a Bronze Medal for good conduct and attendance. Today they would be claiming thousands of pounds in compensation. I often feel very bitter about the whole thing, and

was very nervous in the Second World War, especially as I had two babies.

Letters of sympathy were forwarded to parents by the Chairman of the Education Committee; a special message from the President of the Board of Trade being conveyed in the Chairman's Letter. The minutes of the Council also recorded the receipt of expressions of sympathy from many schools outside London, including two in Western Australia and a donation from the pupils of Clifton Down School in Bristol. The girls at St Columbia School, Kilmarcom also pledged £15.00 towards the fund to help the children who had suffered injuries in the raid.

━ ═ ⚬ ═ ━

Those who survived may have felt neglected, but the eighteen who perished at Upper North Street received one of the most impressive and moving funerals ever experienced in the East End. Thousands turned out on 20 June, when the children were laid to rest.

The funeral was held at All Saints Church, and the service was taken by the Bishop of London with the assistance of the Bishop of Stepney, and Reverend O S Laurie, Bishop of Poplar. Hundreds packed the church, with hundreds more outside standing in hushed silence. A number of public dignitaries joined the mourners, including Lord Crewe, Chairman of the London County Council, Lieutenant General Sir Francis Lloyd and Will Crooks MP. The teaching staff were also present, with the surviving pupils represented by six girls in white dresses and six boys in scout uniforms. Trades Unions and businesses also sent their representatives. In the Town Hall across the road lay over 500 wreaths donated by individuals, businesses, market traders, schools and others.

The bodies lay in coffins which rested upon trestles in the church, each covered with wreaths. The hymns chosen were Loving Shepherd of Thy Sheep, There's a Friend for Little Children, and Oh God Our Help In Ages Past. The King sent a message of sympathy, which the Bishop read out:

> The King asked that you will assure the parents of those children who were killed during the air raid of 13th inst while at school, how His Majesty and the Queen are thinking of them and their homes especially today when the bodies of their little ones are laid to rest. The early ending of young innocent lives, at all times pathetic, is made so more than ever in these cruel and tragic

155

circumstances. Their Majesties pray that the mourners may be blessed with God's help and comfort in their sorrow.

In his address, the Bishop said that during the twenty-eight years he had worked in London this was the most touching sight he had ever seen, and, 'it was only with broken words that he could express what was in their hearts'. He added that it was almost inconceivable that after 2000 years of Christianity war should be made on women and children. Referring to the growing calls for reprisals however, he sanctioned caution, expressing his belief that those who had lost children would not want other parents, whoever they were, to endure the same misery. He added that only strong and decisive military action could ensure that those responsible for the outrage were brought to book. The service ended with the 'Dead March in Saul', played by the band of the Poplar Training School. The tiny coffins were slowly carried outside to the waiting hearses and the solemn procession then made its way past the hushed crowds to the East London Cemetery. Here sixteen of the eighteen children were laid to rest (two had private burials) carried to a special grave by Royal Naval ratings.

A special fund was established to erect a memorial to the children, and money was soon flooding in. A total of £1,455 19 11d was raised from individual donations and door-to-door collections around the East End and from elsewhere in the country. However, it was felt that to spend all the money on a memorial was not such a wise use of the money and that, 'the memorial should be also of such character as to benefit the living'. So part of the fund was used to endow two cots, one in the children's ward of the Poplar Hospital, and another in the Lord Mayor's Home for Crippled Children in Alton, Hampshire. The balance paid for the stones for the three graves in East London cemetery, and a memorial inscribed with the names of the children to be erected in Poplar Recreation Ground.

It was unveiled by Major A B Ashmore on 23 June 1918, when children from the school laid wreathes in remembrance. The memorial, which still stands somewhat neglected and forlorn today, was an inspiring and moving sight; an angel with outstretched wings and hands clasped in prayer, upon a pedestal below which are inscribed the circumstances of the tragedy and the names of the eighteen young victims.

Relatives of the eighteen were presented with a small gold and black-lined sympathy card, the cover of which bore the image of an angel ascending to heaven and below which was the legend, 'Suffer Little

Children to Come Unto Me'. On the outside were lines from an anonymous poem alongside the name of the victim. Below this, and in surprisingly simple and unemotive prose, bearing in mind the emotion aroused by the incident, were a few simple words... 'Who Passed Away June 13th, 1917' and the child's age. Modest cards were also printed in remembrance of the raid itself, with the proceeds going towards the relief fund. Bearing the more stark legend 'In Sacred memory of the Victims of the Hun Death Dealers', they bore inside an account of the King's visit to the London Hospital to visit air raid victims.

In an effort to address the problems of children being at school when an air raid occurred and to prevent the possibility of a repeat of the tragedy, the Borough Council convened on 19 June to approve the publication of two posters which were to be distributed to the borough parents:

> During danger from air raids, all children will remain inside the school buildings; all gates will be shut, and no one will be admitted. Crowding round the school premises only increases the danger. No place is absolutely safe, but experience shows that children are safer in school buildings than if sent out into the streets. The London County Council is doing all it can to secure the safety of the children, and it is hoped that parents will help by leaving their children entirely under the control of teachers until the danger is over.

They could have had little confidence however, that such instructions would be adhered to if there was another raid like that of 13 June. Another matter upon which the Council was called to discuss was the concern of the teaching staff of the affects of the raids and the arrangements which ought to be made to limit them. On Wednesday 27 June, a deputation from the London Teachers' Association met with the Elementary Schools Sub Committee. The minutes state however that:

> The deputation advised us of the subject of the instructions which had been issued, and certain suggestions and dealt with special cases of difficulties which arose on the occasion of an air raid.

The deputation was assured that it had their every confidence during the period of 'abnormal strain' and they were certain that they would be able to cope and to carry out their duties and shoulder them on the occasion of an air raid and meet 'the serious responsibilities suddenly devolving upon them on the occasion of an air raid'. Nevertheless despite such pious platitudes, the Committee did not feel it appropriate for them to discuss the options face to face, and patronizingly asked them to leave the room whilst they considered the matter.

The problems associated with using schools as air raid shelters was further discussed, as it was becoming increasingly common for the buildings to be used as a focus for the local population during an attack, or suspected raid. To prevent this, Regulation 607 was passed, stating that 'the outer doors of schools shall be locked at 10.00 am and 2.30 pm. In connection with consideration of the precautions to be taken in schools in the event of air raids, the Elementary Sub-Committee are of the opinion that it would be desirable for the duration of the war, subject to children who arrive late at school being satisfactorily dealt with, that the gates should be locked'.

On 26 July, the Elementary Sub-Committee took further measures in that they advised the vacation of the upper floors of schools in the event of a warning of air raid or actual raid. They added optimistically that, 'ways of diverting the children's attention during air raids' be found. The discouraging of people to seek shelter in schools was again raised, and to deter this, signs stating 'No Available Cover in this Building' be installed.

Whether or not shelters were the right solution to the immediate danger of air raids, debate was growing as to the correct response to them. Not surprisingly, the single tragedy at Upper North Street raised to a clamour calls for retaliation in kind whilst others sanctioned a more measured response.

Letters published in newspapers illustrate well the kind of emotions running at the time. One correspondent, Bradford Leslie, responded to a writer using the pseudonym Senex, who urged retaliation in kind - 'a salutary lesson'. Leslie stated however, 'does Senex think that the slaughter of any number of German women and children, even if British airmen could be induced to undertake it, would make the Kaiser forgo the pleasure of strafing England?'

Senex however was adamant: 'our women and children are being systematically killed and maimed.. it is time to raise our voices in protest against inaction'. He went on to say that:

>...revenge-in-kind was all these brutes understand... it may go against the grain, but our duty is quite clear... we must be ruthless and strike without mercy... .

Another correspondent, Robert Dona, agreed:

It is not reprisals that we want but retaliation. We are not prepared to take these raids lying down, and we retaliate effectively on the Western front and in Belgium. But we want more than this. We want to carry this war, as well as that on the battle fronts, into the enemy's territory. We have the means of doing so and we must use them.

Another contributor, signing herself, 'A Mother' submitted her views as someone who had suffered first hand, asking:

...I gave two sons in the war (my only two) and they will never come back to me. I gave them willingly and have no regrets. I gave them to help rid the world of tyranny and barbaric savagery... But should I live to see Englishmen sent to murder in cold blood German women and children and harmless civilians, then indeed I should begin to ask, 'have my sons died in vain...?'

Such magnanimity was far from universally held. William Joynson-Hicks MP addressed a crowd at Tower Hill and urged that, 'every time the enemy makes a raid on London, British airmen should blot out a German town'. The meeting was well attended by a number of people, one of whom stated that five raids should be made on Berlin for every one on London. 'We must send over 500 aeroplanes to Berlin,', he insisted. The meeting concluded with a resolution calling upon the Government to 'pay back the enemy in the same way as he has treated this country'.

Inquests too, tended to stray into emotive and rabble-rousing territory. An inquest into the death of a sixty-four-year-old factory worker concluded that the piece of metal found in the nose, the two wounds in the left side of the chest and stomach, and the injuries which caused his left thigh and left foot to be blown away, was as the result of, 'wilful murder against some person or persons unknown, who had ejected bombs from an enemy aircraft'. Other verdicts referred to murder, naming the Kaiser as the culprit.

Nevertheless not everyone was baying for blood. Speaking at the annual meeting of the Royal School for Naval and Marine Officers' Daughters, Admiral of the Fleet Sir Hedworth Meux, counselled restraint, urging his listeners not to go along the road of an eye for an eye. Lord Montague however, suggested that if that were the case, 'if they have the perfect right, we have no right to impose any penalties on its exercise, and the whole of humanity is degraded to the level of the

159

Prussian confusion of might with right'.

The argument raged on between armchair strategists and tea-time theorists while mobs gathered in the streets, smashing windows and assaulting individuals with German-sounding names.

The Government had to act – or be seen to be doing so. On 17 June a meeting was held in Whitehall, with Field Marshal Haig, Lord Trenchard and the entire War Cabinet. It was ventured that by successfully launching an offensive, the very territory from which the Gothas were taking off could be captured. Haig supported this, and happened to be planning a fresh attack that summer. The thorny issue of deterring further attacks by launching reprisals was also raised. But this it was agreed would be repugnant to British ideas:

> But we may be forced to adopt them. It would be worse than useless to do so however, unless we are determined that, once adopted they will be carried through to the end. The enemy would almost certainly reply 'in kind' unless we are determined and prepared to go one better than the Germans, whatever they may do and whether their reply is in the air, or against prisoners, or otherwise. It would be infinitely better not to attempt reprisals at all.

In any case Haig reiterated, that he would need all available air power for his next offensive. He would not tolerate having it diverted to carry out reprisals, 'the diversion of aeroplanes for a bombing attack of this kind would entail such risk to Army operations that I am not justified in recommending it'. In a secret session of the House of Commons, Lloyd George made it clear that the Germans' new strategy would under no circumstances tempt or lure the Government into any operation against the interests of the country to pursue blood-lust or revenge. In any event, it was now felt that sufficient aircraft would soon be available to provide more than enough resources for home defence, and that another raid like that of the 13 June would be repulsed with ease. Until then it was agreed that:

> The first consideration before the Government is to see that the Army in France is sufficiently supplied with aeroplanes... the first duty of the country is to protect its men. The Germans realise the importance of this question quite as much as we do. The second means by which they are attempting to diminish our superiority is by trying to force us to withdraw our machines in France in order to protect our own towns. If the Germans know that by bombing English towns they can force us to withdraw fighting squadrons

160

from France, then there will be nothing that could encourage them more.

The arguments, demands and counter-demands would continue, but despite all the fuss and furore, there were a number of men quite unmoved or fazed by it all. These were the men who witnessed on a daily basis the slaughter and waste of life on the Western front, which made the losses at home seem trivial. Men such as the RFC pilot Cecil Lewis, who had little time for the cries for revenge coming from Britain. By now, there was widespread contempt for the dodgers and profiteers who stayed at home in safety whilst they did the fighting and faced death every day. For them the chastening reminder of what the war meant, was probably a good thing. His thoughts of the time fairly reflect this point of view, recording how:

> One jolly June morning the peace of London Town was disturbed by the unexpected arrival of about twenty German bombers, who laid their explosive eggs in various parts of the comfortable metropolis. They did not actually do very extensive damage; but their appearance was quite enough to scare the civilian population very thoroughly, and raise an outcry. Barbarians! Dastards! Bombing open towns! Waging war against defenceless women and children! The daily hymn of hate rose to a frightened scream. England was, as usual, unprepared. The arrangements made for home defence were quite inadequate. True, a few old [B.E.] 2c's had staggered into the air to attack, but they could not climb up anywhere high enough. They might be alright for Zepps; but against Gothas they were a joke – worse than useless! The complete German squadron returned home triumphant... Agitation in the press! Scandalous neglect of the defence of dear old England! Questions in the House! Panic among the politicians!

—————◦—————

Finally, all talk of the rights and wrongs of the attack and the need for reprisals gave way to the vexed question of warning the population of a raid. Certainly, the people exposed in Fenchurch Street on 13 June would have been grateful for the chance to escape to shelter before the explosions came. But the Government was convinced that warnings were not the answer. Home Secretary George

Cave advised the House of Commons that:

> The occasions when air raids were threatened or impending were many times more frequent than when air raids actually occurred. The result of giving warning would be the immediate dislocation of business all over London. If warnings were given on every occasion the result might be loss for a day of thousands of workmen. This might affect the manufacture of munitions and therefore our fighting forces. The effect on our ordinary occupations and our preparations for war might be such as to give the greatest possible satisfaction to our enemies who would be encouraged to make more raids whenever possible. The wisest things people could do when an air raid occurred was to go under cover; a solid floor was almost certain protection... it was the practice to give warnings to the hospitals, doubting whether it would be wise to warn school authorities, least the result be that the children were sent out from the shelter of the school buildings.

But the Minister's reasoning was flawed, according to the Chairman of the London Hospital:

> Some better organisation for warning hospitals must be devised, because upon us falls the main duty of attending to the wounded. We had our garden here at the time full of patients on stretchers, and the numerous balconies outside the wards were also full of patients... An enormous lot of arrangements have to be made at a hospital to meet a disaster such as a big raid... and all cannot be done in the space of a few minutes.

Newspapers broadly supported the call for some kind of warning system to be implemented, the *Stoke Newington Recorder* among them, calling the Gothas, 'the Orangutans of the civilised world'. Rather untactfully, Secretary of State for War, Lord Derby preferred to labour on the fallacious fact that, 'not one single soldier had been killed'. To appease detractors on the warnings issue, the Government acquiesced on demands for reinforcement for the hard-pressed Home Defence Forces. A memo was sent to Haig telling him, 'You should send over for a week or two one or two squadrons... and the machines would then be returned to you...'.

In the event, two squadrons were requisitioned from front line duties: 56 Squadron, consisting of SE5s under the command of Major R Blomfield, was flown across to England, and 66 Squadron consisting of Sopwith Pups under the command of Major O Boyd, directed to patrol from the French side of the Channel. The two squadrons left their airfield at Estree Blanche on the morning of 21 June, 56 heading for Bekesbourne and 66 for Calais. Haig was promised that he could have them back on 5 July. In the meantime, there were few complaints, especially from the men of 56 when they heard the news. Cecil Lewis was amongst them:

Lloyd George acting quickly! Result: a crack squadron to be recalled for the defence of London immediately, and twelve elated pilots of 56 Squadron packing a weeks' kit into our cockpits... God bless the good old Gotha!... The defence of London was quite a secondary affair. The things of real importance were squadron dances. To fight Hun bombers over London would have been a picnic for us after a month of gruelling Offensive patrols... Good Old Jerry! Good Old Lloyd George...!'

CHAPTER 10

WE ARE ALL IN THIS BUSINESS TOGETHER

Brandenburg and his men were feted throughout the country, heroes of the German Reich. The country's rich and powerful fell over themselves to be seen in the exulted company of the heroic fliers, as the returned crewmen suddenly adjusted themselves to their new roles as superstars. However, the fruits of victory were to be short-lived.

Summoned to the Supreme Headquarters at Kreuznach near Mainz for an audience with the Kaiser, Brandenburg was decorated with the coveted eight pointed gold and blue cross of the *Pour la Merite* – presented to him personally by the Emperor. After spending the weekend briefing his Emperor on the finer details of the operation, he left early in the morning to return to his squadron. Everything went according to plan until suddenly the aircraft, a two-seater Albatross piloted by *Oberleutnant* von Trotha, jolted suddenly, lost power and then went completely out of control shortly after taking off. The pilot fought with the controls, but it smashed headlong into the ground, killing von Trotha and inflicting crippling injuries on Brandenburg. They were so severe that he had to have one leg amputated and spend a year off duty in recuperation. In a matter of seconds, Germany had lost one of its pre-eminent heroes. The squadron would never be the same again, although he would return briefly to command towards the end of the war after its incumbent commander was killed.

The loss of Brandenburg was to prove a body blow to the Squadron. His patient and calm leadership and his careful analytical approach to ensuring the success of the squadron, led to the attainment of its goal. The raid of 13 June proved what could be achieved under the right circumstances and under the right leader. He had been able to ensure both were in place. Now the stunned German airmen steeled themselves nervously for the arrival of Brandenburg's replacement. They did not have to wait long.

The son of an infantry colonel, Captain Rudolf Kleine was every inch the young and dashing Prussian Junker, with his handsome chiselled features, cropped hair and arrogant strut. He had enjoyed a lengthy and successful military career which belied his youthful thirty years, and which found him the proud recipient of two Iron Crosses and the *Order of Hohenzollern*. He seemed the ideal replacement for the beloved Brandenburg and a fortunate one in times when talented leaders of men were growing increasingly scarce.

It was soon obvious that he was determined not merely to match, but surpass his predecessor's achievements – whatever the cost.

Although no one on either side knew it yet, the German campaign had already all but shot its bolt, and the turn of events was to give Kleine only a short time in which to emulate his predecessor. The British response to the Gotha raids manifested themselves in a revolutionary overhaul of the defences. In the interim, true to their word, the British Government had sanctioned the return of the two borrowed squadrons to the Western Front on 5 July, before they had even had the opportunity to demonstrate their ability to thwart another attack. Haig had insisted that the squadrons be returned as agreed, despite Lord French's ill-disguised anger at the decision. He forthrightly articulated his views on 2 July, when he pleaded that:

> The withdrawal of these squadrons will leave the means at my disposal to repel aeroplane attacks dangerously weak, and it cannot be supposed that the danger of attack can be any the less after the 5th instant than it is now or has been in the past. In fact, it is probably much greater, for, as far as is known this new type of enemy machine is now being produced in considerable numbers. Further there is a reasonable probability that the enemy may send fast machines to create alarm on the coast and then induce us to put our machines into the air, following them with a strong attack of large Gotha aeroplanes.

While the British prevaricated, a couple of phyrric victories would have to suffice to massage Kleine's ego.

Leutnant Georgii gave Wednesday 4 July as the best chance for cooperative weather. He was, however, unwilling to risk everything on his first raid and decided to attack the coastal towns of Harwich and Felixstowe in Suffolk. Meanwhile 56 Squadron of the RFC reluctantly began packing their kitbags and return to the Front.

On 4 July, twenty-five German machines took off from their airfields. Before long they were waving farewell to two comrades who signalled engine trouble, and shortly afterwards another five machines joined them with badly running engines. Despite the omens, Kleine was confident that his early start and more northerly route would catch the enemy offguard.

By 7.10 am, the force had divided into two wings, one of whom's objective was Harwich and the other Felixstowe – the former an important naval base and the latter a key RNAS station on opposite sides of the river Orwell.

Despite later German claims to the contrary, neither targets suffered serious damage, but the Home Defence reaction was also typically mediocre. Not a single machine as much as sighted one of the raiders. But, on their return home, the Gothas were to get more than they bargained for from the squadrons on the other side of the Channel.

At 8.00 am, a patrol from 4 (Naval) Squadron at Bray Dunes set off to intercept the raiders as they fled back to their bases. Led by Flight Commander Alexander Shook, the force of eight Camels and two Pups spotted Gothas and their escorting fighters about thirty miles out from Ostend. Inspired by their leader, the British machines tore into the Germans. One pilot, Sub Lieutenant Ellis, later reported how he fired over 300 rounds at one machine which went down in an erratic manner, and reported it as a 'kill'. Shook also reported engaging enemy machines. Berlin however, denied any losses.

Machines from 6 (Naval) Squadron also sortied ten fighters, but found nothing, and 66 Squadron at Calais put in an indifferent performance owing to the fact that they were packing up to return to front line duties and were not warned of the enemy approach until it was too late.

Kleine's victory bloodied the eager commander and gave him a taste for loftier things. He had taken his squadron on its first raid since the loss of Brandenburg, and he was impressed both by their professionalism and skill. The lamentable performance of the British defences would have given him no cause for concern, certainly less than it was giving Lord French. His letter of 2 July still unanswered, French was in no mood for niceties. On 6 July he lamented the loss of the two squadrons, more so now in view of recent events:

Apart from the slower machines which have neither the climbing power nor speed sufficient to make them effective against such machines as the enemy may be expected to employ, the means at my disposal to repel aeroplane attacks are... twenty one [machines].

As unwelcome as the attacks were becoming in England there were people in Germany too, that viewed unfolding developments with grave disquiet. German Foreign Minister Bethmann-Hollweg was having cold feet, and feared the political repercussions the raids could provoke. He warned Hindenburg against anything '...which could impede England's decision to enter into peace negotiations...' adding that:

> ...no English government which was willing to treat with Germany after such an occurrence would be able to withstand the indignation of the nation for a day. As I am unable to believe that such aerial attacks are absolutely necessary... may I be allowed to suggest that they be given up... .

But Hindenburg had no intention of giving up; keep the war going, crush the enemy, grind them into submission – but on no account stop until one or the other side was brought to its knees.

In any case, Bethmann-Hollweg's fears were groundless, if one were to believe Lord French's evaluation that, '...if London is once again subjected to attack the results may be disastrous...'. But this was total war, a war to the finish. Hindenburg warned how:

> ...the German people, under pressure of English starvation and the war, has become a hard race with an iron fist... the hammer is in our hands, and it will fall mercilessly and shatter the places where England is forging weapons against us.

Unlike Lord French, Bethmann-Hollweg received the courtesy of a reply to his objections. Hindenburg assured him that:

> I do not think that England will be ready for a peace of understanding as long as she still has hopes that Germany will collapse before herself... we must therefore prosecute the war with all our resources and the utmost intensity. Your Excellency appreciates the aerial attacks on London... the military advantages are great. They keep a large amount of war material away from the French Front, and destroy important enemy establishments... I should therefore be glad if you would acquaint me with the facts... that the recent raid on London has aroused the passions of the English nation to a disastrous degree.

While politicians and warlords on both sides of the Channel argued with one another, Kleine continued with his preparations for the next raid on the capital itself. An improved window of weather was offered by meteorologist Georgii which suggested that Saturday, 7 July offered the best opportunity. He was further heartened by intelligence reports which suggested the two British squadrons seconded to the defence of London had been returned to duties on the Western Front.

The Gothas, now divested of some of their bomb-load to improve speed and height, were ready.

The German force crossed the Crouch at 9.45 am, and meanwhile the machine allotted to the task of attacking Margate broke off. By the time it reached Manston after scattering a few bombs on the target, six RNAS fighters were taking off from the airfield and two guns opened up, accompanied by another nearby at Pegwell Bay. However the six machines which had taken off were not bothered about one single bomber which now seemed to pose little further danger. They were after the far bigger fish still making their way to London, and headed north. The raid on London had achieved little, except one incident which threatened the operation of the General Post Office's communications hub – The Central Telegraph Office in Newgate Street. A major national communications centre in peacetime, it was especially crucial in war. Two high explosive bombs found their mark, causing extensive but not fatal, damage. Some telegraph facilities on the first floor were ruined, and damage done to parts of two upper floors, but there was only one fatality – a soldier – and three injuries. The building was back in operation within a few days.

In all, the Germans had killed fifty-seven, injured ninety-three and caused damage valued at around £250,000. Certainly far fewer casualties had been inflicted than might have been the case had the raid been on a weekday.

Their return flight to Belgium was dogged by attacks from British machines piloted by men including James McCudden and Second Lieutenants Frederick Grace and George Murray, who dived upon a group of Gothas around the Girdler Lightship. They received as good as they got, but their persistence was to pay off when, turning their attentions on a lone Gotha flying low and without support, Grace poured rounds from his gun into its starboard side. Murray opened fire with the Lewis, and eventually they saw their prey plunge into the sea.

McCudden was at Dover when the alarm came through, having his machine overhauled and:

Made up my mind that I was not going to miss them this time. I arrived over Southend at 16,000 feet, and then flew eastwards along the north bank of the river. Very soon I saw the welcome cloud of British Archie bursting over Tilbury and I could not discern a lot of big machines in good formation flying east. I had plenty of time to determine what to do, and also a lot of height to spare. As soon as the formation had passed, I dived on the rearmost machine and fired a whole drum at close range. In diving I came rather too near the top plane of the Gotha and had to level out so violently to avoid running into him that the downward pressure of my weight as I pulled my joystick back was so great that my seat-bearers broke, and I was glad it wasn't my wings. I remained above again and now thought of a different way to attack the rearmost Gotha. I put on a new drum and dived from the Hun's right rear to within 300 feet, when I suddenly swerved, and changing over to his left rear, closed to 50 yards and finished my drum before the enemy gunner could swing his gun from the side at which I first dived. I zoomed away, but the Hun still appeared to be OK. I put on my third and last drum and made up my mind that I should have a good go at getting him. I repeated the manoeuvre of changing from one side to the other and had the satisfaction of seeing my tracer bullets strike all about his fuselage and wings, but beyond causing the Gotha to push his nose down a little, it had not the desired effect. I was very disappointed, as I had used up all my ammunition and the Huns were only just over Southend.

His ammunition used up, McCudden then bravely decided not to break off the action as such, but to linger within view of the Gotha:

> ...to monopolise the gunners' attention so that some of our other machines, of which there were a lot in attendance could fly up behind the Hun unperceived and shoot at him while he was looking at me.

Instead, the Gotha managed to get McCudden in range and, 'put a good burst of bullets through my machine, one of which went bang through my wind-screen, much to my consternation'. This close-shave indicated the danger of his tactics and,

> I now got rather fed up with acting as ground bait for other people... so I flew a little father away from the... Gotha, whose gunner I decided was a very nasty man.

He then returned to Joyce Green.

Other British airmen from both sides of the Channel also attempted to intercept the bombers, and were later to claim a further four 'kills'. However, it turned out that with the exception of the machine shot down by Messrs Grace and Murray, the Germans' own misfortunes, not British marksmanship, accounted for the additional four casualties. One pilot, RNAS Sub Lieutenant Loft, pursued three Gothas almost as far as Walcheren Island before he was within range of one of them. It was then his guns jammed and his engine began misfiring. He had to get home, but later reported seeing the quarry with its nose down. The Gotha was to limp back to France.

Loft's colleague, Flight Lieutenant Daly, also claimed to have put paid to a Gotha, but here too, the enemy machine appears to have survived – but only just – and to have returned to its base. The same story goes for fellow RNAS pilots Butler and Scott. One machine, its fuel all but spent made it to base, while another crash-landed so heavily it killed two of its crew.

—⚬—

By 1.00 pm the Gothas had reached their airfields. Kleine, the young Junker reincarnation, had realized his ambition and had shocked, horrified and outraged the British more than ever. Within weeks of the last raid, and having given the authorities plenty of time to make arrangements to respond properly in the event of a repeat episode, the Germans had once again 'lorded it' over London. The shame had not been greater since the Dutch had been able to sail up the Medway in 1667, fumed the *Daily Mail*, and *The Graphic* bemoaned the loss of British prestige in the air, following her successes on both land and sea. The 12 July issue of *Flight* lamented how they were,

> ...no dragonflies or fluttering birds...they were huge, sharply defined, mobile magazines of death... their turning movements were masterly, defiantly precise...like ships at a naval review. The manoeuvre was a well-rehearsed triumph for the enemy...but it seemed to us who watched deeply humiliated that such a thing should be achieved unhindered in daylight over London.

The Times expressed the, 'sense of desperation aroused by the apparent ease with which the enemy airmen carried out their mission'. Other, less measured observations were not lacking, 'Oh, for five minutes of Captain Ball to smash this insolent formation', exclaimed a journalist of the *Daily Chronicle* who likened the fall of the bombs, 'with

170

unhastened regularity...to the rhythmic beats of an incredible metronome'.

Sir Hall Caine, Manx novelist and dramatist resented some of the apparently admiring comments of his peers, and wrote scathingly how:

As a display of military prowess I thought it little short of contemptible. Already I see it described as an impressive and terrible spectacle. The squadron of aircraft are said to have come in close formation and brilliant battle array. The manoeuvring under the clear guidance of a leader is said to have been masterly in its plan and execution. Nothing of the kind. It would be difficult to imagine anything less suggestive to the eye of the spectator of the majesty, the unison, the terror and the splendour of war. Flying slowly, astonishingly slowly, the greater body of the formless mass came over the metropolis and hang at poise [sic] there. For fifteen to twenty minutes they did not seem to move. Against the grey bank of cloud, they looked precisely and exactly like a collection of cholera germs on a glass disc... I intended to make some attempt to draw the political and moral lessons of this attack on London, but my heart is too hot for that today. Perhaps I have no such technical knowledge as would justify me in criticising the apparent unreadiness of our air defences.

Perhaps not, but his anger was readily shared by his compatriots, once again manifested in anti-German disturbances. The Hun had gone too far – everything and anyone even remotely German in origin or connection was despised and reviled as never before. So extreme were public sentiments that the name of the Royal House, revered and respected since the marriage of Queen Victoria to her consort Albert had to be reviewed. However, despite the Germans' hopes, there was no anti-government disturbances or riots in the streets. Nevertheless, people were tired of it all, and it was this feeling that a number of avid anti-war campaigners seized upon. Sylvia Pankhurst, editor of the *Women's Dreadnought* the mouthpiece of the female suffrage movement, took up the case. She argued vehemently, 'To Stop the Raids, Stop the War!' in the issue of 11 July, speaking out strongly against reprisals:

In some streets of greatest destruction old posters are on the walls announcing a meeting convened by *The Daily Express* to demand reprisals. From a string across the street hangs a Union Jack and a strip of calico roughly inscribed 'we demand reprisals.' ...the

171

amazing statement is that the way to stop the German air raiders from dropping bombs on London is to drop bombs on German towns!

Yet fringe papers were not the only ones taking up the cry for an end to the fighting. The *Daily Mail* also made the case against reprisals:

We raided Freiburg as a reprisal for the sinking of a hospital ship. The Germans are still sinking hospital ships. The German government instituted the submarine campaign, nominally at any rate as a reprisal for the British blockade of Germany. The great French air raid on eleven German towns last Friday was undertaken as a reprisal for German bombardments of French Open Towns. The German despatches repeatedly describe these attacks as being made in reprisal for previous air raids on these cities.

Miss Pankhurst however, went even further:

Is not London a fortified place of military importance...? Are there not extensive munition factories and stores of military equipment here? Is not London the headquarters of the British military machine? Is not London fortified? The only means of protecting a city from bombs hurled from aircraft are anti aircraft guns and aircraft. The government assures us that London is thus fortified! Reprisals cannot stop the air raids. Nothing can save us from the risk of them except to stop the war.... Stop the war... stop the war, that is the only way to save the lives of brothers, sons and husbands, the only way to stop the misery and hunger that is falling upon the people.

Peace or revenge, the calls for a proper system of warnings and protection remained the same. The inadequacy of defences was the main topic of discussion at 10 Downing Street whilst on the Monday following the raid it was decided to recall a squadron from France again. Two were demanded, but Haig insisted he needed all his resources for his forthcoming campaign and repeated that its success would make the enemy airfields untenable and prevent further raids.

What was generally agreed was that decisive, long-term measures needed to be considered, evaluated and implemented to put an end to this reign of terror once and for all. Lloyd George selected General Jan Smuts to head an inter-service committee with the following terms of reference, to examine:

a. the defensive arrangements for Home Defence against air raids; and

172

b. the existing aerial organization for the study and higher direction of aerial operations.

Lloyd George chose Smuts because it, 'was a question that called for examination by a fresh and able mind free from departmental prejudices' and thus Smuts, a former implacable enemy of Britain, was offered the task on 11 July. While he got to work the question of air raid warnings once more raised its head. On 9 July, Winston Churchill spoke in the Commons on the subject in which he insisted that:

> There ought to be a perfectly clear guidance by the Government and the authorities that when an air raid takes place it is the duty of every person to seek such accommodation in the lower parts of those buildings as is convenient... .We are all in this business together... the important point is to find out what is the best thing to do.

⟫ ⟩⟩⟨0⟩⟨⟨ ⟨⟨

The result of growing calls for warnings were answered by the introduction of the oddly named 'maroons' – in fact maritime distress rockets. Eighty were delivered to selected sites – all fire stations radiating from Charing Cross – on 21 July. The idea was that upon the receipt of a warning from County Hall, each station was to fire off three rockets at fifteen second intervals. But their first use a day later, in response to a raid against Harwich and Felixstowe which it was believed would extend to London, resulted in confusion. Luckily the farce took place on a Sunday so the disruption was minimal. Perhaps it served to support the Government view, but now that the means to issue warnings existed there was no going back.

On 19 July, Smuts presented the results of his findings, which were detailed and far reaching, including the creation of separate zones for fighters and anti-aircraft so that the guns would break up the enemy formations and make the fighters' task easier in engaging individual raiders. A ring of gun sites twenty-five miles around London was proposed. Shortages of guns would delay this measure but, as time passed, more resources would be available to extend and enhance the arrangements. Pilots were also given a swifter and more efficient way of being warned of impending raids, each squadron maintaining a telephone operator on duty twenty-four-hours-a-day who would sound the alarm should the call come through from GHQ that a raid was imminent. Crews could then jump into their flying kit and reach their machines, already made ready by the ground crew, and be in the air within a few minutes. Smuts also suggested an overall command structure, 'specially charged with the duty of working out all plans for the London Air Defences'. By the end of the month the London Air Defence Area had been created under the command of Lieutenant General Edward Ashmore. These somewhat hastily arrived at, but potentially effective measures, now required the return of the Gothas so they could be put to the test.

While Smuts' measures were being put into effect, the British air forces in France grew eager to adopt a more proactive role. On the morning of 29 July, 7 (Naval) Squadron at Dunkirk sent a force of DH4s and the new Handley Page 0100 bombers to attack Ghistelles. It did little to disturb the enemy, but it heralded an increase in future activity adding to the growing woes of the German squadron. As such actions increased, they would compel the enemy to take steps to make themselves less prone to Allied attack, causing them to draw further back behind their own lines and lengthening their lines of communication.

But it was the weather, not the British pilots, who were to dictate German operations, and it was to the forecasters that the fliers looked for guidance. Since the attack on Harwich and Felixstowe, foul weather had kept the impetuous Kleine firmly grounded, though he needed only the slightest opportunity to get airborne.

Kleine selected Chatham as his next objective, with Southend as secondary target, and on 12 August assigned just thirteen machines to attack. This episode underlined more than any the commander's rashness. A vague weather window prompted him to instruct his men to prepare to become airborne with just a few hours notice. Ill-prepared, the smallest force mustered so far, took to the skies, and lost two almost immediately to engine trouble.

Unfavourable weather left the squadron with no choice but to make for Southend, but the manoeuvre also confused the defenders, who guessed they were going for London again and stationed their aircraft in anticipation. The attack on the seaside town resulted in thirty-three deaths and forty-six injuries: 139 aircraft were sortied to intercept them - to the wrong place.

Kleine was still convinced his forces were unstoppable, and as soon as his squadron returned home he was pushing Georgii to sanction another sortie.

The meteorologist insisted the weather would ill-favour an attack, indicating very severe winds and generally poor weather conditions over

174

England, but Kleine would not be told. He scheduled 18 August for another attack on London.

Twenty-eight aircraft left their airfields, the largest force massed for a single operation so far. The ferocious winds actually blew them over neutral Dutch territory, earning them warning shots, followed by serious bombardments from the anti-aircraft guns below. They were flying directly against the wind, reducing their speed to just 50mph, and after three hours of a miserably hostile flight, Kleine learned to his horror that the squadron was forty miles off-target. To add to his woes, the struggle against the elements had seriously depleted fuel supplies, and, despite his certain embarrassment, he knew he had no choice but to abandon the fruitless mission and return to base before his squadron dropped one by one into the sea as they ran out of petrol.

The hapless raiders made it back across the North Sea, but it was too late. Two machines ran out of fuel, one making for the beach near Zeebrugge and the other probably ending up in the grey waters. Another ran out of fuel over Holland, and the other was shot down. The crews of both aircraft landed safely but were soon captured by the Dutch and interned for the rest of the war. Five more machines ran out of petrol and, after gliding for a few miles, eventually crashed. Four more managed to land, but only by writing their machines off in the process. Kleine had lost close on half of his force to the elements. No doubt he received a severe reprimand, and ought to have been replaced, but in the event it seems he failed to learn his bitter lesson.

The filthy weather continued, but once again this only caused Kleine's impatience to burn the greater. The moment he received a favourable weather forecast, he mounted another operation, this time on 22 August. Once airborne, five of the fifteen aircraft broke off with engine trouble. The remaining aircraft were flying into stiffer resistance, and the attack was a failure.

For a Germany desperate not to have their initiative thwarted so soon, this meant that another bombing aircraft development long on the drawing board could now come into its own, the impressively named 'Giant' or R-Plane.

As the Gotha IV began losing the fight, it was to the *Zeppelin-Staaken Riesenflugzeug* that German hopes were pinned, with their enhanced bomb-carrying capacity of up to 2,100lbs. These monoliths dwarfed even the impressive Gothas, with wingspans approaching 140 feet and with four powerful 245hp Maybach engines. They had already seen some service on the Eastern Front, attacking troop concentrations, supply dumps and communications centres and, in the summer of 1917 Rfa502, commanded by *Hauptmann* Richard von Bentivegni was transferred to Germany to equip with newer models in preparation to attack England.

A disappointing series of combined attacks by airships and Gothas produced no significant results during September so, on the night of the 28 August two R-Planes joined twenty-five Gothas in an attack on London. It was totally ruined by the weather. Only three Gothas and the two R-Planes made it as far as the coast, all the others heeding advice to abort the attack if the commanders considered the weather dangerous. A few bombs were scattered around the Harwich/Ipswich area and there were a few reported incidents north of Billericay in Essex and some isolated pockets in Kent. Poor weather also kept the British pilots at bay, but despite the dismal outcome from the German's point of view, Von Hoeppner congratulated the crews with a rousing message:

> To the commander of Rfa502. I congratulate the participant crews on the occasion of the first successful attack with which the R-Planes have begun their important assignment on the Western Front. I am confident that the R-Planes will grow from flight to flight into an ever stronger offensive weapon.

Some evidence suggests that the decline of the Gotha crews' efficacy was beginning to spread and make their colleagues in the R-Planes equally despondent. The campaign had dwindled since the heady days of 25 May, 13 June and even 7 July. Then it seemed their ordeals in enemy airspace were a bold, honourable and valuable contribution to the war effort. Then they were certain it was going to produce something startling and conclusive; perhaps an early end to the war. That sparkle and élan was now a memory.

But they were still loyal soldiers of the Kaiser, and they were required to serve without question. On the night of 29 September, three R-Planes accompanied by seven Gothas (of which only three completed the mission) embarked upon another journey to London, but with the exception of some hits on Waterloo Station, there was little material damage, though forty people died and over eighty were injured. Gothas attacked alone the following night, with London, Dover, Chatham and Margate receiving a sprinkling of bombs. Another raid took place over London on the night of 1 October, when there were eleven fatalities and forty-two injuries.

A brief pause saw some airship raids launched against northern England, and then a return to the south-east on the night of 29 October, with an assault by three Gothas. Either Kleine was desperate to maintain the momentum, or desperate simply to keep the British awake, for not the slightest benefit could be gleaned by even the most optimistic propagandist.

A more reasonable outcome came on the night of 31 October, when twenty-two Gothas took off from their airfields. They were all armed with the newest 4.5kg incendiary bombs and, had they been dropped en masse would certainly have stretched the resources of the London Fire Brigade. However, only half the bombers made it to London, the rest choosing to attack coastal targets and get home for breakfast. Those bombers which reached London failed to achieve the bombing concentrations needed to cause the anticipated conflagration. Another poor performance for Kleine, his prestige was eroded further by the loss of a further five machines crashing before they made it home.

Fortunes took a turn for the better on the night of 5-6 December, when sixteen of nineteen bombers dispatched, penetrated London defences to liberally pepper the capital with bombs including incendiaries. These were dropped around Finsbury, Whitechapel and Kensington, this time starting serious fires to cause substantial damage. As well as further improvements in the number and disposition of anti-aircraft guns, the raiders had to reckon with the new Bristol Fighter whose speed and manoeuvrability put its predecessors like the B.E. models in the shade.

One lucky ground shot shattered the propeller of a Gotha, and gave the crew no choice than to put itself at the mercy of the British, force-landing on a golf course near Rochford aerodrome. On their thirteenth mission over England, crewmen *Leutnant* Schulte and *Vizefeldwebel* Senf were unlucky enough to receive a hit from ground fire, putting the port radiator out of action. The engine overheated and finally burst into flames. The crew eventually made landfall in a field near Sturry in Kent, where they set upon their aircraft, smashing it as much as they could, then surrendered to the first Englishman they came upon – a local vicar who doubled as a Special Constable. A further Gotha was lost over the North Sea, whilst another crash-landed and two more were lost over Belgium.

If Kleine had any ideas to improve the fortunes of his squadron over England then he would never live to see them bear fruit, for he was killed on 12 December leading attacks on troop concentrations near Ypres. He was replaced by his deputy, *Oberleutnant* Walter who was a better aviator and less eager to please his superiors at the expense of his men.

177

Walter's first operation since the death of Kleine was mounted on 18-19 December, and saw thirteen of fifteen Gothas and one R-Plane dispatched, head for London. This was the last time the incendiary was carried and so poor were the results that the Germans abandoned the whole idea until the new 'Electron', which was lighter and smaller and could be carried in greater numbers, promised better results in the spring of 1918. However, the high explosive ordnance of the raid brought the biggest material results since 1915, with some 11,300lbs of high explosive having been dropped on the capital.

Captain G W Murlis Green would garner some payback by achieving the first night-time 'kill' since the Germans began their nocturnal activities. He found his quarry over Bermondsey and gave it a determined pounding, but the craft limped as far as Folkestone, until the bullet-riddled starboard engine gave out at a height of 3,000 feet and ten miles out to sea. The commander *Leutnant* Friedrich Ketelsen, saw it was hopeless and turned round to ditch the machine on terra firma. In the event, the craft fell short, Ketelsen was drowned and his crew picked up by the armed trawler *Highlander*.

The Germans continued with their parlous efforts right up to the end of 1917, and despite the results of 18-19 December, had little to show for them except the loss of good men and a few pinpricks on the sprawling London metropolis.

═══◎═══

The New Year, 1918, failed to stop the rot. The defences were being improved as an ongoing process, and the balloon barrages were installed and sound locators were introduced, enabling raiders to be detected much earlier than before by the noise of their engines. Defending aircraft could be sortied sooner and directed more accurately. In theory it meant bombers would lose the main element of surprise.

From the German leaders point of view, the air attacks were still diverting important resources from the Western Front, and costly resources at that. The development and deployment of bombers had cost a fortune but, like so many military advances, it seems they had come too little, too late. Nevertheless the campaign was to grind on.

On the night of 28-29 January seven Gothas and one R-Plane attacked London. A Gotha was shot down by night fighters, but the R-Plane reached London. It was carrying a single massive 300kg bomb which smashed into the basement of Odhams, the printers in Long Acre

178

(See chapter 4). The resulting explosion killed thirty-eight people and injured another eighty-five sheltering in the works. The following night, four R-Planes were dispatched without Gothas, each with even larger 1000kg bombs. One suffered engine failure; another was forced off-course by heavy ground fire and the two that remained were forced to drop their bombs short.

Five more attacked London and Dover on the night of 16-17 February, one carrying the new 1000kg bomb. Three machines made for Dover when the weather deteriorated, whilst the 1000kg bomb carrier proceeded towards the capital. The north pavilion of the Royal Hospital Chelsea, home of the Chelsea Pensioners, was demolished, whilst the other R-Plane scattered bombs across Woolwich and killed seven people. The raid against Dover was less successful, most of the bombs fell in the sea and one of the R-Planes suffered serious engine trouble and barely made it home.

The following night a lone R-Plane made it to London, under the command of *Leutnant* Max Borchers. Bombs were dropped to the south of the city, and more fell across Lewisham, Peckham and Southwark. The *coup de grâce* came when the machine unloaded eight 50kg bombs which exploded on and around St Pancras station and killed twenty-one people. Another thirty-two were injured. It was the biggest achievement of the night campaign so far, and served as a reminder that, had the weather conditions been more favourable, and larger concentrations of bombers being mustered, they could still create carnage and terror among the enemy when caught off-guard.

Greatly encouraged by this episode, the Germans generated all their resources – six R-Planes for the night of 7-8 March. One was forced to turn back due to engine trouble, but the remainder made it to London and scattered bombs over St John's Wood, Whetstone, Hampstead and Battersea. The raid was disappointing owing to ground fire which forced them high and caused the formation to disperse. Twelve died when a 1000kg bomb fell on a row of houses in Maida Vale. Another twenty-three were injured.

Following this attack, there was a long rest punctuated by small forays against northern England while the Germans mustered their forces for another attack. The opportunity came on the night of 19-20 May and for this effort thirty-eight Gothas and three R-Planes were to be deployed, accompanied by two Rumpler C-type reconnaissance aircraft. Of the twenty-eight Gothas and three R-Planes dispatched, seventy-two bombs were dropped on the City, another thirty-six over Essex and another forty-nine on Kent. Forty-nine people died, but in retaliation the ground defences and the eighty-eight fighter sorties saw the destruction of six enemy bombers – all Gothas in this, the last German bomber raid of the war on London.

— ⚬ —

Minor raids and incursions continued with airships, but the promise of the early days remained unfulfilled. British defences were rendering further efforts foolhardy. Then, the March Offensive against the Allies was launched with much optimism. It was to be the last Germany could muster, and was intended to throw the enemy back before the Americans could field enough men to tip the balance. When the German ground forces began to falter themselves under pressure of Allied counter-attacks, the bombers were diverted to frontline support roles.

This change in fortunes heralded the final blow to the air campaign against Britain. The men of Brandenburg's original bomber fleet were now scattered throughout the skies over the Western Front, bombing British, French and now American troops.

The mighty juggernauts developed with German ingenuity would soon be broken up as scrap under the terms of the Treaty of Versailles, thereafter to be vague memories for slowly-ageing crewmen looking back nostalgically to the days when they briefly ruled the skies over England in that far-off First Blitz.

Germany was perhaps not aware of it yet, but the skill and devotion of their fighting men had made true the musings of men like Francesco de Lana and had indeed brought terror from the skies. H G Wells' prophetic writings too, earn a measure of currency, although it would only be in the years to come that his tales of foreboding would become truly manifest.

For the time being however, an impartial evaluation of the campaign would find it difficult to see such consequences. On a scale of one to ten, the strategic value of the German air offensive against Britain during this period is a debatable four, insofar as it did nothing to influence the way the war went, one way or the other. It is true, that tactically it diverted some valuable Allied resources, but it also took much needed materiel for the Germans. Of the Gotha crewmen sent against England, fifty-seven lost their lives or were reported missing: only twenty-eight British crewmen were killed. Of the R-Planes, none were lost and no crewmen died.

Total civilian losses were 1,414 killed and 3,416 wounded between

1915 and 1918. Here too, the long-term consequences would have been difficult to gauge so soon after the end of the campaign. Compared with the losses on the Western Front they were slight, and would have elicited little sympathy from soldiers acclimatized to casualty rates in which these figures would have been lost during a single days' fighting to capture a single German strongpoint. Hence the rather caustic comments from pilots such as Cecil Lewis. The full significance of the campaign would have to wait a while to be placed in its proper context, but perhaps we can leave this narrative by giving the last word to Lovat Fraser. He summed up his views as early as July 1917, when he passed his judgement on the consequences of the Gotha Raids:

> If I were asked what event of the last year has been of most significance to the future of humanity, I should reply that it is not the Russian Revolution or even the stern intervention of the United States in a sacred course; but the appearance of a single German aeroplane flying at high noon over London.

PERFORMANCE RATINGS OF AIRCRAFT IN SERVICE WITH THE HOME DEFENCE SQUADRONS

Approximate Capabilities of Machines in Order of Merit

De Havilland 4 (2-seater):	Climb - 10,000 feet in twelve minutes Speed at 10,000 feet - 100mph
Sopwith (2-seater):	Climb - 10,000 feet in twenty minutes Speed at 10,000 feet - 90mph
RE8 (2-seater):	Climb - 10,000 feet in twenty-five minutes Speed at 10,000 feet - 90mph
Armstrong-Whitworth (2-seater):	Climb - 10,000 feet in thirty minutes Speed at 10,000 feet - 85mph
B.E.12 and B.E.12a (single seater):	Climb - 10,000 feet in twenty-five minutes Speed at 10,000 feet - 70mph

TEACHERS AND STAFF PRESENT AT UPPER NORTH STREET SCHOOL ON 13 JUNE 1917

Boys

Head Master	Mr F Denner
Assistants	Mr A G Knapp
	Mr A E Strong
	Mrs E J Sommerville
Unattached	Mrs E S Curtis

Girls

Head Mistress	Miss E Eastland
Assistants	Mrs M E Mountford
	Mrs M P Cannington
	Mrs F Prevot
Supply	Mrs A E Allum

Infants

Head Mistress	Miss E Ely
Assistants	Mrs A Smith
	Mrs J Crowhurst
	Miss E W Watkins
	Mrs I S J Moore
	Mrs M H Tietgen
	Mrs G Middleton

Schoolkeeper

	Mr Batt

APPENDIX III

PUPILS WHO DIED AT UPPER NORTH STREET SCHOOL ON 13 JUNE 1917

Child's Name	Age
Louise Annie Acampora	5
Alfred Earnest Batt	5
Leonard Charles Bareford	5
John Percy Brennan	5
William Thomas Henry Challen	5
Vera Margaret Clayson	4
Alice Maud Cross	5
William Hollis	5
George Albert Hyde	5
Grace Jones	5
Rose Martin	11
George Morris	6
Edwin Cecil William Powell	12
Robert Stimson	5
Elizabeth Taylor	5
Rose Tuffin	5
Frank Winfield	5
Florence Lillian Wood	5

BIBLIOGRAPHY AND SOURCES

A number of books and other publications have been consulted in the preparation of this work. The list is by no means exhaustive, but represents those publications which have proven most useful in my research and reading.

Baring, Maurice, *Flying Corps – 1914-18*, G Bell, 1920.
Bishop, William, *Winged Warfare*, Grossett and Dunlap, 1918.
Bowen, Ezra, *Knights of the Air*, Time Life Books, 1980.
Boyle, Andrew, *Trenchard*, Collins, 1962.
Castle, H G, *Fire Over England,* Secker and Warburg, 1982.
Chaumier, J A, *The Birth of the Royal Air Force*, Isaac Pitman, 1943.
Chitto, Walter Raleigh, *The War in the Air*, Windus, 1922.
Churchill, Randolph S, *Winston S Churchill, Companion Vol. II,* Heinemann, 1969.
Churchill, Winston S, *The World Crisis, 1911-1918,* Odhams Press, 1938.
Clarke, Reverend Andrew, *Echoes of the Great War*, Oxford University Press, 1985.
Cole, Christopher and Cheeseman, E F, *The Air Defence of Britain*, Pitman, 1984.
Collier, Basil, *A History of Air Power*, Weidenfeld and Nicholson, 1974.
Coxon, Stanley W, *Dover During the Dark Days*, John Lane, The Bodley Head, 1919.
Cuneo, John R, *Winged Mars, Volumes 1-11,* Military Services Publishing Co, 1942.
Emme, Eugene M, *The Impact of Air Power*, Princeton: D Van Nostrand, 1959.
Fredette, Raymond H, *The First Battle of Britain*, Cassell, 1966.
Gamble C F, *The Air Weapon*, Longmans Green, 1947.
Gilbert, Martin, *Winston S Churchill, Vol III*, Heinemann, 1977.
Gilbert, Martin, *Winston S. Churchill, Vol IV,* Heinemann, 1975.
Goble, Bill, *Bill Goble – Lifelong Rebel*, Shepherds Bush Local History Society, 1984.
Hogg, Ian V, *Anti-Aircraft – A History of Air Defence,* Macdonald & Jane's, London, 1978.
Hook, John, *They Come! They Come!, The Air Raids on London*

During the 1914-18 War, London, 1987.

Hunt, E H, *British Labour History, 1915-1914,* Weidenfeld & Nicholson, 1988.

Jones, H, *The War in the Air*, University of Arkansas, 1990.

Jones, Neville, *The Origins of Strategic Bombing*, William Kimber, 1973.

Lewis, Cecil, *Sagitarrius Rising*, Greenhill Books, 2000.

Lloyd George, David, *War Memoirs*, Odhams Press, 1938.

Ludendorff, General Erich, *My War Memories*, Hutchinson, 1919.

Ludwig, Emil, *Kaiser Wilhelm II*, Putnam, 1926.

Maddow, G W and Grosz, Peter, *The German R-Planes – The German R Planes 1914-18*, Putnam, 1988.

McCudden VC, Captain James, *Flying Fury – Five Years in the Royal Flying Corps*, Greenhill Books, 2000.

Munson, Kenneth, *Bombers, 1914-1919*, Blandford Press, 1968.

Millin, Gertrude, *General Smuts, Volume III*, Faber & Faber, 1936.

Morison, Frank, *War on Great Cities*, Faber and Faber, 1937.

Neumann, G P, *The German Air Force in the Great War*, Cecil Chivers Ltd, 1969.

Pankhurst Sylvia, *The Women's Dreadnought, 17 July 1917, Vol IV, No.16,* pp 800-801.

Poolman, Kenneth, *Zeppelins Against London*, John Day, 1961.

Reynolds, Quentin, *They Fought for the Sky*, Cassell, 1958.

Rimmell, Raymond, *The Zeppelin: A Battle for Air Supremacy*, Maritime Press, 1984.

Robinson, Douglas H, *The Zeppelin in Combat*, G T Foulis, 1961.

Sassoon, Siegfried, *Memoirs of An Infantry Officer*, Faber and Faber, 1930.

Scott, J D, *Vickers, A History*, Weidenfeld and Nicholson, 1962.

Stevenson, John, *British Society, 1914-45*, Pelican, 1984.

Turner, E S, *Dear Old Blighty,* Michael Joseph, 1982.

Turner, John, *Britain And The First World War*, Hymen, 1988.

von Bulow, Hilmer, *Die Angriffe des Bombengeschwader 3 auf England, in Die Luftwacht*, 1929.

von Hoeppner, Ernst, *Deutschland Krieg in der Luft,* von Hase and Kohler, 1921.

von Tirpitz, Alfred, *My Memoirs*, New York, Dodd, Mead, 1919, Hurst and Blackett 1919.

White, C M, *The Gotha Summer*, Robert Hale, 1986.

Winter, Denis, *The First of the Few - Fighter Pilots in the First World War,* Allen Lane, Penguin Books, 1982.

East End News, Various.
Flight Magazine, *vol. ix. No.28*, 12 July 1917.
The London Times, June-July, 1917.
The New York Times, June-July, 1917.

PUBLIC RECORD OFFICE, KEW

The Public Record Office at Kew, London, contains a considerable amount of primary information relating to pilots and guns stations reports and other relevant information.

GHQHF (General Headquarters Home Forces), Air Raids 1917-18, Volume 1A PRO/ADM1/8464.
PRO/AIR1/177.
PRO/AIR 1/2123.
PRO/AIR1/258.
PRO/AIR 1/588.
PRO/AIR 1/589.
PRO/AIR 1/614.
PRO/AIR1/668.
PRO/AIR1/691.
PRO/AIR1/2126.
PRO/AIR1/2312.
PRO/AIR1/2319.
CAB/23/2.
CAB/23/3.
CAB/24.
CAB/24/20.

INDEX